At the Butcher Counter of Life

Adventure, Chaos, and Illumination in New Zealand

To LaLa —
My first editor
(with the bird's-eye
view) and little
dancing star.
I love you.
XO
Mama Suma

Janet Parmely

At the Butcher Counter of Life: Adventure, Chaos, and Illumination in New Zealand

Copyright © 2018 Janet Parmely. All rights reserved. No part of this book may be reproduced or retransmitted in any form or by any means without the written permission of the publisher.

Published by Wheatmark®
2030 East Speedway Boulevard, Suite 106
Tucson, Arizona 85719 USA
www.wheatmark.com

ISBN: 978-1-62787-552-3 (paperback)
ISBN: 978-1-62787-553-0 (ebook)
LCCN: 2017952071

rev201801

"Life is like a butcher counter."

That's what they told me at the pub. "You can have whatever you want. You just have to ring the bell."

But suppose you don't know what to order when you step up to the butcher counter of life? Lamb chop or pork knuckle, ma'am? What then?

Chances are, the universe will hand over what you need instead.

CONTENTS

Part I: The Leap... The Landing

Chapters

1. We were riding on the bones of our asses, on top of the world and feeling dangerous 3
2. Untold annoyances comfort and rumble around the world 12
3. When I call into port, the first thing I do is stake out my pub. . . 19
4. Love at first sight is only lust, worth not much more than diamond dust 33
5. It's hard to look both ways when you're standing at a blind bend in the road 40
6. At the heart of every pearl is an irritant, mate 58
7. Most of us are victims of our own self-destruction 65
8. Who wants given fruit when stolen's sweeter— Mrs. MacElroy's peaches, Mrs Taylor's plums 72

Part II: Bolter in Paradise

Chapters

9. The busy gremlin with a pint-sized voice goading you over the cliff while you rejoice has a name—and that is Choice 83
10. The main thing to keep straight if you're a ventriloquist is which one's the dummy. 89
11. Everything was perfect and complete, it was. 94

v

CONTENTS

12. Everyone thinks he can be a train driver just because it runs on rails. Maybe he can drive a locomotive, but he can't drive a train . . . 101
13. All you need, luv, is a dry bed, full tummy, and family who loves you. 106
14. What fun's the fruit without a worm? 117
15. If the romance isn't perfect, it damn well better include confit of duck. 124
16. A whistling woman and a clucking hen are neither use to God nor men 130
17. Become one with the stumble. 139
18. A full hitch of Clydesdales is nothing compared to what two tits on a woman can do. Rosy Promise doesn't even need tits 146

Part III: Seeker in the Shit

Chapters

19. When all else fails, take the next sensible step: the pub 153
20. The whole lot was planned out, not one damned thing worked, and it all turned to custard 163
21. There comes a time to depend on the parachute not the plane . 167
22. It's not terrible to want to go back to the way things were. It's just unlikely 172
23. I had this starboard/port confusion, no paddle, no bailer, and was night-blind as well 176
24. I was happy just to hear her voice, like a maiden's sigh or the pop of a champagne cork 185
25. Life can be easier if you weasel out of things, at least for the weasel 192
26. There are things to miss wherever you are 197
27. The man will fail before the boat 210
28. It's a balls-up, God save the queen, but there's no way back . . . 216

CONTENTS

29. Fish the scum line on the outgoing tide 224
30. On the night you need one, any torch will do,
    even if it came from the $2 Shop 232
31. There is no substitute for billable hours 242
32. To get two versions of truth, put a man and woman under one roof
    for six decades. If you want more renditions, add offspring . . . 252

Part IV: The Tide Comes in at the Speed of a Galloping Horse

Chapters

33. Sure he's a decent bloke at the pub, but who is he at home? . . . 265
34. You'd be amazed how fast the tide comes in
    once it makes up its mind to 273
35. There is one solitary order you cannot dodge, no matter
    how many underpants you refuse to fold up and put away . . . 280
36. What kind of parents order a bologna sundae for their kid
    at the butcher counter of life? 288
37. Many things that couldn't ever happen have. 295

Epilogue
Hope, gratitude, and underpants: that's what it's all about 305

Glossary
A list of curious Kiwi terms and more 311

Part I

The Leap
The Landing

Chapter 1

We were riding on the bones of our asses,
on top of the world and feeling dangerous.

—#28, God's Holding Paddock

Keep in mind this happened some time ago. I'd know better now. Fifty had tapped me on the shoulder. The birthday got my attention, of course. But I had no inkling that this trickster, the Big Five-Oh, was ushering in a decade about to do a number on my romantic notions and change the lay of life as I knew it. Furthermore, the bugger didn't even bother to leave a revised map behind.

It happened before smartphones with GPS. If I could have asked Siri for directions, I might have resisted the siren call to adventure in a faraway land: "Come to New Zealand—idyllic, untouched, at the edge of the world. We have sixty million sheep, but we're short on audiologists."

Come! Yes, you.

With a one-year contract in hand, I wouldn't have left my newlywed husband, family, friends, dog, and cat behind on the other side of the equator, the International Date Line, the world. So it goes. Try to rectify a few bad decisions with an extreme one and pretty soon you're a charge audiologist selling hearing aids in a country with sixteen times more sheep than people.

In exchange, I would not have met the skipper of a fifty-two-foot sailing yacht, a riddle of a man with a mind of his own. Nor would I have gotten clobbered upside the head with the cosmic-wake-up-call skillet. But then, with reverberations still ringing in my ears, I would not have come to understand that the guys at the pub had been half right.

If I'd been prudent, I wouldn't have rented the house on the slope of the mountain at Whangarei Heads, a spot so dear that its name may as well be tattooed over my beating heart. In the shadow of Mount Manaia, tuis whistled, belled, and chuckled in the flax bushes. Angel's trumpet ramped its hallucinogenic way in the subtropical air and bloomed after dark. Its lemony musk mingled with the heady scent of lady-of-the-night and lingered until dawn. Across the tangle of vegetation, over the rooftop of the widow Ngaere's dairy, past Taurikura Bay, and beyond the mouth of Whangarei Harbor, a sliver of the Pacific Ocean shimmered when the sun was just right.

If I hadn't gotten the job in New Zealand, I would never have walked into the pub that uncommonly sunny June day and been invited to join God's Holding Paddock, a table at Parua Bay Tavern where the regulars swapped yarns and advice. I would have missed out on the best bunch of fellows ever assembled from a disappearing generation of Kiwi men.

If this seeker hadn't left home to find it, I would never have come to love a country despite the incessant rain and perplexing fondness for beets.

Crocuses were blooming when I left Kansas City in March, and in New Zealand, autumn had just begun. Metaphorically it was wrong. It's customary to run away in search of greener pastures. Sensible women don't leave spring behind. They don't forgo the company of a brand-new six-foot-three husband, wafting head notes of mandarin and heart notes of sandalwood, fresh from the shower. They don't leave him holding a box of 365 cotton swabs that he has bought to mark the days and console himself, "When I clean my ears with the last Q-tip, you'll be back home in my arms." This was no bubblegum stretch for a civil engineer.

Levelheaded women do not begin the millennium at fifty-one, seven and a half thousand miles from home, with a kunekune pig in a paddock below the front door and a mountain looming out back that is sacred, forbidden, tapu.

The pig weighed as much as three kegs of nails, and its snout looked like it had rear-ended a bus. It was black and bristly, and where it wasn't bristly, it was bald. Something swung between its legs in the mud. It might have been its belly, or maybe not. The pig didn't move about enough to catch a breeze, but it rooted in its trough with determination. Rats scampered and magpies swooped for the potato peels and onion skins it scattered to the wind. When the pig wasn't eating, it slept, and when it wasn't sleeping, it et.

The freighters that came into harbor looked as if they would run headlong onto the sandy shore of Taurikura Bay, up the hill, over a cow or two, and right into my kitchen sink, where water swirled wrong-wise down the drain. Instead, at the last minute, they veered broadside around a dogleg, and the tankers docked at the oil refinery on the flatlands across the channel.

The day I moved in, two tugs maneuvered the coastal freighter *Taiko* through the narrows. The pilot, a speck, swayed four stories down a rope ladder back to his bobbing boat, and the vessels in the vignette outside my window went their separate ways. The tugs and pilot boat returned to shelter. *Taiko* boomed three energetic blasts, left for sea on the tide— and the catamaran *Jingle Bells*, diamonds and Krugerrands in the hold, must have sailed unnoticed past the Heads on her way to the Town Basin in Whangarei.

A crown of mist burned off Manaia, and the sun did a turquoise tap dance across Taurikura Bay, but soon the rains would set in, a mizzle and a drizzle, then cats and dogs, and wash away the boundaries once so clear between earth, sea, and sky. The northeasterlies would gust to thirty-five knots and send flames leaping in the wood burner I stoked to heat my home. The stovepipe would clatter beneath the mountain where a god had turned a stolen wife to stone. And one winter day, Manaia would vanish behind a curtain of rain in Aotearoa, the Land of the Long White Cloud—New Zealand.

Date: April 9, 2000
To: Jack B.
Subject: All Who Wander Are Not Lost?

    We shall see, my sweet husband. We shall see. You are a patient man, and I love you all the more for your generous spirit. Few husbands would be willing to see off a wife of three months on a plane to New Zealand for an escapade of her own making. With the good-bye parties behind me and sparkle off the glitz of anticipation, tonight my "year abroad" seems like a very long time without you by my side.

    It's rained for two weeks straight, horizontally. But at least I am finally online. So far, no revelations in the job department. I just got back from my traveling clinic in Kerikeri. Across a fern-green world speckled with Belted Galloway cows and Polwarth sheep, past fine horses wearing blankets against the morning chill, it's a two-hour drive from my house at Whangarei Heads—on the wrong side of the road, invariably behind a tandem logging truck, and usually in the rain.

    I bought a used car at Ellerslie Racetrack in Auckland, where I trained in the corporate ways of Bay Audiology before they sent me up north to the clinic in Whangarei. Went to the Sunday Car Fair, stood by a sign in my price range (under $5,000), and made a deal with a Scottish lass who was heading home. I gave her $4800 in a wad of Kiwi twenties I had pulled from my USA account at the ATM. And she slipped a note in the glove box that I found a week later: "May you be as happy in New Zealand as I have been. Kind regards, Gillian."

The car has a tape deck, but the audiobook selection at Whangarei Library is pretty sparse. No Mark Twain but plenty of Maeve Binchy and Tolstoy. I settled on *Anna Karenina* and *War and Peace*. That should keep my brain in gear on the drive to work. Lord knows if it's my right brain or left; the poor hemispheres are so confused.

Twice a month, I load up "the boot" with a prehistoric laptop, an audiometer as old as my degree in audiology, a briefcase bulging with files, a box of programming cables tangled like spaghetti, hearing aids to be fitted, pottles to hold hearing aids to be repaired, and a Dremel to modify hearing aids that pinch. Something essential, like the otoscope, always gets left behind at base camp in Whangarei.

I take everything out of the boot in Kerikeri and set up for the day at the pharmacy in a back room that Bay Audiology timeshares with a podiatrist and a cosmetologist. It has one small window, stuck shut, and someone has left a No Bugs bomb on the sill. I presume it's to finish off any blowflies that might congregate there in the warmth of the sun. Judging by the weather so far, it'll never get detonated.

My equipment barely fits on the exam table, and I have to set the audiometer in the sink. The podiatrist leaves toenail clippings and callous scrapings behind, scattered like confetti from a hobgoblin's parade. The cosmetologist has hung an advertisement two meters high featuring a naked woman's derrière (without cellulite) on the wall behind the chair where my patients sit.

Today dapper old Mr. Curnow, with a dab of shaving cream in the notch of one ear and oblivious to the larger-than-life ass towering behind him, assured me, "You forgot the cables to program the new aid? No worries. I'll wear my old one until you come back. There's not much I need to hear in the next two weeks. I've got my glasses. As long as I can see, I won't miss a thing."

Nighty-night,
I love you,
Your Wife

AT THE BUTCHER COUNTER OF LIFE

Date: April 9, 2000
To: Laura P.
Subject: The Gossip from Ngaere's Dairy
Attached: Mount Manaia from the plane into Whangarei

Zip-a-dee-doo-dah and hallelujah Hotmail, your mama's online!

I just got back from Ngaere's Dairy. (A dairy is a Kiwi general store.) Ngaere has the wiry physique you see in women of a certain age who refuse to give up life's little pleasures and continue drinking and smoking at a rate that would kill a twenty-year-old. She wears her graying hair in a profusion of soft curls that is incongruously coquettish, given the remarkable bags under her eyes.

The dairy also serves as the local post office, "Private Bag Taurikura." Ngaere sorts the mail that the postie delivers into twenty-five cubbyholes behind the cash register and consequently knows everybody's business.

"*Tsk tsk.*" She gave me an envelope, knowing full well it contained my gotcha-by-the-speed-camera from the New Zealand Police. "That'll cost you eighty quid," she said, and she was right.

Handing over a padded mailer, she griped, "Took me a week

to track that one down, luv." It was stamped with Stars and Stripes and addressed in spidery script:

> Private Bag Taurikura
> New Zealand

That's it. No name. To her credit and my relief, Ngaere never opened the package from my doddery old friend. It contained three *Playboy* magazines "for reference" and a note recommending I spice up my emails.

Cats prowl the dairy. Kamikaze races across the beer chiller and bait freezer—a nuisance to anyone provisioning to fish at Whangarei Heads. You have to shoo away Shadow to get at the pork pies in the bakery case.

The back room smells like guano. Parakeets chitter from cages that line the walls. Turtles lounge in a pool of algae in the midst of it all, unperturbed by the ruckus. Pretty Boy, Ngaere's sulfur-crested cockatoo, sits on his perch and greets customers.

I made a fool of myself last week bobbing up and down, trying to get the bird to return my "Hello-Hello-Hello." Finally gave up, and as the screen door slammed behind me, Pretty Boy called out, "See ya, mate-See ya, mate-See ya, mate."

Ngaere told me there was trouble here long before the mountain was called Manaia, the bay Taurikura, or the harbor Whangarei. There are Maoris, still, who so respect the mana of Mount Manaia that they won't let the sun set upon them anywhere near it. I received this information right after signing a one-year lease for a house at its base.

As usual, the difficulties started with a man and a woman. Then another man. Chief Hautatu married Pito and moved his bride, as pretty as the fantail that flits in the bush, right under the paramount Chief Manaia's nose. That's Ngaere's story, but Maori legends have as many versions as the words they have for rain, from a drop to a day's worth. There is a name for weather leading up to rain, another for the moment it stops, and for all the showers and torrents in-between.

From the stronghold of his mountain *pa*, Manaia cast a jealous eye across the harbor to the flatlands where Hautatu and Pito lived. He fumed and hatched a plan. Fickle Manaia decided to take care of two birds with one stone.

Ever since he had conquered the distant Bay of Plenty tribes, they had given Manaia nothing but trouble. He gathered now a band of men from his ranks and the lesser chiefs', and appointed Hautatu to lead an attack that would crush the rebels once and for all.

While the warriors paddled south along the eastern coast of Aotearoa, Manaia built a causeway from the bay at the foot of his mountain across the harbor to Hautatu's village. Over it he led a war party of his own. Manaia slaughtered what decrepit men had been left behind and stole Pito away in the moonless night.

When he got the news, Hautatu was horn-mad at Manaia and none too happy with a wife who had let herself get stolen. He rushed back from the Bay of Plenty, scrambled up thirteen hundred feet across the gnarly roots of the pohutukawa trees, over the palisades, and laid siege to Manaia's *pa*.

They fled across the headland ridge, Manaia in the lead, Pito hurrying his two children along, Hautatu on their heels, about to smite Pito with a club. The sky turned black. Thunder pealed. Lightning flashed. Rangi, the great sky father, irked by all this earthly foolishness, turned the Maoris to stone where they stand today—five legendary peaks at Whangarei Heads.

Chapter 2

Untold annoyances comfort and rumble around the world.

—#39, God's Holding Paddock

The wind shifted into the south mid-April. The rain let up. A waxing moon rose over Mount Manaia, and a string of clear, still nights unfolded under the stardust luster of the Milky Way. This bliss was disturbed only by a din that grumbled through my bedroom window. The infernal noise persisted. I told my right-hand woman at the Whangarei clinic about the Big Snore.

"It's probably just a possum, luv."

"No way, Mary, that noise is coming from an animal the size of a house cat."

"New Zealand's little speed bumps."

"Oh, I thought those were dead foxes in the road."

The brushtail possum, it turns out, is far more handsome than its northern hemisphere relations, a cutie with a luxuriant coat from head to tippy tail. It's also a kitchen raider and opportunist that flourished after its introduction in 1837 for fur trading, into a country without native predators. When I arrived in 2000, there were seventy million of them doing particular damage to the native totara, kowhai, and pohutukawa trees, not to mention the eggs of the national bird. Possums threaten the dairy industry because they carry bovine tuberculosis, and to add insult to injury, the brushtail possum is an import from Australia.

AT THE BUTCHER COUNTER OF LIFE

Sodium monofluoroacetate, brand name 1080, has been used for years to keep the population in check. The possums devour the controversial if effective poison concealed in tasty bait, go haywire, and die. So do nontarget birds, amphibians, insects, and scavenging mammals like cats and dogs.

With typical Kiwi ingenuity, they started knitting apparel from possum fur, which sounds disgusting, until you get your mind off the image of a rat-tailed Virginia opossum playing dead on your shoulders and don a merino/brushtail possum cardigan that feels like cashmere. They even make nipple warmers out of the fur, although that's more of a tourist artifice because you have to sell so many to dispose of one possum, and the average woman has no idea how to keep them on. Yes, the brushtail possum was an Aussie infiltrator fit for nothing but cardies, socks, and nipple warmers, but was it really cranking out the Big Snore and keeping me up at night?

Maybe I had a neighbor whose poor wife hadn't gotten a good night's sleep in thirty years. Maybe there was a big fat hobo in the bush. (Kiwi culture was already working on me. I wasn't worried that an ax murderer was prowling around.)

After two weeks of whoever it was, I'd had enough. I grabbed a flashlight and a cheese sandwich—the hobo might be hungry—and took the shortcut to the dairy, out the back gate and down the lane that ran along one side of the paddock.

An hour ago, the plumes of toetoe grass had looked like lamplights in the setting sun. Now it was moon-not-yet-risen dark. Kiwis duetted on the slopes of Manaia. A schnarfle crescendoed above their whistle and screech. I followed it to the fence, stretched the barbed wire with my boot, and slipped into the paddock. I was halfway out of the USA in my expectations and halfway into a kinder, gentler Kiwi mind-set, betwixt and between. But either way, this was trespassing.

The cozy aroma of frying onions whiffled from Ngaere's quarters at the back of the dairy. A wheeze filtered through the datura. I was on the trail of the Big Snore! I chased after a snort and a grunt, and in the beam of my flashlight, snoring in the kikuyu grass, there it was—the kunekune pig. I giggled. I whooped. I tossed it the sandwich.

My love affair with New Zealand began with that pig. Who wouldn't embrace a country where an expedition in darkest night didn't lead to a hobo or an ax murderer but just an ugly porcine mug?

Like a cat's purr or the wag of a dog's tail, the snore was a comfort. It made me smile at three o'clock in the morning when it hit just how far away I'd flung myself from my daughter, now years past the first word, first step, first joint, and blossoming into an upright member of *Homo sapiens*. It took my mind off my aging parents, independent still, but who knew how much longer they could totter along? On account of the pig, I stopped by the Whangarei Town Basin one night, and that changed history for a couple of people, maybe three, more like four.

I romanticized the pig. Friends asked after the pig, and it became a sort of international celebrity. "Is your pig snoring tonight?" I attached photos to emails, and they begged for more. "*Ewww*! It's so big! It's so gross! Send me another shot!"

The pig helped me stick it out during those awkward months that were so lonely my skin ached, when nothing was done by rote, when I careened thirty kilometers from Whangarei clinic to the Heads, winding along the harbor on an unaccustomed side of the road without guardrails, hugging the cat's-eye reflectors in the centerline to guide me in the rainy darkness to home by Taurikura Bay.

The sweet snoring pig seduced me to stay in New Zealand longer than advisable, past all harmony with the northern hemisphere and into a vulnerability that led to a spot of bother, a world of trouble, and a decade of doing the splits across the equator. It was all the pig's fault, you see, and my undoing.

AT THE BUTCHER COUNTER OF LIFE

The pig snored for the hamlet of Taurikura. Sawing logs, it paid homage to Manaia and the Man in the Moon, who would smile down seventeen hours later on my family and friends, who were thinking, I hoped, of me. It hailed the vessels that rounded the crook in the harbor channel, so it must have snored for *Jingle Bells* and her skipper on their way to Whangarei.

Date: April 26, 2000
To: Jim C.
Subject: The Soft Side of Hard Men

Easter and Anzac Day don't always coincide to make a long weekend, so I am one lucky worker bee. I had a choice to spend the holiday writing or visiting a real Kiwi dairy farm. Being a writer yourself, you know I picked the field trip. I pinned a red felt poppy to my lapel, like everyone else who donated a gold coin to commemorate the landing of the Australian and New Zealand Army Corps in Gallipoli during World War I, and drove eighty-seven kilometers west to Dargaville, near a shipwreck-strewn coast on the Tasman Sea.

Adrienne, who works at the corporate office, invited me to lunch at her friend's spread. She's built like an opera diva and has refined Auckland tastes. Peter's a Napoleon-size man of few words, a "meat and three" guy. That's standard fare here: a trio of root vegetables roasted with a lump of meat until it's gray. He has very unruly eyebrows.

Adrienne made quiche and salad for lunch, which horrified Peter into a torrent of conversation. "That's rabbit tucker! Where's the good wholesome bachelor food, the deviled sausages, my toad in the hole?"

"Well I don't think much of your cheese cutter, so there!" Adrienne pointed to a cap hanging by the door.

"It's a bloody good hat."

"It makes you look like Steptoe."

Peter grinned and warmed to this comparison to some rag-and-bone man from an old British sitcom. He's been separated from his wife for a while and is heading for divorce.

It was raining horizontally by late afternoon. North of Auckland, the driving's all two-lane, whipping up and down hills and around hairpin curves. I wasn't prepared to negotiate the trip home with zero visibility, so I spent the night.

Adrienne woke me up at four thirty. Peter had already had first breakfast. "Cups on at five!" he shouted, took one look at my city shoes, and said, "Won't do." He lent me gumboots, and I jumped behind him on the quad, a position of honor normally reserved for the dog. We fishtailed down to the milking shed as dawn broke through a smokestack of clouds and turned the puddles pink.

I got to see a cattle dog work. To ear-piercing whistles, Peter's huntaway, Track, barked and moved the cows accordingly: stop, get away back, come in, walk up. (Track used to be called Mack until he got run over, which hasn't appeared to slow him down.) Over morning tea, I told Peter I was impressed.

"Nah-ow-oo," he protested. That's how they say *no* here, with as many vowels as possible. "You shoulda seen me other two."

"Tell her about Tommy and Meg," Adrienne said, and added in a stage whisper, "They went everywhere with him. He treats his dogs better than his women."

"Maybe the dogs are easier to talk to," Peter suggested.

Adrienne ignored this. "They were up at the new dam, and Peter didn't take any notice when the dogs buggered off up the gully."

"I just give 'em a pat now and then to remind me they're there—"

"That night Peter fed and watered them, tied the dogs to their kennels, as usual."

"Come out the next morning to find Meg stretched out at the end of her chain. Tommy had dug himself under the fence. It's a horrible death by 1080, just horrible—"

"Regional Authority had laid bait and missed one of the carcasses."

"Didn't know they'd found the possum. If only—"

"Murray came by, remember, Peter? He asked you what the hell happened—"

"I told Murray, 'I just lost me two best friends.'"

I saw seven rainbows in one day in Dargaville, and Peter let me keep the gumboots. He and Adrienne are going to drive over to Taurikura next weekend with a load of macrocarpa firewood. Adrienne called and asked if I had a good time and what I thought of Peter.

She said indignantly, "He's not even fifty, and he's making himself an old man!" I knew she was itching to trim his eyebrows and domesticate him.

Date: April 27, 2000
To: Anne B.
Subject: *Z-Z-Z-Z-Z*
Attached: The culprit behind the Big Snore

My snooping paid off, and the mystery's solved. Pig's the game. Highway's the name—ever since Ngaere rescued her from the side of the road seven years ago. It took five men to transport her, and when they tried to shift her into the paddock, Highway escaped from the front-end loader, charged it twice, and walked through the gate on her own.

I don't know if it's the beginning of a beautiful friendship. We probably won't go out to lunch like you and I used to do in Kansas City, but it's nice to have her in the paddock next door.

Chapter 3

When I call into port, the first thing I do is stake out my pub.
 —#6, God's Holding Paddock

At Parua Bay, conveniently located halfway between Whangarei clinic and the Heads, there was a pub. It sat on a blind curve, sandwiched between the water and the road, and had sat there since the 1880s in one form or another: dairy factory, hotel, restaurant, tavern.

Parua Bay Tavern's two white stories were spruced up with red trim, and petunias grew in boxes on the balcony under the beer advert, Lion Red, the Measure of a Man's Thirst. Rounding the bend in autumn, I could see its jetty stretching into the bay. In winter, the windows of the ground-floor bar shone with genial light, an altogether welcoming sight between a long day at work and no one waiting at home except a snoring pig. But I only rubbernecked and passed up the pub for three months. Was it the kind of place a lady could happily drop in unaccompanied?

Until the 1970s, a woman's traditional place in New Zealand was at home, a man's, the paid workforce and pub. It was men-only in the public bar of hotels and taverns. Women were allowed in the more upscale lounge bar (it had chairs), but beer cost more, so it was a show of commitment for a fellow to take his girl out for a drink. Respectable women didn't drink solo when they went out. If ladies nipped sherry, they nipped at home.

Change, however, was a-comin'. The women's liberation movement rumbled onto the horizon. New Zealand feminist Sue Kedgley informed the Labour Party Conference in 1972, "It is not your penis we have been envying all these years, but your freedom." Women stormed the stag bars at the Great Northern Hotel in Auckland and Wellington's Victoria Tavern in pub liberations in the early 1970s and demanded service. Other bastions took longer.

It's known on good authority that "the endangered males of Northland Club in Whangarei fell victim to women seeking the long-term misery of men in 1996. It was the third to last male-only club in New Zealand to allow ladies membership, and it's been downhill ever since. All the poor bastards wanted was to drink in peace, free of female company and ringing phones. We loved them, but this replaced the silken cord around our necks with barbed wire someplace else."

It was the repeal of the six o'clock swill, however, passed by referendum on October 9, 1967, that really paved the way for equal-opportunity drinking. With its demise, the pub took on a more civilized spirit because it resembled a lavatory less.

For fifty years the six o'clock swill had defined New Zealand public drinking, crammed into one meager, manly hour starting on-your-marks-get-set-go after work and finishing when the pub closed at precisely 6:00 p.m. The restriction started out as a temporary wartime measure in 1917, prodded along by temperance enthusiasts who reasoned that "a well-ordered, self-disciplined, and morally upright home front was a precondition for the successful prosecution of the war." The intent was to encourage patriotic sobriety. The effect, naturally, was just the opposite.

Beer cascaded at the pub. It sloshed. It swashed. It spilled. It slopped in the attempt to guzzle as much as humanly possible in one hour. Husbands might have come home early, but they arrived reeking of beer and stinking drunk. It's rumored that in more expedient establishments, a man had only to dip and slide his handle through a trough of beer to fill 'er up, although the oldsters protest, "Never in New Zealand, mate. Maybe *Australia*." The Kiwis who were actually there will tell you more cunning than that was involved in the six o'clock swill.

"As soon as I got to the pub, I ordered three jugs up front and set them between my legs. All I had to worry about was emptying them into my glass before the six o'clock bell." (There were five "sevens," a seven-ounce glass, to a jug. When you do the math, it boggles the mind.)

For those less inclined to plan ahead, the barkeep replenished glasses from a barrel of no-name draft chained behind the bar, or when the system got streamlined, from a permanently cocked beer gun. Trays of refills got passed through the crowd like laurelled athletes. A man rarely got his own glass back, and no one cared as panic mounted and the clock ticked toward the bartender's cry, "Last call! Drink up!"

"Then you ordered a flagon, threw it over your shoulder, and staggered off to your place, joyously, happily pissed." Nod to the home front, no doubt.

The police often stopped by to make sure there was no sly grog. They were less strict in country pubs, and you can get one version or another of this story from any man on the North or South Island:

"I was sitting with this bloke after six," at Aratapu or Parua Bay Tavern, say.

"'How about another, mate?' he asked me.

"'I don't know. What if the cops surprise us?'

"'They won't.'

"'How can you be so sure they won't?'

"'Because I'm the constable.'"

I finally stopped at Parua Bay Tavern in early winter with a prod from my daughter, the first of only four visitors from home in the next nine years. (It's something to consider if you decide to move seven and a half thousand miles away to find yourself: family and friends will have difficulty finding *you*.)

"Come on, Mama, I can't believe you could pass up a pub." Laura had ulterior motives. At nineteen, she was still a minor in the States. The novelty of drinking legally (eighteen in New Zealand) must have appealed to her. She was a college student, after all.

We parked in front of the pub, where spaces were usually available on a quiet afternoon, poked our noses into the vestibule, and read the guidelines, clearly posted:

NO CHILDREN ALLOWED ON THESE PREMISES AFTER 7 PM
REMOVE YOUR MUDDY GUMBOOTS PLEASE

The patrons had dutifully left their gummies at the door. Back then Parua Bay Tavern was a "rough pub," a workingman's pub.

We stepped into a dim barroom that smelled of old ashes and fresh beer. The bartender called out, "G'day," and two men conversing with him raised their brews in modest hello. One had a magnificent nacre-white beard. He looked like Father Christmas, except for the bare feet and coveralls. This immediately set me at ease, indicative of my starry-eyed thinking back then. Because a guy resembles Santa, the bar where he is drinking must be a safe place to take my daughter?

His companion wore paint-flecked shorts, a nubbly sweater his wife had likely knitted, and jandals, the New Zealand equivalent of flip-flops. Both were typically attired for labor in Northland, the northernmost governmental region of New Zealand, the "Winterless North."

An elfish man at the end of the bar gave us a big smile, but we got no notice from a pair of craggy guys with eyebrows that would have done a schnauzer proud. The terriers each had a pitcher of hard cider in front of them, deep in discussion over their sevens in a smaze. The smoking ban in pubs would not be enacted for three and a half more years, in the summer of 2004, another landmark day for pub goers.

No one was at the pokie machines in a nook off the barroom. The back room was empty except for two men shooting pool. Through the mullioned windows, the reflections of the yachts and fishing boats at anchor did not quiver—it was that still—and Parua Bay had the verdigris shimmer of an exemplary cold and sunny June day.

"Won't you join us?" the older of two men at a table near the door offered. "We're harmless," he said with a roguish smile, and his glasses and dentures were so large in relation to his gaunt face and sagging dimples that the overall effect was indeed innocuous.

Laura and I shrugged. *Why not? They're harmless.*

Little English John introduced himself and then his dimpled companion, who hauled milk for Kauri Dairy. He was a horse whisperer as well and on account of all the sex appeal that attends the métier, or the dimples, had earned the nickname Sexy Rexy.

"I'm not just a pretty face, Johnny."

"You're not even a pretty face, Rexy."

This spindle of a man with a persistent cough and gray hair cropped in a midcentury cut must have had his nickname for a very long time.

"We'll shift to God's Holding Paddock once Dick gets here." Rex gestured to a table in front of the cold fireplace. "His wife makes him go to the pub every night." He reflected a moment to give the generosity and intelligence of this act due respect. "'It's good for you, Dick,' Joan tells him, 'but it's better for me.'"

"God's Holding Paddock?"

"Been an institution here for donkey's yonks, so long that no one can remember who started it. I think maybe Dick. Come by some night, darlin', and check out the average age of the men sitting there. We're getting on. You never know whose chair might be empty the next time you stop by, but can you think of a better place to wait for roundup day?"

I told Rex I could not.

"What more could a man ask for? Spend a night at God's Holding Paddock, wake up, and you're still in God's Own, New Zealand." Rex picked up his beer and thumbed the blue plastic tag labeled #9 on the handle while he contemplated his good fortune. Overcome, all he could say was, "Sweet as."

The conversation turned to men and women as it usually does. "We'll never win the war between the sexes. Too much fraternizing with the enemy."

"No, Johnny, you've got it wrong. It's about the shoes."

"How's that, Rexy?"

"Say a couple goes to a dance. The woman frets over her hair and what she'll wear and consequently misses the whole point of dancing. When a man looks back on the evening, he remembers the slow dances, and the woman wonders, 'How did I look in my dancing shoes?'

"Put any group of men together the next day, and the first thing they'll ask their mate is 'How close did you get to hold her when you danced?' That's the real question." It was such a sensitive observation that I had to reconsider my benchmark for sexy.

I returned to Parua Bay Tavern a few weeks later with my husband, Jack, who had scheduled a visit when he was hit by the overwhelming number of Q-tips still left in the box. We parked in a lot across the road. Rain drowned out the sound of traffic, and any approaching headlights were invisible around the bend through the trees.

"Safe?" he asked.

"I think so."

He took my little hand in his, and we crossed the road in a leap of faith.

The scene in the pub was lively compared to that first sleepy afternoon. The crowd had swelled to a full contingent of regulars whose conviviality gained steam as they commenced their third and fourth beers.

"Here, you can sit here, girl," the man at the head of God's Holding Paddock said as he rose, and motioned to a seat on the bench next to him, facing the fireplace, now ablaze with the heat of a single massive

Kauri log. His face was wind-battered red, and he was about seventy, although he moved with the square-shouldered grace of a navy boy.

I slid in next to him at the head of the table. "Thank you. You must be Dick."

"You must be the American girl. The bush telegraph said you might come back."

Rex offered a chair to Jack, and they introduced themselves around the table, each man in his customary spot with his numbered "handle," or beer mug. Big English John had a fine Yorkshire accent. Lenny, a diminutive fellow with white, bristle-brush hair, said something about "born in Fiji," although he looked to be of European descent, like the rest. He mumbled so earnestly that I made that rolling gesture one does with the hand to encourage him to elaborate on certain startling bits like "so painful a man will beg to have his foot cut off." In fact, I had no idea what he was talking about.

Dick later interpreted what was definitely a pet peeve, this story he had heard a hundred times. Many years ago in the islands, Lenny had trod on a stonefish, the most venomous fish in the world, and lived to tell about it, again and again and again.

Ron was coordinator of the pub's fishing club. Parua Bay Tavern was the first weigh-in station in Northland. Boats and fishing figure prominently anywhere in New Zealand, a country with more than nine thousand miles of coastline and no spot more than eighty miles from the sea. He had organized that night's raffle and held out a butcher tray of mixed grill for inspection—"Meat pack tonight, mates!"—while everyone enthusiastically searched his pockets for a gold coin.

Kevin, "the bean counter" with one blind eye, put down his handle (tagged #28) and shook hands. Then he got back to bemoaning the repeal of a rule of thumb that allowed a man, for purposes of moderate correction, to beat his wife with a stick under one inch in diameter. Pete, "the train driver," lifted his beer (#21) in a cheerful hello and confirmed that the biggest advantage of his job was that he couldn't take his work home.

"I always get here at seventeen hundred hours, more or less," Dick said, "so I can hold the table. Don't want to lose it to some family stopping by at the end of the day with their sprats and sprogs. Some people don't understand this is no place for kids, and most of them can't curb the little buggers, anyway. I don't drink and smoke in their kindergarten, so why should they run and shriek in my pub?"

"Dick has the best seat in the house. He's got the fire in winter, and in summer he can see through their dresses when the girls come in the door."

"But they don't wear dresses much anymore, do they, Rex? A shame.

"I had my honeymoon up there"—Dick pointed to the ceiling to indicate the story above us—"back in 1952 when it was a hotel. I'm the oldest member of God's Holding Paddock . . . now that's a worry!"

Lenny was about to say something. These two clearly went way back, and seniority was a bone of contention, but he didn't push it. Dick sat at the head of the table in more ways than one. Instead Lenny scooted back his chair, went to the bar, and bought a jug of takeaway beer. Hobbling off, pockets jangling from an apparently successful run at the pokie machines, he bid us, "Good night, children."

Jack and I stopped by the pub most nights after that. Before he returned to the States, Dick promised him, "We'll look after her, mate," and that was that. I was a junior member of God's Holding Paddock. I had my own handle (#39) and a bodyguard who showed up with his wife's blessing every night at five o'clock sharp, showered, shaved, in a pink singlet, dress shirt, and pants pressed with military creases.

From then on, my car never seemed to make it past that bend in the road without pulling into Parua Bay Tavern. No matter how tired, I said to myself, *Oh, just one*, and I was never disappointed, ever. Shivering that winter, like the little matchstick girl in a story with a happier ending, I burst into the radiance of the fellowship and the fire as Dick or

Rex called out, "Look what the gale blew in!" Or six months later on a balmy evening, a mere eighty degrees, Dick confirmed from his catbird seat, "It's hotter than the hobs of hell here in summer, didn't we tell you? Better sit down, girl, and cool off with a beer."

Dick might offer some terse comment on the passersby: this one's got deep pockets and short arms, or that one acted the right maggot last night. He'd complain after Lenny went home, "He comes in with dollar bills and has the bartender change them for coins to play the pokies. Then he's impressed with how much money he made because his pockets are noisier at the end of the night."

Pete might launch into an ex-mother-in-law story. "It was a sad indictment of my marriage: I think I was falling in love with her. She was the only one in the family who watched the news. We stayed on good terms even after the divorce. I told her once, 'I'd like to come back as your cat, Thelma,' and she said, 'Sure, Pete, but you must realize the first thing I would do is get you neutered.'"

The men at God's Holding Paddock rarely swore in front of women. (On their own, it was a different matter.) Ngaere's son, Max, ear studded and head shaved, parked his motorcycle in front of the pub one night and came in with a pet possum hidden in his leather jacket. Dick thought he was "mad as a gumdigger's dog," but he welcomed Mad Max at the table because he knew, the Harley and marsupial aside, that he would behave like a gentleman. Dick once asked a foul-mouthed Australian to leave "because you don't talk that way in front of a lady," and that lady was #39, God's Holding Paddock.

Dick had one rule as head of the table: an evening at the pub is meant to make you feel better when you are already well. He kept people to it. Bellyachers, snivelers, and whingers were not tolerated. If I got carried away recounting the woes of the day, Dick put a quick stop to it: "You'd worry sheep." It may have been thirty-three years since the last six o'clock swill, but the deep-rooted tradition of pub as male sanctuary lingered. Somehow I understood this and tried to act accordingly. That is why I got to sit at the right hand of Dick at God's Holding Paddock. That, and Dick was a gentleman.

Now as to harmless. A wise friend of mine told me that women get carried away trying to understand men. Really, it's pretty simple. They just want to feel dangerous. And what is danger after all but opportunity with a buzz, a cloudburst brewing with the promise of hail to put some marble-sized dents in the monotony of the good life. It's horseplay, tall tales, fish stories, and long shots parlayed into endless possibilities. It's the havoc a man thinks he might wreak, with luck, and especially the havoc he thought he wrought. It's the get-my-blood-pumpin'-sweet-mama exhilaration of youth.

Hearsay had it that Rex had jumped the fence, but Dick defended him. "Never when he and his wife were living together, although I wouldn't rule out a hop-on after they separated."

"A hop-on?" I asked.

"That's a bonk after a break-up, but you'd never pay to take her to Australia."

Rex might have had hop-ons. Dick might admire the view through the flimsy dresses. Pete loved to recall the days when he was "wandering around dangering everyone." Kevin went on about the ideal tidy woman. But in the end, these were men of honor who loved their women. They adhered to simple codes like, as Dick put it, "Somewhere along the line, you've got to dig a latrine."

Another might elaborate, "But you need to be aware that some people won't."

Someone would add, "And you had better take that fact into account when you choose your friends."

Dick would take a draft from his handle, #6, and round off the discussion, which was getting too weighty, "But a lot of people don't go that deep into human relationships." Then he would light up a cigarette or excuse himself for a smoke outside, depending on which side of December 10, 2004, it happened to be.

Date: August 1, 2000
To: Laura P.
Subject: Leather Balls

I watched my first rugby game on TV at the pub, our All Blacks vs. the Australian Wallabies. As you know, I've never been a fan of organized sports. Until tonight. I saw the light.

Tana Umaga scored in the first three minutes. Two hundred twenty pounds, six feet of tempered steel constrained only by short shorts and a black jersey bedecked with a silver fern. No helmets, no shoulder pads—and definitely no cups—for our men. When they packed down the scrum, close and deep, steam rising in the frosty air, I had my athletic revelation.

They should have sung the "Hallelujah Chorus" as far as I was concerned, but the All Blacks performed the haka before the match as the team has done for over a century, and as Maoris kicked off wars long before that. It would scare the bejesus out of anyone: three thousand pounds of foot-stomping, thigh-slapping, eye-bulging, tongue-wagging, testosterone-charged oomph, fifteen drop-dead splendiferous specimens of sportsmanliness (fair, courteous, good-tempered too!) grunting, shouting, chanting, trembling from the sheer concentration of all that choreographed brawn.

The Wallaby fans responded with "Waltzing Matilda." "Waltzing Matilda!" How pathetic. Even a convert could tell who was gonna win.

Date: August 16, 2000
To: Anne B.
Subject: A Tidy Woman
Attached: REMOVE YOUR MUDDY GUMBOOTS PLEASE

Kevin is a bantam of a man and resident misogynist at God's Holding Paddock, in spite of the fact that he is happily married, in spite of the fact that his wife drove her car in a fit of anger into the wall of their basement garage and knocked the house off its foundation. Tonight he was extolling the virtues of a tidy woman.

A tidy woman? This intrigued me because if it's been that easy all along to please a man, and a misogynist at that (what, brush your teeth and comb your hair), I could have saved myself a lot of time and trouble.

"What exactly is a tidy woman, Kevin?"

"It's a female who is useable, and I can tell you they aren't thick on the ground. She has huge attributes."

"Oh, I see—"

"No, not a scrubber. A tidy woman is never a scrubber."

"So it's about more than sex?"

"Definitely. A tidy woman never tells a man what to do. If she's an all-around natural nester, it's a real bonus."

"But she has to be attractive, right?"

"She doesn't have to look like a double-dip strawberry ice cream cone, but there shouldn't be any ass hanging over the barstool. If you check out the front versus the back, it should indicate which way she's going. The main thing is she shouldn't make you a more miserable bugger than you already are. She makes you happy, not delirious, but happy enough. She's good value, you see?"

I was beginning to think that Kevin was just an old softie.

"She can pick you up or drop you down," he continued.

"And if she drops you down?"

Kevin paused. "My usual solution to relationship problems: elephant gun at twenty paces. It's all bullshit and jelly beans, anyway."

Chapter 4

Love at first sight is only lust, worth not much more than diamond dust.
—#39, God's Holding Paddock

Dick was born in 1930 and raised in Devonport on the North Shore of Auckland. He met his wife when he was twenty. Joan must have bowled him over, ten years his senior, a grenade assembler fresh off the boat on a relocation plan for work after World War II. She was a £10 Pom, one of thousands who paid ten pounds sterling for a one-way ticket to Australia or New Zealand in search of a better life than postwar Great Britain. Joan figured, "If I stayed in Wales, I'd be a spinster the rest of me life." She embarked on the S.S. *Atlantis* and steamed eleven and a half thousand miles from home—a long way to go to find a sweetie, but it worked.

Joan wasn't a regular at the pub, but the men at God's Holding Paddock adored her. How could they not? She danced on tables. The woman made her husband go to the pub. She appeared to be lost at the Honolulu airport once and, when queried by some well-intentioned busybody if she had ever traveled before, responded tartly, "How the bloody hell do you think I got here from Wales?"

Dick earned his chief engineer's ticket in his twenties and must have had ample opportunities in a maritime career to stray. He got nostalgic one night at the pub remembering a certain barmaid at Aggie Grey's in Samoa. "It was like the sun came up when she took your order. She was plain, but she made your day beautiful."

Rex jumped in. "Now when Dick talks about going ashore, I want to make it clear he was straight up in regards to his wife, God's truth."

Joan never learned to drive, which must have limited the prospects for any monkey business on her part. Dick had tried to teach her but gave up after the first lesson.

"Would you be comfortable driving down this metal road at eighty Ks?"

"Well of course not, Dick."

"Then you'd better slow down, girl."

I went over for a cuppa one Saturday afternoon to meet Joan. The visit got the ball rolling for many invitations to come—"Let's continue on continuing on"—with Dick and Joan after I left the pub.

They had built a spacious, no-frills house on a coastal section at Parua Bay and named it in Welsh, Sound of the Sea. From Sŵn y Môr, it was a ten-minute drive to the pub—along a lane where Tom the goat kept the grass under control, past a shingle beach, up Ritchie Road, and down Darkey's Hill. Dick's car probably knew the way by heart.

On the back deck with a bag of bread, Joan was tossing bits to the pukekos, and I got introduced in a flurry of dopey swamphens making a fuss. She suggested that Dick show me the barbie (his pride and joy) and offered to make coffee after that.

Crooning, "Here, eelie, eels," she headed with the last two slices to a pond damned on the hill.

"She has them trained to come when she calls," Dick said with a fondness implying that the eels admired her as much as he did—and the bread was immaterial.

"Instant, Dick, or shall I get out the percolator?" Joan called back.

"By all means, get out the percolator!"

On a grass verge, there was an old city bus where Dick and Joan had stayed when they built their home, with two sons grown up and out and two more to raise at Sŵn y Môr. Dick had tacked on a barbeque shed made from corrugated iron, cinder blocks, orphan windows, and surely countless pieces of farm wire, the foundation of Kiwi resourcefulness. Give 'em a piece of number 8, and they can do anything. It was easy to imagine Dick stoking the fire, sausages sizzling on the big griddle, and most of the smoke curling up the flue.

On special occasions, they roasted a pig on a spit or put down a hangi in Maori fashion, steaming baskets of meat, fish, and veggies in a pit oven while they drank copious amounts of beer. "Once in a while, we unearthed the damned thing and discovered it wasn't hot enough to steam a mussel," Dick said. "Then we had to bring up the sober drunk to drive to the dairy for fish 'n' chips. Sausages are more dependable."

Joan, in her best housedress, joined us in the second-floor lounge, took a dramatic look around, and said, "I did a big tidy up. I didn't know the place was so nice, Dick." We sat down to coffee and biscuits on chairs that were covered with skins from sheep raised in their paddock and sparse from years of use. Dick pointed to a picture on the wall.

"That's Kidwelly Castle in Joan's hometown in Wales. When we visited her twin sister and husband, I found an exceptional pub in Kidwelly. By the end of the first night, everyone knew my name. The relatives weren't drinkers, and they had tea at six o'clock." He repeated "six o'clock," and shook his head in dismay. "I never eat until I'm done with my beer. Fortunately they were very hospitable and set out a plate for me to heat up when I got back from the Boot and Shoe. It was a wonderful visit, just wonderful. There is a fellowship among drinkers around the world, and it's easy to feel at home once you stake out your pub."

Dick had just buried Meg, a seventeen-year-old cocker spaniel, and could not speak of her without tearing up. They were left with Bess, a seventy-pound German shepherd mix beginning to falter in the hindquarters, and Jed, a sweet-tempered Rottweiler that got ice cream for lunch and an entire Butch Dog Roll for dinner. Jed used to take blind old Meg's lead in his mouth and guide her home from the shores of Parua Bay, and Dick described the scene with such reverence, it was as if he had seen it for the very first time.

The dogs patrolled the table, and now and then Dick tossed a Butternut Snap to one of them, and Joan said with mock reproach, "Dick!" before she did the same.

"Lucky dogs," I said.

"No," Dick said. "I'm the lucky one. They don't owe me anything. I owe them."

I asked Joan how she and Dick had met.

"My girlfriend and I went to a dance the Masons had sponsored six weeks after I got off the boat. We were talking when Dick and his pal walked in. Dick said to Harry, 'I'll take the tall one,' and I said to Nell, 'I'll take the one on the left,' and he's been me toy boy ever since.

"We still shower together—so we can check and make sure all our parts are still there. Sex is the spice of life." She was eighty then, with a puckish grin, if not a full complement of teeth, and smiled at Dick for confirmation.

"And it's free if you put your mind to it," he added, putty, even now, in the old grenade-assembler's hands.

I asked Joan if it was true that she danced on tables.

"Aw, I only did it once. Had to stop. It scared the fellas. They were terrified I'd do a striptease every time I came to the pub. 'What's it gonna do?' someone would ask.

"'It's gonna get on the table and take off its gear,' someone would answer, and they'd all shudder and get up for another beer."

It was common knowledge at the pub—and further cause for esteem—that Joan served Dick breakfast in bed every morning. I asked him what that entailed.

"Scrambled eggs and devilled kidneys, Weet-Bix and cream, steamed fruit, black Doris plums from our tree out back, fishy things."

"Fishy things?"

"Like kippers."

Dick noted the flamingo sunset over Parua Bay, and said, "Sun's over the yardarm." He poured Joan and me each three fingers of homemade gin (concocted by Ron of the pub) and mixed it with a fruit drink reminiscent of Tang. Joan brought Dick a Lion Red, put out soda crackers, crunchy, home-pickled onions, and an economy block of Tasty Cheddar carved into neat cubes. It was the stuff of a pensioner's budget and laid out with enough generosity to make a heart high-jump.

Dick recalled how Joan had panicked before their wedding when it dawned on her, "Where are we going to live, Dick?"

"I said, 'Joan, I've bought us a house!'" Forty-eight years later, he still lit up at the surprise he had organized for his bride. "I bought that house on Takapuna Beach for eight hundred pounds, sight unseen. There was no indoor plumbing, but it had a long drop. I sealed the deal in the pub at the Marine Esplanade. Drew out cash from the post office, put it on the bar, took the key from the man who owned the house, and then we shook hands. That's how it was done in those days, easy as that."

"That's pricey real estate now. Imagine what it would be worth today," I said, and Dick looked at me incredulously, like the dumb American I was, ignorant about the fishy things on your breakfast tray and who was really the lucky dog, missing the whole point of life. With a sweep of his hand, Dick indicated all the riches and memories that Sŵn y Môr was and ever had been: the spot where the boys had pinched the family dinghy to smoke pot in the mangroves, the barbeques, Meg's grave, the showers together to check each other's parts, how nice the place looked after a big tidy up.

"All the beachfront property on the North Shore doesn't compare to this. The only color in Auckland is the taillights." Dick took out a new pack of Pocket Edition and scoffed at the Health Department warning:

SMOKING KILLS
Ka mate koe i te
kai hikareti

He refilled his battered tin with enough left over to lay a line of tobacco down the center of a Rizla Yellow paper, snug against a Boomerang Slim Filter, licked the glue strip, and rolled a cigarette for Joan. Then he cupped his hand over an intricate brass lighter that number-two son had given him, and leaned in to give her a light—with a look that any woman, any age, would like to be on the receiving end of.

He lit his own cigarette, dropped some ash on the floor, and said, "Bollocks."

And Joan told him, "I'll have none of your engine-room talk in my house."

Dick reached to the buffet for a plush-toy Shar-Pei that one of the grandkids had given Joan. He pushed a button in its paw, and it bounced and rapped "Who Let the Dogs Out" in a battery-operated falsetto until Joan got so tickled she said, "Stop it, or I'll wet me pants!"

When Dick finished his last beer, Joan got up and surreptitiously removed the plastic wrap from two plates sitting by the microwave, divided the steak-and-kidney pie into three portions, and asked me to stay for dinner.

Dick went over to the turntable, pulled out an LP, and put on some Louis Armstrong, "What a Wonderful World."

AT THE BUTCHER COUNTER OF LIFE

Date: August 19, 2000
To: Laura P.
Subject: One More for the Swing of the Door
Attached: Joan and her toy boy the night they met

At God's Holding Paddock this evening, Rex inquired about Joan. Dick said, "She was fine when I left her last night. I rolled her four cigarettes and poured a gin like I always do, and then I put the phone on the dining table, so she could call her sister in Wales. But I got a fright when I came back from the pub. She was lying on the floor under the table. When I said, 'Joan!' she didn't answer, so I crawled down there with her. She woke up, and I asked her what she was doing there, and do you know what she told me?

"She said, 'I dropped me ciggy, Dick, and when I got down here, it was so comfy, I decided to stay for a while.'"

Dick shook his head. "I might as well be sitting on the blowhole of a whale. Now let's have one more for the swing of the door, and then I'd best get home and see what my girl's been up to tonight."

Chapter 5

It's hard to look both ways when you're standing at a blind bend in the road.
—#9, God's Holding Paddock

Getting the mail at Ngaere's was as good as a trip to the zoo, but I flinched at the sight of the raw-grated-beet pile that lurked under the bun of every hamburger I ordered. The dissonance of Kiwi cuisine was beginning to outweigh the novelty of visiting a talking bird down the lane. I was sick of kumara, New Zealand's adored and anemic sweet potato, and had listened to *War and Peace* five times. I couldn't find a new dress that wasn't made of polyester. There is a trade-off for the simplicity of midcentury lifestyle, and it is midcentury fashion. The double rainbows and fogbows of New Zealand winter had ceased to astound me. Bracing for each chockablock day, it soon became evident that I had replaced a banal and stressful job with—ta-da—a banal and stressful job, although the scenery on the way to work had certainly improved.

Granted, no one had told me to fuck off yet, like that old man in Kansas City who had been dragged in by some well-meaning family member. My patients here were far more entertaining: plucky grandmothers, wild-boar stalkers, possum trappers, nine-fingered farmers, skippers eager to get back to their boats, woolly-capped codgers who fished in the surf. They all had tales to tell.

"Used to inseminate elephants . . . freeze the sperm . . . it'll last a hundred years . . . now dog sperm . . . quite resistant . . . you can store that in your pocket . . ."

"Grandad was a Dali... came out from the Adriatic Coast to dig for Kauri gum... fossilized in swamps for tens of thousands of years... key ingredient for varnish in the day... talk about living rough..."

"He might have been Champion Axman to the rest of Northland, but he was gentle Jack Murray to me... sitting on a log shooting wild goats... I was sixteen... asked him what he'd do with the money he'd saved... why, Ruth, I'm going to marry you... almost shot my foot off... started married life on Great Barrier Island... and did you know a cork is handy to push a needle through the scalp when a logger cracks his head...?"

The worst anyone had to say was, "The missus died since I saw you last, just when I had her trained up right." These Kiwis cocked their heads and reminisced because they had all the time in the world to tell me, "You know, I've had a good life." It was beginning to dawn on me, however, that I had merely succeeded in trading a dilemma back home for a boondoggle abroad.

Before I left for New Zealand, I had been teetering on the apex of middle age, as muddled, full of puff, wind, and rabbit tracks as a teenager. It felt like the last-chance summit. I wanted security. I wanted adventure. I wanted to matter on this planet, dammit, before the lights went out. I was brimming with panic and perimenopausal glee. In short, I was crazy as a loon. And the padstones of my childhood had already proven to be puny foundation for life in general, let alone bearing the weight of this midlife stretch.

My family had moved around when I was growing up. My parents bickered. They bickered in Massachusetts. They bickered in Tennessee. They bickered across California and New York State. They had even bickered in southern France. Bickering was my nursery rhyme.

"Babes in the Wood" was my lullaby. Every night, with a soprano chirp, Mom spun out the tale, pretty much a downward spiral: two wee children, names unknown, left in the forest all alone, the sun went down, how sad their plight, the moon gave no light, they sobbed, sighed, bitterly cried, and finally—enough already—they lay down and died. No wait, not finished yet. The robins so red, strawberry leaves over them spread. Then she tucked me in with "Sweet dreams!" and left me in the dark.

In the obscurity, I brooded. At five, I knew that wolves prowled behind the attic walls of our house in Nashville, and if they slipped off the bare joists into the dusty, dirty insulation, they would crash right through the ceiling onto my bed. The bully next door had told me so. I dreamed—just once—that they did. Fangs bared, slavering, the pack jostled and circled, poised to pounce. I woke up before they attacked, but there was no relief in that. The scariest nightmares stick, not because of their preposterous scenarios, but because the feelings they conjure up are so real. The beasts may not have torn me to pieces, but the wolf dream stuck fast and implanted itself as a leaden kernel that weighed in somewhere between homesickness and dread.

I doubt that Dad was even aware of my dream, and Mom pooh-poohed it, having been dreamed only once, after all. Or maybe the wolf dream was flawed because it wasn't set to music.

One bedroom alone, in Aix-en-Provence, recalled any fond memories. Its ancient window sweated when Dad stoked the coal stove, a behemoth in the hall. Droplets coursed down the wallpaper below and added to the generations of stains. My brother and I slept on mattresses stuffed with straw, and it was all a great adventure for us. Our father was happy. He was teaching at the university and learning French, in his element, immersed in life. Our mother took her anxiety and regret with her wherever she went. But they were difficult to put a finger on, polished as they were to a mirthful veneer.

The field outside the bedroom window had just been planted in garlic, and a hint of it lingered. There was a boy across the lane, a boy who made my heart skip a beat when he swooped in on his bike with a flourish, home from school for the midday meal. He was called Jean-Pierre, and I wrote his name in my diary twenty times a day.

I was learning French too. I was beginning to notice things. Like boys. And how good food tastes, with all the sautéing and simmering that goes on in Provence, the farm-fresh produce, a riot of color at the market. My mother was a pressure-cooker cook and had for years delivered mounds of pallid meat and unidentifiable vegetables to the table without zest. In France, I discovered how wonderful peas can taste, lowly little green peas popped out of their pods right into the pan, with a knob of butter, dash of salt, and white pepper. And oh, the gutsy cassoulets and blancmanges light as a pinfeather, with a kick of kirsch!

When our family had arrived several months earlier at the house in the country outside Aix-en-Provence, my mother had laid a suitcase on my bed of straw. She opened it with gravity. It was lined with Kotex, taken out of the boxes and neatly stacked, in the manner of a bank-robber's cache.

"We need to be prepared. It could happen any day," she told me. Like war. Like women in France had no supplies to deal with a period. Like there was nothing more to the nebulous world of love and sex taking shape before me than bleeding monthly.

At night, when the bickering stopped and everyone was asleep, I got out of bed and crept to the sweating window. Being careful not to wake my brother, I turned the big brass knob to release the shootbolt, pushed open the panes, and slipped out. It was a ground-floor bedroom. Not a difficult maneuver. This was my first window on the world, and I was climbing through it.

Jean-Pierre was waiting for me under a chestnut tree. Our breath haloed in the frosty air. We kissed. The moon was full. It didn't worry us. There was nothing clandestine about this, except the trick of escaping before someone found out and derailed the fun. There was no shame—

this was France, after all. We were completely in the moment. It was all about the kissing, which seemed to go on forever. There was no escalation to fumbling or groping. There were no missteps. Just body-out-of-time bliss. It was the kind of kissing that is only possible when all you know about sex could fit in a Kotex-lined suitcase.

We returned to the States the following year, and I hit adolescence like a wall. My mother had started tinkering in earnest with family alliances. "It's inconvenient enough you're a good student. Now you want piano lessons?" *Tap-tap-tap.* "No, you're not taking music away from your brother too. Hell's bells, you're as bad as your father." *Tap-tap-tap* on the wedge.

I collected presents for the Christmas stockings. I made the stockings. As December 25 approached, if Mom or Dad or my brother fell short in the final count, I put my allowance in a red plastic coin purse and pedaled my bike to the shops to buy a bottle of Evening in Paris, a pack of unfiltered Camels, a cap gun, whatever it took to keep the love and loyalty titer up and even all around. (In my own stocking, big enough to accommodate better gifts, Santa left one apple in the toe, a pair of scratchy woolen shoe socks, and underpants bearing the names of the days of the week.)

Trailing anxiety and regret behind me—even my spoor was not my own at this point—I married young. Neither my husband nor I had been gifted by parental example with much of a marital skill set. Moreover, at nineteen, no one knows the stuff they are made of, even if they think they do, and the stuff probably hasn't been made yet anyway. Given all this, the marriage lasted surprisingly long, seventeen years. Six years after the birth of our daughter, it ended in divorce. By the time I was fifty, I had not made another successful attempt to climb through any more windows on the world.

But I did hit my stride and carved a niche in Kansas City as a single, working mother. For a decade, I had dated the love of my life, a classical music enthusiast with a degree in economics who decided early that he didn't want to sit on the twenty-sixth floor of Commerce Tower and watch the big rigs roll by. He wanted to drive one.

The truck driver wore a Scrooge top hat on Christmas Eve and played the curmudgeon all year long, but in truth would give a down-and-outer his last dime. He wept when dogs died, and he heard the bell. This used to be my all-time favorite expression for getting it, what life on this big blue marble is all about—hear the bell! It sprang from a concoction of Christmas stories, a broken bell off Santa's sleigh that chimes if you just believe, the jingle-bell ring of true love when a couple swaps sacrifices as precious as gold, frankincense, and bitter myrrh, that sort of thing.

Then, in 1999, one by one in quick succession, the fundaments of my cozy niche vanished. The doctors who had employed me as their audiologist for twenty years retired. I had dabbled at several reinventions and settled on writer but was constantly wrenched out of the fictional dream, late for my day job. Now I didn't even have a day job.

My daughter went off to college. I was still a mother, but my role was transforming at lightning speed. For thirteen years, I had baked bread from scratch. Why? Did I really believe that life after divorce would tick along smoothly as long as there was home cooking to be had? Did I not hear Laura moaning by third grade, "I want Wonder Bread like everyone else"? Maybe it was the era I was raised in, when Dick had seven rockets and Jane had five pies. Dick's eyes might have been on the stars, but the best plan I could come up with was to stick my head in the oven. Who was I cooking for now?

I realized early that the stork had dropped me off at the wrong address and consequently had invested a great deal of time yearning for something that felt like home. Seeking without directions for a place where you've never set foot is bound to be only marginally successful. What's more, it often plays mischief with those you meet along the way in your quest. The dithering and posturing that go along with the journey make it difficult to foster robust relationships. The truck driver was as close as I had come to finding true love and home.

But he never left so much as a pair of socks behind after he spent the night. He carted a change of clothes in a gym bag, and we broke up over it. We got back together because we missed the near-perfect fit, then he distanced himself, so did I, and we started the to-and-fro all over again.

Fifty looked like the end of the line back then. I needed the business of "I do" behind me, so it wasn't "I do today," which only makes a woman worry about tomorrow. There's more to life than hearing the bell, isn't there?

I gave up on the man who put rubber roaches in my bathroom sink and built a condom machine for our Truck Stop Hop. (Don't Be a Diesel Daddy! Tarp Your Load!) I walked away from the old curmudgeon who set up a train around the Christmas tree for the little girl in me who wanted the Lionel set her brother got, not a damned piece of fruit in a Christmas stocking's toe.

I married a big quiet engineer who said he'd like to see the world through the light in my eyes—and had used the same barber for thirty years. It was a mismatch conceived in blind optimism and the glow of the only happy surprise of midlife, its best-kept secret, the one that baffles the dewy ingénue, annoys the satyriscus in his cups, repulses your children, and alienates your celibate friends: you can still have hot sex. It was a decision that was fair to neither one of us.

I sold my 1950's bungalow, its rambling backyard graced with a stand of Scotch pines, Christmas trees planted before the divorce. I said good-bye to the musty basement where my daughter had set up camp during her Goth phase. I bid farewell to the Victorian treehouse that the love of my life had built, entwined in the branches of a hedge-apple tree. Reeling, I closed the door on all the laughter and heartache that are bound to seep into the walls of a home you have tended for years and know like the baby you diaper or the flesh and bones of the man you love.

AT THE BUTCHER COUNTER OF LIFE

I moved into a taupe split-level in the crabgrass suburbs with my new husband and rejoiced briefly, like a pack mule whose solitary burden has been lifted on a long and dusty trail. Then I took a good look out the window.

The backyard was fenced. The only exchanges between neighbors were the squirrels that scampered from yard to yard along the high branches of dying elms. The peeling siding next door was close enough to reach out and touch from the window over the kitchen sink. But most disturbing of all was the hulk of a woman who paced the sidewalk in front of the house, avoiding cracks. Her skin was the color of a Nacho Cheese Dorito, her hair, the shade of stale ballpark mustard. The overall effect was, well, very orange indeed, a downright unnatural tint for a happy human being.

This woman appeared every morning at nine o'clock sharp, applied sunless tanner that deepened her carroty hue as the weeks progressed, and walked up and down the block for an hour, haunting the pavement in front of our incommodious home. She is the one who pushed me over the edge. The orange woman—that specter of the worst to come if you yoke yourself to security and routine—made me bolt to New Zealand.

Yikes. I had my "I do," but somewhere along the line I'd lost the bell. I mourned my bungalow, underestimated the support of friends accumulated over decades, and saw only a tsunami of change crashing down upon me. I wanted a deus ex machina. I wanted my mommy. Not my real mommy. That mommy was already my brother's deus ex machina, always swooping in with a checkbook to rescue him from debt, despair, inconvenient wives, whatever.

What were my options now? Slip into moth-eaten oblivion? Nurse grudges and recite a rosary of regrets? Set people straight? They all seemed to be popular old-lady routines.

How about denial? That looked dandy. My mother's outlook on life had been framed early by movies that starred the likes of Deanna

Durbin, and she still peered at the world through a Vaselined lens. The cheery haze had enabled her to recall her childhood with a schizophrenic mother as chock-full of surprises and to take her son's chronic unemployment as the mark of a real free spirit.

Mom rewove family tragedy into a legend that kept us on the edge of our seats. As tales go, it was a good one, with regal bloodlines, heroism, gruesome death, and the callousness of a major airline in time of need. She revamped her childhood memories so effectively that she and her sister might have grown up in different homes. When Patricia looked back, every picnic had a pall over it. Joanne jumped into the Ford with suicide doors, off on an idyll in the Kansas sun.

Mom had even rolled with the punches when Dad, after bickering with her for more than half a century, tossed up his hands at eighty and announced that he was moving to the office—a one-bedroom apartment overlooking two Dumpsters and the University of Arizona's experimental goat farm.

"I don't understand what happened. Your father was so amorous after the war."

"The Second World War was a long time ago," I reminded my mother.

"I shouldn't have married him, but it was wartime. People did a lot of crazy things back then."

"Back when *One Hundred Ways to Please Your Husband* was a cookbook? Maybe that had something to do with it."

"Nonsense. But your father's going to give me a heart attack if I let this bother me. So I won't."

Mom was a pro when it came to denial, but I wasn't a natural. Overoptimism was more my gig. Maybe I could settle into herding the minutiae of daily life with the engineer, wait for grandchildren, and deprive the next generation of Wonder Bread. I could slap a smile on my face and keep my big mouth shut, as my aunt used to recommend. (Aunt Pat failed to elaborate that a lobotomy is necessary if a woman intends to maintain this strategy over the long haul.)

My closest friends were several years behind, still raising children. I had no role models. But I did have a motivational calendar. In October, Joseph Campbell had promised I wouldn't break my nose running into a wall if I followed my bliss. Doors would open just for me. In November, W. H. Murray egged me on. If I got my butt in gear, Providence would too. By December, Goethe had me in the palm of his hand. If I could dream it, I could do it, but I had better start toot sweet.

Anyone familiar with the story of the wizard of Oz knows you have to leave home to find it. New Zealand was as far away as I could go without a spacesuit, but hadn't the calendar savants virtually guaranteed great rewards for gutsy if irrational behavior?

Running off to the Antipodes, however, does not ensure security or adventure, and it sure as hell doesn't prove that you matter. It suggests you have a screw loose. It costs more than a one-way ticket to New Zealand to find yourself and tighten your hardware.

Looking back, it is incomprehensible to me that I did all this, let alone that my newlywed husband had the grace to cooperate with an adventure that was far more than seven and a half thousand miles outside his comfort zone. But the decisions a woman makes sliding into her fifties are not the decisions she made in her forties, and certainly not the ones she will embrace on the backside of sixty.

When a woman is between fifty and sixty, anything can happen, or everything, usually all at once. Children leave. Maybe they marry PhD candidates. Maybe they run off with tattoo artists and return with children named Moonbeam Belou and Patchouli Peace. Aging parents take on a life of their own and may take hers with them. A sister-in-law drops dead at fifty. Obsolescence and insinuations of mortality are about to collide at an unmarked intersection. Can she swerve and avoid the wreck? If she can't, where's the air bag!

The voice that whispered to me in my forties, *Someday it might be too late*, was coming through a megaphone in my fifties, and the conversation went like this:

Oh my God, you're too old to be a prima ballerina.

Well of course not. I'm not that stupid.

Did you ever consider that the end of the game of life might not be death?

Death sounds pretty final to me. If you're breathing, aren't you still in the game?

Naïve and overly optimistic.

I know. I have a problem with that. The love of my life warned me about it.

'Toogoodtobetrue'?

Toogoodtobetrue.

There are many ways for it to end, you know.

For instance?

Death of choice. Worst-case scenario, lingering death of choice, dwindling options, the petering out of pastimes waiting over the horizon, if you can push your walker that far. It's usually fatal: not enough ozone, the bracing sea breeze of change. And dearth of time. Remember what Georgia O'Keefe said about how long it takes to see a flower. Quality time is hogwash. A sufficient quantity of time to be in the moment is the issue. And that is precisely the time you are running out of.

Oh dear.

You want to climb out that window into the world? You want one last adventure? Then put on your Indian moccasins, Scout, your hiking boots, your walking Oxfords, your bowling shoes—well maybe not your bowling shoes. Although when opportunity knocks, it doesn't care if you open the door barefoot in your underpants.

AT THE BUTCHER COUNTER OF LIFE

Oh my.

You want to write? Then start tappin' those keys, baby, because soon, very soon, it will be too late.

A woman in her fifties begins to understand that she is different in more ways than bye-bye menses, and her world is different. By sixty, she's too bushed to make any more stupid choices, let alone live with the consequences. This accounts for the wisdom-that-comes-with-old-age booby prize.

But the hell-bent fifties can be every bit as crazy as adolescence. Middle age is no summit. It is not some trickle of time though the hourglass. It is a refractory vessel that must withstand temperatures high enough to alter and purify its contents. Middle age is a crucible.

Date: August 26, 2000
To: Laura P.
Subject: No Freaking Out in Paradise

Yes, you are right. I have no business freaking out when I live in paradise. But would you please send your mama a jalapeño double cheeseburger? I worked up an appetite climbing Mount Manaia and would kill a man for something spicy that a Kiwi hasn't garnished with raw grated beets.

Date: August 27, 2000
To: Jack B.
Subject: You're Never Fully Dressed without a Smile

    Kevin asked me tonight at the pub, "You know where Montana is?"

    I said, "I do."

    "You've heard about the talking dog then?"

    "No, but I bet you're going to tell me—"

    "Since you asked. A guy was driving around the backcountry of Montana, and he saw a sign in front of a broken-down home, Talking Dog for Sale.

    "He stopped and knocked on the door. The owner appeared and told him the dog was in the backyard. The guy went out back and saw a nice-looking Labrador retriever sitting there.

    "'You talk?' he asked.

    "'Yep,' the Lab replied.

    "After the guy recovered from the shock of hearing a dog talk, he asked, 'So what's your story?'

    "'Well, I discovered that I could talk when I was pretty young. I wanted to help the government, so I told the CIA. In no time at all, they had me jetting from country to country, sitting in with world leaders. No one figured a dog would be eavesdropping, so I was one of their most valuable spies for eight years running. I uncovered some incredible dealings and was awarded a batch of medals. But the jetting around really tired me out, and I knew I wasn't getting any younger, so I decided to settle down. I got married, had a mess of pups, and now I'm retired.'

"The guy was impressed and went back to the shanty to see if he could work a deal with the owner.

"'How much do you want for the dog?'

"'Ten bucks.'

"'Ten bucks! This dog is amazing! Why would you sell him so cheap?'

"'Because he's just a bullshitter. He's never been out of the bloody yard.'"

Why not hop a plane and meet me on the sheepskin in front of the fire? I will be wearing nothing but a smile.

X's and O's in all the right places,
Your Lonely Wife
P.S. If you can't come, can I buy a dog?

JANET PARMELY

Date: August 28, 2000
To: Anne B.
Subject: Rethinking My Old Age
Attached: Marewa Ki Te Rangi Toto (also known as Kaimaha), aged 101

Photograph taken circa 1930s by John Frederick Louden (1888?–1967) possibly in the Waikato Region. Ref: ½-045769. From the H. Ault Collection, Alexander Turnbull Library, Wellington, New Zealand.

I ran across this image, a wee treasure of a Maori uber-elder, nesting in the H. Ault Collection, in turn housed in the Alexander Turnbull Library, in custody of the National Library of New Zealand in Wellington. Like a matryoshka doll. I'm wrapping my head around Kaimaha.

Her hair is white. Her fingers are knobby with decades of manual labor, and her nails are dirty. Her face is lined like a topographical map of her one hundred and one years, and her chin is engraved with an elegant and symmetrical moko (although her tattoo would have been carved with chisels not punctured). She has paused from her pipe puffing to look straight at the camera and beam, broadly. The four teeth I can count in her grin are decayed.

If someone had shown me this photo when I was forty, I would have been appalled. Even five months ago, I was probably too full of delusions and busy making decisions based on them to appreciate Kaimaha.

She was born around 1830, a different time and place of the human heart. I bet Kaimaha didn't run halfway around the world to find herself when she was fifty-one. (Given life expectancy then, it might not have been an issue.) She looks like a gal who had an authentic view of herself early on.

And tonight she looks pretty good to me. I have a sneaking suspicion that by the time I have skidded through midlife, I will be stripped of much that I once held dear and thought permanent, including teeth, it seems. Maybe that's part of the bargain for the privilege of a long life?

Anyhow, she's clearly still enjoying herself. She still has vices. I could do worse than Kaimaha at 101. I'd like to hang on to my teeth, though.

Date: August 28, 2000
To: Sheryl O.
Subject: Not Out of Africa Yet
Attached: Bird's-eye view from Mount Manaia: little Taurikura, home for seven more months

The cat I am trying to steal from the neighbor is curled up on the love seat I bought at King's New and Used. All you need to steal a cat anywhere in the world is a bowl of food. I discovered that they sell kindling at the grocery store, so I don't have to gather sticks in my backyard like a crone anymore. I have a humdinger of a fire going, and the rain on the metal roof sounds like a machine-gun *rat-a-tat-tat*. The Kiwis would say, "It's bucketing!"

I am so grateful to Mary for helping me find this house. The Pacific Ocean is at my front door and Black Angus are grazing out the back. So far nothing about this insane move feels right but this: the view is great. (It didn't take long to realize that if you are unclear about what you're up to, you will likely end up engaged in something else. I should have bought a Yogi Berra calendar instead of that inspirational piece of crap.)

The daily grind, unlike the weather, is sucking me dry. We groused about it all those years we worked together, and what did this dunce do? I got a full-time job. I expected some *Out of Africa* experience, but my days are consumed with work, or driving to work, flying to meetings for work, learning some new task at work, or mastering some new way to perform an old task at work. I wouldn't notice Robert Redford if I had to step over his body to get to work.

Running a coffee plantation sounds like a heck of a lot more fun than sticking amplification devices in hairy ears. But I do enjoy having a natter with my patients. Last week Mrs. Anderson told me that her son took her skydiving a few years ago.

"When the pilot asked him how many jumps he'd made, he said, 'This is my second.' You should have seen the pilot's face. Of course, he's done it hundreds of times. What novice would strap his mother to his back and jump out of a plane?

"I'm too ancient to do it anymore, eighty-two years old, for goodness' sake. I was probably too ancient then, but it was wonderful. You have no sensation of falling until your chute opens, and then you tug on the ropes and soar like a bird."

Chapter 6

At the heart of every pearl is an irritant, mate.

—#28, God's Holding Paddock

In December, the directors of Bay Audiology asked me to extend my contract. It was coming to an end in March, and I agreed to stay a few more months. Jack grumbled but took a leave of absence from his job (and barber) to join me at Christmas, forced by practicalities to choose between transporting his golf clubs or my sewing machine. When he disembarked in Auckland lugging a thirty-seven-pound Bernina, a few more stars were certainly added to his crown. My househusband quickly discovered he liked his new line of work. It had heaps of fringe benefits: weekends off, honorary membership in God's Holding Paddock, snoring-pig serenades, and certain other perks we both had keenly missed.

After our mates at the pub assured us that sharks weren't a problem—"It's not bloody Australia"—we headed one Saturday to Ocean Beach, a ten-minute drive from Taurikura. Whangarei Heads Volunteer Surf Lifesaving Patrol watches over the summer crowds—as many as thirty! (It's deserted in winter except for an occasional beach walker, dog retrieving sticks tossed by the beach walker, and a hardy surfer or two.) Ocean Beach looked like an eight-hundred-meter stretch of paradise from the top of the dunes.

We carted the chilly bin and bodyboards gaily painted with cartoon fish down to the shore. Here, the wind sent our umbrella somersaulting, beach blanket flying, and blasted the ham out of the picnic sandwiches.

In the surf, the riptides and side currents intimidated our Midwestern souls, and the water in high summer was still frigid enough to shrivel goolies, if you had 'em. All the while, the sun bit through the hole in the ozone layer and sunblock too. And no one else at this seashore was riding kiddie boards, not even the kiddies.

Plainly not energetic enough to compete with the sports-mad Kiwis, Jack and I retreated to more domestic pursuits. We learned how to work around kumara and beets. For a gold coin dropped in the honesty box, we collected Haas avocados from a stand at the end of the neighbor's driveway. And no meat-and-three. Tail-end salmon filets dusted with dill and delicate racks of lamb chops basted with clarified butter smoked on the grill.

We called ahead to the dairy at McLeod Bay for fish and chips. In the time it took to drive there, the takeaway was ready, a warm little bundle of pure anticipation. The butcher paper conveniently served as a tablecloth upon which to lay crispy filets of hoki, tarakihi, or succulent John Dory, and chips gilded only as potatoes can be when deep-fried in oil just the right temperature and frequently changed.

Scallops were in season when Jack arrived, and Bluff oysters when he left. The town of Bluff at the southern tip of the South Island hosts an annual celebration for its little bivalve, dredged out of the stormy Foveaux Strait. Bluff oysters are scrummy but ungodly expensive by New Zealand standards (fifteen dollars a dozen then). The exchange rate, however, was in Jack's favor, so we cheerfully ordered, "A pottle of Bluff oysters, please."

Like the purists, we slurped them raw, or poached them in lemon juice and butter, finished off with a cream reduction. New Zealand butter comes in five-hundred-gram blocks and is the color of a King Alfred daffodil. New Zealand cream leans more toward the paper-white of narcissi, coats spoons with a lusty sheen, and can be had in liter containers, if your arteries are so inclined.

For an autumn finale, we flew to Nelson in April and rented a car to tour the South Island. The guys at God's Holding Paddock had been right: "You'll find it's a whole other country down there, luv." It was the New Zealand of picture postcards and soon to be *Lord of the Rings*.

We zigzagged down the east coast, past pilot whales, dolphin acrobats, and colonies of smelly, bachelor fur seals. Ruddy South Islanders put us up in B and Bs that used to be sheep shearers' cottages. Full English breakfasts were left at the door on doily-covered trays: back bacon, free-range eggs, mushrooms, and tomatoes ready to cook on an old gas hob. We whizzed across the Canterbury Plains in the frosty air past golden poplars standing sentinel along the road in the setting sun. Slowing for towns with names like Windwhistle and Geraldine and skirting the Southern Alps, we headed to Fiordland. The mossy cliffs of Milford Sound leaked waterfalls and rainbows. The long white cloud hung over Doubtful and Dusky Sounds.

Jack hired a guide to trout fish at the headwaters of the Upukerora River, wending its way to Lake Te Anau, and I tagged along. On the way back to the lodge at the end of the day, the true-blue sky over the tussocky banks of the river faded, and a full moon rose out of the gauze of a pink-tulle sunset behind us.

When I saw Jack off in Auckland after the South Island trip, I would think about what Pete had said at the pub: "Doing things with someone you like is terrific." Certainly was. It's entirely possible that my husband, sporting the ball cap he'd bought on his visit, was thinking back to his conversation with Kevin about oysters and pearls.

We might have been working around kumara and beets, but the rest of New Zealand was worming its way into my heart. Mine. This was my adventure, my quest, not Jack's. He already had a home, Kansas City, with a banner flying by the front door on game days to prove it. And he wanted his wife there by his side. The good times we had together during his four months' leave had underscored what we were missing. When I blithely extended my stay in New Zealand, I went too far. I asked too much of a green sprout of a union and of a man who simply wanted his wife by his side at home where a Chiefs pennant fluttered. I did not hear it yet, but the death knell was softly tolling for our sweet, ill-conceived marriage.

Date: January 12, 2001
To: Jim C.
Subject: Bugger!

Jack seems to be settling right in. Already he's gone out and bought himself a new ball cap, spin-off merchandise from a popular Toyota Hilux ad here.

The TV's on most nights at the pub. Unless there's horse racing or seasonal sports, no one pays it much attention, but we all get a kick out of this commercial every time it comes on.

Here's the gist of it. With his trusty ute, a Kiwi farmer bears down on a fence post to straighten it. The rest of them fall like dominoes and pull down the entire fence. "Bugger!" the Kiwi farmer says. He goes on to hitch the pickup to a stranded tractor and pulls off its front axle. "Bugger me!" Then he ropes a stump to his Hilux, whips it smartly out of the ground, over the vehicle, and into the long drop, sending the chickens flying. "Bugger!" When he surveys the cow he tried to haul out of a ditch, he can only say, "Oo-oo-oo, bugger." Back at the farmyard, as the bloke peels out for more adventures, the dog jumps for the truck, which spatters mud all over his wife and the laundry on the line, the dog misses the bed of the Hilux and lands in the muck, yelping what sounds distinctly like "Bugger."

We were back deep in discussion when the TV spotlighted another commercial featuring a chorus line of dancers in thongs and not much else. Beers suspended in midsip, every head at God's Holding Paddock, including my husband's, swiveled in unison to gape at the screen. They couldn't help themselves. At the end of the night, not one of them could tell you what the scantily clad girls were advertising.

Embarrassed at being caught in the act of ogling, Pete tried a diversionary tactic, turned to Lenny, and asked, "Have you ever worn a thong, Len?"

The image of grumpy, Lilliputian Lenny in a thong was so hilarious that it broke the tension, and finally, we all lost control when Len replied, "Well, of course."

Pete said, "Not jandals, Lenny! Not the bloomin' thongs you wear on your feet!"

Lenny mumbled, "Bugger." The very same word that is neatly embroidered above the bill of Jack's new hat.

AT THE BUTCHER COUNTER OF LIFE

Date: March 4, 2001
To: Laura P.
Subject: Gordy's Flytrap

Mary and I spent the weekend drumming up business at Field Days, Northland's annual agricultural fair in Dargaville. A large part of our work involves fitting hearing aids through ACC, the Accident Compensation Corporation, a government program that covers, among other things, work-related injuries like hearing loss. Farming is a noisy business.

Jack helped us haul over all sorts of advertising—Hear Now Brown Cow! Free Wax Checks!—and set up in the Federated Farmer's tent in a space marked off by hay bales. It's the best tent to be in because all day long here they fry up sausages, enfold them in a slice of white bread with fried onions and "toe-mah-toe sauce" (Kiwi ketchup), and hand them out for free. After hours, someone might throw some homekill onto the fire, which means that one of the Federated Farmers was on a first-name basis with the beast that went into the snarler. You cannot imagine how good it all tastes when you have been on your feet all day, hawking hearing aids, the scent of rain and manure in the air, wondering if you won the free-semen draw or guessed the correct weight of the Red Devon bull with balls the size of Arkansas.

It was like Old Home Week. Our clinic has fitted many of the farmers up here, and Mary remembered the name of every single one who stopped by to say hello, an impressive feat when you consider she's been with Bay Audiology for thirteen years. While she nattered and manned the booth, I did a walkabout and inspected the Rocky Bay Alpacas, tractor pulls, pole-climbing competitions, sheepdog trials, and commercial offerings, like Gordy's Flytrap. As you know, the flies at Taurikura have driven me crazy (something to do with my Aberdeen Angus neighbors), so I stopped to talk to Gordy.

"So you set your flytrap on a bucket like this, and the flies buzz right in?"

"Mmm," Gordy said. This is Kiwi for anything you want it to be. Maybe yes. Maybe no. Maybe you're buying time. Or just need to have a think.

"Why would they fly into the trap? How do they get suckered in?"

"Attractants—bait. One-hundred-seventy grams per liter of water. That'll last about a week. After that, the dead flies serve as bait. Very economical."

"What sort of lure do you start with?"

"Rotting meat's good, fish offal, squid, rabbit, possum, roadkill."

"Probably not for home use then?"

"Could do," Gordy replied.

And I said, "Mmm."

Chapter 7

Most of us are victims of our own self-destruction.
—#21, God's Holding Paddock

It had been easy to say yes to Bay Audiology in December when gossamer-sunshine days tint Whangarei Harbor absinthe, old sol slips over the horizon like a fertilized egg, and it all starts over again at dawn. When Monarch butterflies catch a lift on thermal columns and glide lazily over swan plants. When shags sun themselves on rocks in the harbor like runway models throwing open designer coats. When the wise little morepork roosts unseen in the bush and hoots *more pork* in the still night. When horizontal rain is just a distant memory.

No one in her right mind would have agreed in the middle of winter to extend a sojourn in Whangarei, because then it's just Whanga-rain. Kids might run around in bare feet all year long, but kids will go barefoot until their toes freeze off unless an adult says, "Put on your socks and shoes."

Central heating is nonexistent in Northland—because it's winterless—so I spent my evenings after the June solstice scurrying between oases of warmth. When I got home from work, I started a fire using all sorts of non–Girl Scout shortcuts, striking an entire box of matches to ignite a month's worth of *The New Zealand Herald* or adding a dash of mineral spirits to really get things going. After particularly trying days, I simply turned on the space heater Mary had lent me and had a double gin.

Mary had also put me on to the hot-water bottle, which in my American youth had been an icky device hanging on the back of the bathroom door. It had attachments whose intimate functions I was too young to understand but knew intuitively I didn't want to hear about. The New Zealand hottie is entirely different and comfy-cozy, associated with caring friends, mothers, and grandmothers who cherish you enough to knit a cover for it and slip it into your bed a half hour before you crawl in, snug as a bug in a rug.

What Kiwis call the "electric blanket" (a heated mattress pad) works fine too. And it's a better option if you're all alone. The point of the hottie is to remind you that someone in the house loves you. The rigmarole of putting on the jug to heat the water, filling the bottle without scalding yourself, and tucking it into your own bed only highlights that you don't.

To avoid major disappointment—discovering you failed to preheat the bed—some wastrels might turn on the electric blanket as soon as they get home, so after a dash from the dying embers of the fire or last blast of air from the space heater, they are sure to be toasty in dreamland. Until they have to get up before dawn to catch an early plane so they can fill in at some distant clinic and arrive punctually in the rain.

Yes, the directors of Bay Audiology knew exactly what they were doing when they inquired in the splendid month of December if I would like to extend my stay. By June, rain was Irish stepdancing on the pig and the paddock by Taurikura Bay.

One Sunday morning, I put on a slicker and headed down the back lane, ostensibly to check the mail at Ngaere's, but really just to get out of the bloody house. Through the dripping shroud, I saw that a section of the paddock fence had been removed, that there were tractor tracks in the mud, that the kikuyu grass was flattened where something had been sledged out—that Highway was nowhere in sight.

A crowd had already gathered at the dairy to offer condolences. You can't sneak a three-hundred-pound porker out of a paddock in a small neighborhood without word getting around.

Ngaere was so upset she was barely intelligible. Apparently Highway had simply reached the end of the lifespan for a morbidly obese kunekune pig. Ngaere wiped at tears with an arthritic finger, ocher from years of rolling her own. "You have to keep going," she told me. "That's all you can do, luv, just keep going.

"I loved that pig" was all the more she could say.

Now Highway wasn't exactly a merrymaker. She didn't do anything but guttle and snore, but she was dependable about it. Highway had given me strength when I needed it most, and the pig made me smile. The animal got one cheese sandwich and never asked for anything more in return. If that's not love, what is?

I had rocked in the cradle of the swine's faithful rumble under the Magellanic Clouds for over a year. Now Highway was dead, and winter had arrived again in Whanga-rain. I was homesick all over again.

On impulse, I dropped in for Yachties Night, a happy hour every Tuesday at Reva's Restaurant in the Town Basin, a marina with about three hundred berths. Whangarei is a jumping-off point for yachts catching the trade winds from New Zealand to the islands. The town therefore boasts more chandlers, diesel mechanics, electricians, and sail makers, more tins of bully beef, pails of cabin biscuits, and cartons of long-life milk at PAK'nSAVE than you might expect for its population of some fifty thousand inhabitants.

Cyclone season in the South Pacific runs from November through April. By October most yachties are looking to catch a weather window out of harm's way back to New Zealand, with some trepidation. It can be a daunting passage, beating against the wind through a succession of highs and lows across a vast expanse of open ocean, save the Minerva Reefs, two nearly submerged atolls in the middle of nowhere. Sailors and gimbaled tables and stoves are often put to the test. Additionally the coastal blow around New Zealand, although nothing like the screaming katabatic williwaws of Tierra del Fuego, is unpredictable.

Exhilarated to make landfall, the cruisers arrive in Whangarei: among them, Americans in their bright, shiny vessels; Germans, more functionally decked out; Canadians and Kiwis, less persnickety; the French, generally acknowledged not to give a stuff; and South Africans, some of them in very big boats.

But first, before anyone lands, Biosecurity New Zealand, an arm of MAF, the Ministry of Agriculture and Forestry, boards and confiscates fresh meat, eggs, fruits and veggies, as well as any tinned items that weren't originally packed in New Zealand. Anyone crazy enough to bring in a cat or dog will quickly discover that this island nation values its rabies-free status and intends to keep it that way. Most cruisers approach the Land of the Long White Cloud pet free and subsisting on rice and beans.

The yachties transfuse little Whangarei with gratitude, hustle, bustle, and cash as they prepare to set off the next season, blasting off barnacles, applying antifouling on the hard, and meeting for drinks with kindred souls at Reva's.

There are always live-aboards and stragglers, so even in June, Yachties' Night was the epicenter of a little social whirl. It was an energetic if hardheaded crowd, which you have to be if you are going to put a thousand nautical miles between you and terra firma and sail to Fiji or Tonga.

At Reva's, I met Daisy from Australia and her husband, Colin, a Pommy doctor working as a locum in town. They were about my age and had a sloop they day sailed. Petite and devilishly sociable, Daisy was a right pixie and took me under her wing. If I didn't have Highway anymore, at least I had two watering holes now.

Daisy and I were gossiping by the bar at Reva's one Yachtie's Night. Colin was across the room talking to a slight man in his fifties. "That's Adrian," Daisy whispered.

The man she pointed out did not lean into the conversation but stood with a forearm across his midriff, palm up, where he rested the elbow of the other arm, beer in hand. The pose might have come off as casual—even Johnny Depp as Jack Sparrow—had he not appeared to be carved out of stone. Ramrod straight, shoulders back, stray animations under control, it lent him instead the air of some English aristocrat in a BBC miniseries.

"He owns *Jingle Bells*." Daisy nodded toward the biggest yacht moored on Cat Alley where the multihulls floated in shallow water. "He's been living on it over a year."

"Where's he from?"

"South Africa. Emigrated here with the wife and family, but they're in Auckland. He told me he just got divorced. Said she was a real dragon."

"Really?"

"And I think he's interested in you." This man's behavior had been so circumspect in general, his communication downright reticent, that I had hardly noticed him. He'd certainly shown no particular interest in me that I could recall.

"Well, I am gobsmacked," I said to show off how Kiwi I had become.

Daisy, being an Ozzie, wasn't impressed. "Actually, I think he's besotted."

The skipper of *Sea Eagle II*, a thirty-nine-foot monohull, overheard our conversation. "I'd be careful, if I were you," he said sourly. "That one's the kind of man who would hold the lantern while his mother chops wood." I chalked it up to boat envy.

Date: June 29, 2001
To: Sheryl O.
Subject: Bibbidi-Bobbidi-Boo
Attached: Whangarei Town Basin

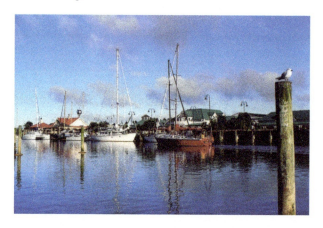

There's going to be a ball in Whangarei, and this Cinderella has been invited. The hospital is sponsoring it, and Daisy has set me up with some stuffy South African who's got a big boat. She knows I have a man back in Kansas City, has determined him to be the Empress's New Husband, and is proceeding as if he didn't exist.

The date doesn't worry me one way or another. But finding a pair of stockings in town that aren't reinforced for industrial support does.

I was directed to a lingerie shop called the Blue Room. (Surprisingly, here in the Country of Call It What It Is—Big Fresh, Liquor Land, Hammer Hardware—it wasn't Knocker Locker.) I could have bought a dozen and had them couriered to me from the States for what one pair of sandal-foot sheers cost me, but I am ready for the ball and don't have to depend on birds, mice, or magic.

Leaving the store, I did a double take at the window display. How had I missed that on the way in? A svelte mannequin stood there in sexy knickers and a matching bra with trap doors. Suspended by fishing line, a baby doll hovered at her left nipple—or where the nipple would have been had it not been a mannequin—like a little naked angel. Above the display was a foot-tall sign in bold pink letters, NURSING BRAS. It restored my faith in forthright Kiwi advertising.

In the attached photo, you can just see Reva's, where I got asked to the dance.

Chapter 8

Who wants given fruit when stolen is sweeter—
Mrs. MacElroy's peaches, Mrs. Taylor's plums.

—#21, God's Holding Paddock

When you hop on that bike or straddle that mule, you should log off the Internet, power down the phone, and forget about writing home. That's travel writer Dervla Murphy's advice. How different my New Zealand experience would have been if I had followed it. But whoops, I had left a husband, daughter, dog, cat, friends behind in Kansas City, and two old parents in Tucson. That tactic would have been difficult, if not perverse. (If you go looking for yourself, it's best to do it before you have accumulated all those people you have to send postcards to and certainly before you adopt cats and dogs.)

One of my many visits back to the States was scheduled in September 2001, coincidentally to arrive in time for 911. Adrian offered to drive me to the airport. I was skeptical about the besotted business. Daisy was loads of fun, but she was a stirrer. We had spoken a few times at Reva's before the ball, but Adrian hadn't been particularly forthcoming.

"You're from South Africa?"
"Uh-huh."
"And you're divorced?"
"Almost."
"How did your boat get its name?"
"Every day on board's like Christmas."

Wow. He was a man of few words, but those were hard to beat. Sounded like someone who might hear the bell.

He said he had been such a disciplinary problem at school that they caned him, and this sounded so titillating that it impressed me. But I had to pry the details out of him.

"Caned?"

"Every week."

"What on earth did you do to get caned?"

"Nothing."

"They caned you for no reason at all?"

"Wasn't my fault."

"Not your fault?"

"I discovered cigarettes, booze, and girls all at once. It was too much for me."

"Yes, I suppose it would have been too much for anyone. Who caned you?"

"Prefects, teachers. Gym teacher was best."

"The best?"

"He could lay the stripes on top of each other in one big welt."

"And the worst?"

"Math teacher. Bad breath and bad aim. When you don't know where it's going to hit, you can't prepare yourself."

"So you mended your ways after all that caning?"

"No. The headmaster told my parents I could do anything I set my mind to, if I were interested. If not, I'd do nothing, or cause a lot of shit." A scamp who heard the bell. Even better.

Adrian evidently decided to build boats instead of causing shit—or maybe he did both—and then he sailed around the world twice. And then he moved to New Zealand with his family. Now he was getting a divorce.

The word around the Town Basin was that he had money. Although he dressed like a ragamuffin and went barefoot when he could, he drove a Mercedes Benz built like a tank and sailed a fifty-two-foot yacht. No one had any idea where the fortune came from. Was he retired? A day trader? A dot-com mogul? Trust-fund baby? He came from the sort of upper-crust family who rarely dined together: tots in the nursery, Mother and Father downstairs, served by the kitchen maid after the nippers went to bed.

He had evidently owned his own company in South Africa but didn't elaborate if his business was building boats or something else. There was only one point on which he was clear: "I have worked my whole life not to have a boss. No one is going to tell me what to do."

He seemed to be leaving out some critical transitional details, but don't we all? A life story makes more sense that way, especially if you're telling it to someone in a bar. It sounded very Leonard Cohenesque, like birds on wires and drunks in choirs, a scamp who heard the bell and only wanted to be free.

There had been some discussion at the ball about driving up the coast to visit the Rocky Bay Alpaca Farm, but the evening was memorable, more than anything else, for the hangover I had inflicted on myself. Two weeks later, Adrian and I set out, and it started blowing a gale before we got to Rocky Bay. At the farm, the seas heaped up beneath the steep paddocks, where dozens of alpacas stood impassively, their limpid eyes inscrutable under crimped forelocks in the mounting rain. Drenched and as impassive as the alpacas, Adrian discussed their investment potential with the owners, while my nose, fingers, and toes turned blue.

He had set the air conditioner in the Mercedes on high on the drive back to Taurikura. I presumed he was trying to defrost the windows and shivered in silence. Adrian was oblivious to the discomfort. Maybe stoicism was part and parcel of the sailing life, or years of getting flogged.

I changed into dry clothes at home and lent Adrian my bathrobe while his wet things were in the wash. He had built a fire, and okay, he got stuck at my house that night, but no one had any business being on the road in that weather, let alone after all the Cab Sav we had drunk waiting for the laundry to finish. I told him there were clean flannel sheets on the guest bed, but he said flannel was too bloody hot and it made him itch.

It was July, and brume was tumbling off Mount Manaia. I quit arguing over flannel sheets but warned him that nothing was going to happen when we climbed into my bed—"and no fooling around, I mean it"—even though it made me sound like a nincompoop in an after-school special. I was just so damned cold. All I wanted was a warm body next to me, not a measly hot-water bottle at my feet, not an electric blanket irradiating me, but a flesh-and-blood man willing to be reasonably inert and noninvasive. A cuddle would do. As it turned out, nothing much happened in bed that night, which I took as the mark of a real South African gentleman at the time.

Although I was foggy about what I expected the universe to deliver after this running jump, I didn't think it was a man. I had one back in the States, although our daily lives were eighteen time zones out of synch. I was already in tomorrow while my husband was stuck in yesterday. You can't work around that kind of discrepancy forever. Peter the dairy farmer understood it long before I did, when he gave his dogs a pat now and then. You have to be able to reach out and assure each other without a word: *You are there.*

Being there. It's the glue that holds relationships together when men won't talk and women won't listen, a stalemate that can occur up close or seven and a half thousand miles away. A kiss, a hug, a hand to hold: without them babies fail to thrive and grown-ups wither. In Harry Harlow's laboratory, infant rhesus macaques picked a terrycloth mom with an empty breast over a chicken-wire surrogate full of milk every time. They clung to an Iron Maiden, the evilest of all stand-in mothers. She rattled, poked, and jabbed them, blasted them with cold air against the bars of their experimental-monkey cages, and still the babies held on for the comfort of touch—and any denier from a snuggle to a wallop would do.

If you are not sharing a bed, sitting together in companionable silence, or exchanging the chit-chat of day-to-day life, sooner or later you will end up in someone else's car because he was the one who was there to ask you what time you had to be at the airport.

The Whangarei airport is in Onerahi, on the outskirts of town. The only connections to Auckland then were in an eleven-seat Air New Zealand Link prop plane. The terminal building was a one-room, one-story affair, with a welcome mat at the door, mailbox, vending machine for the *The New Zealand Herald*, and a rubbish can marked Thank You for Putting Your Butt in the Bin.

Inside there was one gate (a door to the tarmac), a check-in desk with a bowl of free lollies to help you pop your ears (Air New Zealand cared), four short banks of chairs, five café tables, and a takeaway service offering, most notably, crocheted baby clothes and cheese-and-pickle sammies. You left your keys with the ticket agent, who passed them on to a motel owner down the road. He picked up your car from the airport, stored it for five dollars a day, and returned your car and keys to the airport the day you returned.

Mary had laughed her head off—"What a dag!"—the first time I flew to Auckland for a managers' meeting and arrived two hours early for a 7:00 a.m. flight. I learned three things that day: one, a "dag" is a real character; two, it is also the dung-matted wool that hangs off the back end of a sheep; and three, at Whangarei Airport you boarded fifteen minutes before takeoff. I sat in my car for an hour and a half until they unlocked the front door. One can still slide through the gate at the last minute (with a sixteen-ounce bottle of shampoo in hand), and certain people from Whangarei Heads have been known to call the airport to tell them, "I'm running late. Would you please hold the plane?"

Adrian and I stood in front of the Passengers Only Beyond This Point notice fifteen yards from the aircraft. He handed me something neatly folded in tissue paper. "Just so you know I'm serious," he said, and gave me a brisk hug. "You can keep it, regardless."

On the runway, the wind lashed at my raincoat, whipped my hair into my face, and almost blew the tissue-paper package out of my hands. I gave the boarding pass to the copilot, not much older than my daughter, held on to the bouncing cable railing, and climbed the airstairs.

Adrian stood soldier straight outside the tiny airport. He was still there after the puddle jumper taxied to the end of the short runway and clattered back past the terminal. As it took off, he gave a shy salute good-bye before the squall closed in, and his solitary figure disappeared below the clouds.

I had the impression that he stood there for a long time after that, looking for all the world like a quiet, lonely guy coming out of a bad divorce with passion smoldering for just the right woman. All indications pointed to his good sense in choosing me. There's not a better aphrodisiac in the world.

When we leveled off, I took a closer look at the gift and could see now that it was wrapped in white parcel paper, waxed on the inside and folded into a sort of envelope. At first I wasn't sure what I had unwrapped, glinting in the high-altitude sunshine, flinging rainbows against the cabin wall, because I had no experience with loose diamonds, really not much experience with diamonds at all.

I think this is a diamond . . . a very big diamond . . . probably a South African diamond . . . holy crap!

And just like that, my headlong leap into the southern hemisphere was vindicated. All my Christmases came at once with Santa Claus and Prince Charming bundled together in a boyish, blue-eyed package deal that had been sent to me—me!—on a fifty-two-foot yacht named *Jingle Bells*.

Oh my gosh, Jingle Bells. If this isn't a sign, what is? Hear the bell!

No, but I smell something fishy.
What do you mean?
I'm thinking of fish offal.
Fish offal?
Rotting squid then, rabbit, possum, roadkill.
What does Gordy's Flytrap have to do with diamonds?
Mmm.
You're such a skeptic. I think the guys at the pub are right: life is like a butcher counter. You can have whatever you want. You just have to ring the bell.
Ding-a-ling.
That's what I did when I came to New Zealand. I rang the bell!
But don't you need to have some idea what to order when you get up to the butcher counter of life—lamb chop or pork knuckle, ma'am?
Obviously not. The universe will hand over what you need instead.

I barely knew this guy, but I didn't care if the diamond had strings and a star-studded wackadoodle had lassoed me. I was ready for the fairy tale. I had been looking for it most of my life: not just a prince but the whole picture-book kit and caboodle, the white horse (a boat would do), the castle (certainly yet to come), the crown (with diamonds), the kingdom (rainier than I had imagined, but didn't that keep everything clean and green?).

This diamond was a pledge—isn't a diamond forever?—and the ultimate call to adventure. It promised salvation for a square peg who had spent a lifetime trying to squeeze into or out of a round hole. This chunk of carbon was my last chance to thumb my nose at a lingering death of choice. It was the antidote to what I really feared: if I returned to the house in Kansas City, I would morph into an orange woman avoiding cracks in the sidewalk in the crabgrass suburbs.

This diamond means happily ever after.
It might also be toogoodtobetrue.
Nah. Huzzah, Herr Goethe!

AT THE BUTCHER COUNTER OF LIFE

As the bell clinks, so the fool thinks.

Date: October 13, 2001
To: Anne B.
Subject: Optimist for Sale

I've been here a year and a half and have seen in that time only three weather forecasts for "long sunny spells." Mostly they predict "thundery rain with gusty northerlies" or "a few showers about Northland"—in the dry season. You can imagine how heartening it was to turn on my computer, open Xtra's home page this morning, and see the forecast, "Tomorrow: fine."

Last week I walked down to Ngaere's Dairy in the thundery rain and gusty northerlies to pick up the mail she had held for me while I was in the States. Someone had posted a sign at the bottom of the back lane, Optimist for Sale.

When I called Laura to tell her about this, she said, "How awesome is that, Mama? You live in a country where you can buy an optimist. Don't you just love New Zealand!"

Ngaere told me later that my neighbor was selling a single-person sailing dinghy, similar but easier to handle than the P-Class in which virtually every New Zealand yachtsman from Sir Peter Blake to Russell Coutts learned to sail. The "Optimist for Sale" was a sailing pram.

Okay, so I can't buy a Kiwi to follow me around all day caroling, "All good, no worries, mate, she'll be right"—but at least my Internet provider will reassure me now and then that tomorrow will be fine.

Part II

Bolter in Paradise

Chapter 9

The busy gremlin with a pint-sized voice goading you over the cliff while you rejoice has a name—and that is Choice.

—#39, God's Holding Paddock

I left New Zealand in a quandary and returned with a setting for the two-carat diamond. Surely it was safer in a ring while I made up my mind? The fact that I searched every antique shop in Kansas City for the perfect white-gold caprice meant, of course, that it was a done deal. I had picked an enigma dropped from the Southern Cross, shaking diamonds out of his silver hair.

Jack didn't have a chance. The orange woman was still prowling the neighborhood. September 11 had changed the States for good. When I flew back to New Zealand, the mailboxes at the airport had been sealed so you couldn't post a bomb or a letter. A surly Amazon stuck a metal-detecting wand up my skirt and ran it over my crotch for the sake of national security. (We have acclimated to such insults now, but in 2001 it came as a shock.) The smog was so thick in LA that it looked like the plane was taking off in gruel.

Auckland Airport was bathed in abalone mist at dawn. The passport controller checked my work permit and said, "Kia ora. Welcome home, luv." The *tomokanga* had yet to be unveiled and blessed by Maori King Te Arikinui Kiingi Tuheitia, but its message was already loud and clear. The gateway would be installed seven years later for arrivals at the Jean

Batten International Terminal, as a symbol of the threshold on the spiritual journey from darkness into light.

Truth was I wasn't ready to say good-bye to New Zealand. I could not bear the thought of driving for the last time out of the shadow of Mount Manaia away from the ebb and flow of the tide at Taurikura Bay. The way into town was mapped in my soul: hugging the rocky shore of McLeod Bay where oystercatchers perched patiently waiting for the water to recede; descending into bush on Darkey's Hill past the infamous spot where Dick had once stopped on the way home from the pub to put out a fire under his Ford Sierra's hood, by peeing on it; taking the blind curve past God's Holding Paddock and Parua Bay; slowing through Tamaterau because there was often a speed trap there, and clowns, yes clowns, were known to divert traffic for school fundraisers; accelerating along the flats of Waikaraka by the hillside of grazing sheep, sometimes woolly, sometimes shorn; skirting the mangrove swamps outside Onerahi and pausing at the yield sign where I had turned right into Whangarei hundreds of times. If I departed now, I would have to take an easy left to the airport instead. But I did not have it in me to fly up, up, and away over a patchwork of rolling green paddocks and white horses on the sea below and leave Whangarei Heads behind forever. And so, I returned to New Zealand. The diamond was just a nudge.

Adrian went into full courting mode. Anchors aweigh! Daisy the Stirrer advised him on chocolates to tuck under pillows and lavender sachets to hide in my underwear drawer. He filled the house with roses, balloons, and Chinese lanterns that luminesced like outsized blood oranges. It looked as if the big top had come to town, and I half expected the clowns from Tamaterau to show up.

By November I was overwhelmed and asked Adrian for space. He backed off but kept in touch. One evening he drove from the Town Basin to Taurikura to track me down on my daily walk, found me on the footpath by the main road, extended an umbrella through the window—

in case the showers had caught me unawares—and drove straight back into town, thirty minutes away. While I was at the pub one night, he slipped out to Taurikura and stole my laundry, to take to the lady who did his own. He left Mrs. H.S. Ball's Chutney and Nederburg Shiraz on the counter, Biryani and curry Vindaloo in the microwave. When I got home, coriander and fenugreek perfumed the air. I found a note taped to the stereo: "Press Play," and I did. Jim Croce told me that every time this man tried to tell me, it came out wrong, so he'd have to say I love you in a song.

My tight-lipped court and sparker might not have had the words himself, but he knew how to leverage someone else's. He had burned a playlist, drafted Bon Jovi to say he wanted to lay me down in a bed of roses, recruited Elton John to tell me it was enough for him, a wide-eyed wanderer, that we had gotten this far. Adrian stuck a CD in my boom box with a score for the romance I was already playing in my head, and I fell for him, damn the torpedoes, full speed ahead.

Date: November 6, 2001
To: Jim C.
Subject: Makes You Feel Better When You Are Already Well

The visibility driving home in the fog last night was nil, so my car decided to stop at the pub until it lifted. I had just sat down with my handle when Bill burst through the door, cursing. His wife, Pete's sister, had been driving in front of him and braked at the last minute. (It seems everyone's car has a mind of its own when it passes the pub.) Bill ran into Rae right in front of Parua Bay Tavern.

Rae stormed in. "So here come Bill right through me boot in his pussy four-wheel drive!"

"If it's in my way, it's history!"

Dick gave Bill and Rae the hard look and reminded them that the goal of our evening was to make us feel better when we were already well.

Pete took the cue. "Remember miniskirts and go-go boots?" he said to get us back on track. He got all misty-eyed, and so did the rest of the guys, remembering, presumably, that felicitous convergence of the days when the skirts were short and they were dangerous.

He collected himself and continued. "I was driving down Rathbone Street back then and noticed this girl walking in front of the post office. She was wearing white go-go boots, a microscopic skirt, and she had on a top that was a beautiful shade of green like—like—"

"Like a bottle of Heineken beer?" Kevin suggested.

"Exactly. Like a bottle of Heineken beer. She was carrying a stack of mail very precariously and dropped the letters all over the sidewalk. When she bent over to pick them up, I got so distracted that I drove right up the ass of the car in front of me.

"I got out to apologize to the guy I'd run into. He looked at me and rolled his eyes. 'I knew you were going to do that,' he said. 'The minute she bent over to pick up that mail, I knew you were going to run right up my ass.'

"And do you know what the worst part of the whole thing was?" Pete grimaced. "That girl is now me ex-wife."

AT THE BUTCHER COUNTER OF LIFE

Date: November 15, 2001
To: Sheryl O.
Subject: Caravans

It was a nearly perfect night at the pub. (Most of them are.) Rex remarked on how blustery it's been, and Dick agreed. "The sea's been lumpy all day, and the wind is boxing around." I told them that Mrs. Peterson would have blown over had she not grabbed on to the trellis of jasmine by the clinic door. She flapped around like a flag and then settled safely on the front step.

Ron had a beer with us while he tallied the money for the meat raffle, $139.50 for seventy tickets at two bucks apiece—pub math. Big English John said he went to the new Hot Spud Shop and truly planned to give the quiche a manly try. "But when I got up to the counter, I just couldn't do it. Settled for a loaded baked potato instead. You can't shag on Weet-Bix and you can't shag on quiche."

We paused to watch a vintage Crumpy and Scotty ad on TV. (Barry Crump was a Kiwi icon and rough old fart.) It entailed the usual scenario: dog in the bed of a Toyota Hilux, Scotty cringing in the passenger seat, Crumpy all fired up at the wheel. Taking a shortcut, they hurtle through the bush, off a cliff—"Tell you what, she's flyin', eh!"—and land in one piece. Crumpy lights up a smoke and says, "We'll have a wee breather here, Scotty. Have to wait for the dog." At last there's a *thud* in the bed of the pickup, and away they go!

To top off the evening, we heard shouting out back—"Quick, come look!"—and rushed to see a pod of dolphins frisking off the jetty. Their leaping silhouettes slipped noiselessly in and out of the water, the spray as delicate as snowflakes under the new moon. The barmaid dove into the frigid water to swim with them, not even bothering to take off her clothes, and Dick exclaimed, "Incredible! Fully booted and spurred!"

I arrived home with a nice beer buzz to find a fresh supply of vacuum-cleaner bags and new rubber gloves in the closet, and in my CD player, a disc of love songs, including Roy Orbison's assurance that I could have anything I wanted, baby. I'm hoping the offer includes more than housekeeping supplies.

A note—"Light Here"—was tied to a tail of twisted newspaper hanging, like dynamite cable, from the wood stove where Adrian had stacked kindling and logs from the fresh stack of macrocarpa that Peter and Adrienne brought. To "Caravans," I struck a match and lit the fuse. I have no idea where I'm going, but I'm on my way.

Chapter 10

The main thing to keep straight if you're a ventriloquist
is which one's the dummy.

—#39, God's Holding Paddock

Christmastime in Northland is a fantails-pirouetting, swallows-swooping, pohutukawas-blooming, Santa's-wearing-a-Speedo-and-the-elves-are-going-surfing fiesta. It's not that it stops raining, but there is less of it. It might, for example, rain outside your back door while the sun shines out front. There is alarm over drought, and not being a native, you shake your head and remember that rain swamped the cat's bowl every night for a week. A diaphanous light fills the air, and the panorama of the Heads from hilltop barbeques takes on the look of a watercolor.

Tents sprouted in the paddocks by Taurikura Bay as families came to fish and swim over school holidays. Pohutukawa trees, those venerable coastal evergreens, lined the shore, laden with spidery, scarlet blossoms they would quickly shed into a carpet of crimson filigree.

Taurikura hummed while the campers gutted fish and quaffed beer in the balmy dusk. The Christmas gnome that Adrian had tucked between the books nodded from the top shelf, the fairy lights he had strung up in the lounge twinkled, and I blathered on.

"Back in Nashville, there was a mouse hole in the children's section of the public library. Can't say if it was real or not, but it had been trimmed out and looked to be quite homey inside. A trail of tiny paw prints had been painted leading from it, across the floor, and posted with a sign: Mouse Crossing. I always stopped and looked both ways in case the mice would scurry by. Can you believe it! I could check out a stack of books as tall as I was. Doubt they'd let you do that now. And you probably couldn't find any Dr. Seuss except *The Cat in the Hat* anymore. Whatever happened to *The Five Hundred Hats of Bartholomew Cubbins*? And gosh, what a coincidence—it never occurred to me before—I'm a Sagittarius and love the archery booth at Renaissance Festival!

"And since I'm going to stay in New Zealand a while longer, why not learn to fly-fish? I want to go back to the Upukerora River with a fishing pole of my own, not trail behind the men in waders, picking my way tentatively across the riverbed, scaring away brown trout with my shadow. Do you know what the guide did? He lifted me up by my backpack and skipped me across the bouldery run. 'Confidence, woman, confidence!' he said. 'You'll never get anywhere hesitating like that.'"

I was three sheets to the wind in fool's paradise. I was pickled on optimism, drunk as a skunk on supersize expectations, crocko-blotto-boozy-woozy with the possibility of it all, and Adrian was my pusher, the guy at the bottle store down the road. Heck, he was the genie in the bottle.

And what precisely did Adrian say that night? He certainly didn't comment on the impossibility of wading through the same river again, let alone the double trouble of leapfrogging the equator. No, the wisdom of Heraclitus did not come up: no man steps in the same river twice, for it's not the same river and he's not the same man. He did have a knack for making a recollection sound like a promise, a daydream a done deal, or maybe it was just me throwing my voice around.

"The world is my oyster—now it's yours too! I always flew first class—and so will you! I schussed in Austria. I windsurfed in Hawaii. I cruised the Galapagos—you'll swim with the Blue-footed Boobies, whoop-de-doo! We could buy a canal boat—and eat and drink our way through France—and then we'll raise alpacas, oo-oo-oo!"

"I certainly don't want to sit around and watch TV like my wife."

Wife? This got flicked off like a gnat that was pestering me at what was otherwise the best garden party of my life.

"Now let's finish off the act with a little song and dance:
Wanna llama pajama?
Alpaca for you!
Hanker to weigh anchor?
You can have a yacht too!
And when sailing won't do?
A canal boat, *mon chou!*"
Wife?
Flick.

When Christmas rolled around, I opened my prezzies on a mimosa cloud: a copy of *The Five Hundred Hats of Bartholomew Cubbins*, an English longbow, a quiver of arrows, a fly-fishing rod and reel. All I had to do now was bide my time at the Mouse Crossing and sing my own ditty until every wish I ever made upon a star came true:

"Heraclitus?
Fuck it!
The oyster?
Shuck it!
Too late to chuck it?
The bait's in the bucket."

My daughter and boyfriend had arrived for the holidays the week before, crowned in dreadlocks (one of Laura's many reinventions). As we sat in the jumble of gifts and wrapping paper, I noticed the familiar pull of the wrinkle between her brows but wasn't sure if it was vegetarian rumblings and righteousness or something else.

I helped myself to more of Adrian's Christmas caviar. Such merry colors! I had never felt so merry, so awash in hope, and even now—even now—I wonder if the trade-off wasn't worth it to feel such anticipation once in a lifetime.

Date: December 25, 2001
To: Anne B.
Subject: Christmas Caviar
Attached: Pohutukawa sprig

Arrange these ingredients in festive serving dishes, start with a good base of butter on the bread, and pile on the rest in any order you please:

Black lumpfish roe
Hard-boiled eggs, whites and yolks separated and finely grated

(especially merry if you've got New Zealand free-range—the
yolks are the color of marigolds)
Lots of chopped curly parsley
Red onions, finely diced
Lemon wedges
Westphalian pumpernickel

Serve with mimosas all day long for a very Merry Christmas!

Chapter 11

Everything was perfect and complete, it was.

—#6, God's Holding Paddock

On December 30, the four of us—daughter, boyfriend, Adrian, and I—set sail to usher in the New Year on Great Barrier Island. Adrian hoisted anchor, and *Jingle Bells* motored out of Taurikura Bay, past the causeway, which is a volcanic dike, or maybe, just maybe the remnants of Chief Manaia's mischief.

My first day sail was uneventful, although Laura and I took Dramamine, so we may as well have been in a coma. The boyfriend and Adrian, like a selkie fresh out of his sealskin, scampered across the pitching boat, winding winches and pulling sheets. *Jingle Bells* glided down Whangarei Harbor, past little bays with Scottish names like McKenzie and Urquharts, then south by east off the coast near Waipu township, and out to the Pacific Ocean, course set for pristine and possum-free Great Barrier.

The first Europeans to settle at Whangarei Heads were Scots led by Norman McLeod, a Presbyterian minister who claimed to be so full of the Holy Spirit that he couldn't button his coat. His schooner landed in New Zealand in 1853, a full thirty-six years after he and his wife, Mary, had begun their circuitous journey.

Their first stop after leaving the Highlands had been Nova Scotia. Ice barricaded them there most winters for three decades. When Canada was inundated by immigrants fleeing the Irish Potato Famine, a third arriving in "coffin ships," McLoud had had enough. He sailed with his family and flock to Australia. All they found there was gold-rush sin, drought, and water that cost two shillings six pence a bucket and still had to be strained through muslin and boiled before they could drink it. The Normanites set sail again, for New Zealand. McLeod was seventy-three when he arrived, and he and Mary had left behind in Australia the graves of three sons lost to typhus. When a woman hitches up to someone else's star, she is never assured a day sail.

Date: December 31, 2001
To: Anne B.
Subject: Old Year's Night, 2001

We put Whangarei Heads behind us yesterday and raised the mainsail off Waipu, probably right where Reverend McLeod was preaching a sermon in a dinghy one day, and one of his parishioners, most likely a Dolly or a Flora, fell overboard and would have drowned had her petticoat not ballooned and acted as a life preserver.

We're now safely anchored under Orion's Belt in Whangaparapara Harbor on Great Barrier Island. Silver clouds are skittering like flying fish across the full moon. The waves are lapping, *splish-splash*, at *Jingle Bells*, and a jazz band of crustaceans is clacking in the shoals.

It feels like a pinch-me-am-I-dreaming miracle, all my wasted years fished out of Whangaparapara Harbor and showered back upon me in their right and proper form in an infinite geometric progression of moonbeams.

May your New Year begin as auspiciously.

JANET PARMELY

Date: January 1, 2002
To: Jim C.
Subject: The Pigeon Post

No possums, stoats, goats, power grid, or broadband here on Great Barrier. So I'll save my New Year greetings to disc and email them when I get back to Taurikura. As if conversation across the International Date Line weren't confusing enough. Try phoning, always a day later but how many hours earlier? You just get used to a seven-hour start on Kansas City in winter, five on Tucson, and then comes Daylight Savings Time (except in Arizona because they are loftier and remain on God's time). Since summer and winter don't coincide, the switch to DST is not simultaneous for New Zealand and the USA. There's that complication as well.

The letter, that archaic little tie to home, emissary of the lowdown, the scoop, the inner life, is still the best form of communication, I reckon. With the whiff of days gone by when there seemed to be more time to reflect, written in a hand that loved ones would recognize long after its author is in the grave.

Emails serve the purpose, except for the handwriting. Mine is crap, so they have the advantage of being legible. But printing and collating them certainly doesn't have the romantic appeal of bundling letters in satin ribbons and stashing them lovingly in drawers.

When I heard the story about the Great Barrier Postal Pigeon Service, however, I decided to stop whining about my defugalties communicating with home.

The world's first official airmail express, the pigeon post, started right here in response to one of the worst shipwrecks in New Zealand history. On its way from Sydney to Auckland in 1894, the

SS *Wairarapa* ran off course on a black night in high seas, bow on, full steam into the cliffs on the north coast of the Barrier. One hundred twenty-one people perished, and the sixteen horses crated on deck were lost. It took three days for news to reach Auckland that the ship had come to grief, and the ordeal dramatized just how isolated the Barrier was.

The ever-ingenious Kiwis came up with a messenger that could cover the ninety-three kilometers to Auckland in an hour if the wind was right: the humble pigeon. Homers were shipped to Great Barrier on the weekly steamer. They flew back to Auckland with up to five letters, or "flimsies," under a waterproof legging, "security and absolute secrecy guaranteed." By 1898, the pigeongrams were franked with an airmail stamp.

Except for an occasional snafu, the system worked well. A doctor was summoned in time to save little Charlie Osborne's life. After the Le Roy house burned down, the Kauri Timber Company put the pigeon-dispatched order for lumber on the next steamer. Christina Cooper's provisions were delayed for several weeks, however, when the pigeon that carried her grocery list landed on a ship bound for Sydney.

Pigeons flew both ways by 1901, and a pigeon carried news of Queen Victoria's death to the Barrier. When the first telegraph cable was laid in 1908 between Great Barrier Island and the mainland, the birds were out of a job.

I promise to be more grateful. I might have to do some math, but I can, in the end, pick up a phone and call home. I can post an illegible letter. I can send an email, even if it must be saved to disc for a while—instead of worrying where my pigeongram might have gotten waylaid.

JANET PARMELY

Date: January 5, 2002
To: Sheryl O.
Subject: Carnival at Kiwiriki Bay

We motored from Whangaparapara Harbor yesterday and anchored in Kiwiriki Bay, set to attend the Great Port Fitzroy Mussel Fest with the JAFAs (Just Another Fucking Aucklander), backpackers, ragged flower children, and those children's children. We took the dinghy over today and sampled green-lipped chowdered, skewered, frittered, barbequed, steamed, chopped, and diced over grated-beet salad.

The Barrier used to be known as a haven for the three *A*'s: anarchists, alcoholics, and artists. My impression is that eccentrics and hermits are still overrepresented in its thousand-some permanent inhabitants, as well as devotees of the alternative cash crop of Northland, which grows up there, shall we say, like a weed.

Before we left Whangaparapara Harbor, Adrian armed everyone with spatulas and kitchen scrubbies and threw us overboard in the cold, choppy water to scrape off the barnacles. It seemed like more than a day-sail's worth of limpets, winkles, worms, and green slime had accumulated on the bottom of the boat, but he is feeding and watering us, so we have to earn our keep.

Laura, being PADI certified and able to hold her breath, but not her tongue, the longest, got to scour the keel. She is prickly today, says that Adrian doesn't validate her, whatever the hell that means. Not wishing to rock that boat, I tried to tease her out of it.

"If you get angry, you'll get wrinkles."

"I'm not angry. I'm just right."

Something else riles her. Maybe it's Adrian's protocol not to batten down the hatches, because "it's not a bloody monohull." On Cap'n Adrian's boat, you let everything sit on top of the fridge until it falls over. Only then may you pick up the olive-oil bottles, pepper mill, salt and chili-flake shakers, and sugar and coffee-bean canisters that rolled off the top of the refrigerator, as well as the lamp whose chimney miraculously did not break when it fell off the saloon table and spilled kerosene all over the floor. Then and only then may you stow it all in the galley sink of the not-a-bloody-monohull for the rest of the bumpy sail.

Of course, the status of "Mom's new lover" confers a priori the allure of a red Texas chigger. There is something unseemly about it, all four of us emerging at noon from our respective berths, me with my own mini-dreadlocks on the back of my head and stubble burn on my cheek. Add to that the likelihood that certainly has not escaped my astute daughter's notice: this man is going to detain me longer in the wrong hemisphere. And then there is the issue of honor and timing. Perhaps Mom should not be acquiring lovers at all until her husband is officially ex.

Reputedly boys love their mothers, and girls love and judge them. Since I'm unlikely to bring forth more children, boys or girls, into this world, I'll never know. To further complicate matters, the daughters become mothers, the mothers become grandmothers, then hindsight butts in, and perspective does its fun-house-mirror trick. No wonder the bond between mothers and daughters is fraught with such complexity.

If Laura had criticized Adrian four days ago, it would have really ticked me off. Everything felt absolutely perfect on New Year's Day. John Lennon and the tui sang a duet at noon, and then Adrian switched the sound track to Gershwin or something classical like *Afternoon of a Faun*, or maybe *a Snapper*. I dozed in the hammock, read, and roused to snuff the air. Had he put the chops on the barbeque yet? Must be time for my gin.

But acrobats, jugglers, and tumblers woke me in the small

hours this morning, a three-ring carnival of worrywarts in my head. Isn't that how the New Year goes? You slide into it with high hopes and good intentions, but in no time at all, Father Time tick-tocks down the road, and that old bat Mother Verity rears her trusty head on the horizon like a badass sunrise. I hope this is not all toogoodtobetrue. I hope bad karma is not circumnavigating the globe, looking for a place to anchor in Kiwiriki Bay.

Chapter 12

Everyone thinks he can be a train driver just because it runs on rails. Maybe he can drive a locomotive, but he can't drive a train.

—#21, God's Holding Paddock

Wife?

Certainly Adrian had meant ex-wife? By the end of January, the question was looming like a sci-fi mutant I couldn't brush off with a couple more gins.

"EXACTLY WHERE DOES IT STAND WITH THE WIFE?"

"There are just a few details I have to wrap up."

Adrian carved the roast chicken, fed one of the oysters to me, and ate the other. He was borrowing scenes from *Amélie* and cooking regularly, South African recipes like sosaties and bobotie, in addition to more recognizable fare. Triumphantly, he set ravishing platters in front of me. Frenched chops sizzled. Broiled tomatoes drizzled with grassy New Zealand olive oil arrived on a bed of glistening saffron rice. He elevated the humbler dishes with salty chips hand cut from Red Rascal potatoes and deep-fried in ghee. The aroma of leg o' lamb roasting drove the cat mad.

We were ravenous for the kapow of anything short of law-enforcement-grade pepper, spice deprived in a country where garlic was considered bold and hot chilies unthinkable. You couldn't break a sweat with the local hot sauce, Kaitaia Fire. Adrian introduced me to Nando's Peri-Peri Sauce, made from the African Red Devil pepper. He turned up the heat at Kama Sutra, smug as if he were ordering more at the restaurant than a chili joyride. *I can make her weep and send perspiration trickling between her breasts with a snap of the fingers. Waiter, Indian hot!*

We snuggled and nuzzled and Eskimo kissed. Lights out, he spread-eagled on top of me, skin to skin, and we soaked each other up like baby monkeys deprived of a mother's touch. Chili sneezes addled our brains. Eros and alchemy were in the air. Tossing boules on Daisy and Colin's lawn, we giggled and beamed.

"Look at you two lovebirds," Daisy said in disgust. "Honestly, perched in the bow of the tender last night, motoring into Reva's with Adrian holding an umbrella over your head, and barely a drop of rain? Madame arrives like a specter from *The African Queen*—and Colin drops me off at the curb."

"You're the one who set us up for the ball," I reminded her.

"Well, I didn't know I was creating a monster."

Mindful of inflicting our new, true love on couples married for decades, we retreated to Taurikura on to Nederburg Pinotage now. I listened, rapt, while Adrian recounted how they delivered fresh French bread to the yachts in Papeete. He spoke with authority about dead reckoning, celestial navigation, and the practical relation between watts, amps, and volts and was so thrifty with words otherwise that what he did say had an air of validity—the gospel according to Adrian. Hours disappeared behind the love-seat cushions. He sent me off to work with "The Battle Hymn of the Republic" and went back to *Jingle Bells* to catch up on his rest.

On weekends we took up Adrian's schedule, which he said was a sailor's rhythm: twelve on, twelve off. We banished mornings and slept past noon. All the while, he looked at me exactly like Dick had looked at Joan that first night I had seen him lean over to light her cigarette, and I said to myself, *This will last forever because it feels so good.* Now what kind of thinking was that for a fifty-three-year-old woman with a Phi Beta Kappa key?

Date: January 25, 2002
To: Jim C.
Subject: Ngaere Died on Her Wedding Day

The widow Ngaere got remarried, and the dairy is up for sale. She took a drag on her fag, raised her glass for the wedding toast, and dropped dead. The reception was held at Manaia Club just up the hill from the fire station at McLeod Bay, so the volunteer brigade arrived swiftly. They got the bride's heart beating again. Ngaere was taken to Whangarei Hospital for observation but checked herself out and was back at the dairy next day.

The snoring pig has only been gone seven months, and now it's good-bye-good-bye-good-bye to the talking cockatoo, and my husband, as well.

Papers from Jack's lawyer regarding annulment were waiting on my desk at work after the trip to Great Barrier Island. Excuse me, annulment? Neither of us is Catholic. There's certainly no question of consummation. It has something to do with "an error of fact." Evidently I misrepresented myself. (As what, a sane woman?)

He seems to be claiming that because I overstayed my audiology contract, the marriage, our contract, is therefore null and void. He wouldn't have married me if he had known I was going to stay in New Zealand more than a year. Give me a break. I didn't know. Or might he be insinuating something worse? Is he implying that I undertook this folly with the intention of screwing around all along?

Last weekend I swam across Taurikura Bay at sunset, and a gannet plunged into my wake. Two years and what do I have to show for it? An impending annulment, a couple of swims in paradise, and a few morning pages. What did I expect? A rollicking sabbatical and ticker-tape welcome home, that's what. Manuscript in need of little or no editing tucked under my arm. Literary agent in the throng. Jack and my faithful dog, Molly, in the motorcade. And even that mean old cat that used to prop itself on my rose-velvet settee, hunch over, and lick itself to ecstasy (a maneuver any man would envy).

Instead my husband wants to put the marriage down and the cat to sleep because she is old and has socially inappropriate habits. And the only creative thing I have done after breathing all this clean green New Zealand air is to hack it back up in my journals, which is not much more productive than a masturbating cat.

I have my own theory. Neither of us set out to mislead anyone, unless you want to talk about the self-deceit of optimism. It's hard to willfully misrepresent yourself when you don't know who you are. Eventually it will come down to choosing to be yourself, even if you're feeling your way in the darkness on all fours trying to figure out who that is, look up, and realize that the light at the end of the tunnel isn't just a locomotive. It's a train.

Jack's a homebody. Maybe he wants to see the world through the light in someone else's eyes, but he wants to do it from his recliner. At this point, he seems to have a better idea of who he is than I do, and he's willing to honor it with action. I'll give him that. All I know is that I want to commune a little longer with the idea of a writing life, which is all tied up now with a country where widows remarry, die, and are resurrected. In the end, we are all just searching for a place to call home, and no one has the right to annul the quest.

AT THE BUTCHER COUNTER OF LIFE

Date: February 25, 2002
To: Laura P.
Subject: A Goat Will Do What a Goat Will Do

The topic of goats took up much of the discussion at the pub tonight. Everyone agrees that Dick's new one is far superior to the old one, Tom. He's a better lawn mower, grazing at a more consistent height and ranging farther. He hasn't rammed down a cabbage tree to defoliate it, pulled the laundry off the line to eat it, or nudged a wallet out of someone's back pocket to chew on the pretty Kiwi money, yet.

Kevin has no time for goats. "Hell, you can't tell what they'll do. They're like women."

Pete, on the other hand, has a lot of respect for goats. "Now sheep, they're stupid. If you go roaring through a tunnel, they scatter willy-nilly, and you'll run over a lot. But goats know what they're up to. They stick to the side of the tunnel and lean away from the track.

"Once the train did hit a goat, and it left him with one leg dangling by a piece of skin, so we stopped, figured we'd better put the poor bugger out of his misery. I got a ball-peen hammer and whacked him on the head. And you know what? He got up and ran off faster on three legs than any other goat could go on four good ones.

"Eventually the leg rotted off, and I still see that goddamn three-legged goat up Maungatapere way to this day. But none of them will ever hold a candle to Esmeralda. When we were kids, we'd climb on that goat and hang on to her horns for dear life. She'd race around the paddock, and soon as she threw one of us off, the next took his turn. No bloody carney ride in the world as good as our Esmeralda."

Chapter 13

All you need, luv, is a dry bed, full tummy, and family who loves you.

—#9, God's Holding Paddock

In March, that fateful month, I stopped working at Bay Audiology and moved with my stolen cat and Adrian to Darch Point, a minute as the tui flies from Taurikura Bay.

He had stumbled onto a property there for sale and deemed it a perfect match: my offbeat antiques (in limbo in the States) and this home nestled in the bush, with that most coveted exposure in the Winterless North, the sunny northwest, looking right up Whangarei Harbor.

The Fellowship of the Ring, the first of Tolkien's trilogy filmed by Peter Jackson, had just been released in December, and every quaint corner and lofty peak in New Zealand was straight away imbued with the aura of Middle Earth.

"It's right out of *Lord of the Rings*," Adrian said.

"Here's the castle to go with the fairy tale" is, of course, what I heard.

We did a drive-by that night, turned toward the harbor by the fish-and-chips dairy at McLeod Bay, and skirted Mount Aubrey, across the saddle from Manaia, a smaller-scale vestige of the same volcanic arc. Just after a rise with a magnificent view of Marsden Point Oil Refinery lit up like Mordor, we dipped and took a right onto a dead end, Darch Point Road. We saw nothing of the house, however, except a security light of prison-yard wattage behind a hedgerow of dying pittosporum, lanky oleander, and kikuyu grass colonized by glossy karamu and rampant fools beech.

On our way to view the property the next day, the refinery looked frankly industrial, belching flames with a roar that cannonaded off Mount Aubrey. At the top of the drive behind the hedge, we left the Mercedes in a clearing and set out on foot. The path was choked with native vegetation and remnants of abandoned landscaping higher than a man: agapanthuses; impatiens; a snarl of jasmine vines; a niagara of bougainvillea; a web of silver ferns; and more pittosporum, an indigenous shrub whose genus may be as old as Gondwana, the supercontinent from which little New Zealand drifted some eighty-five million years ago. We could well have been approaching Sleeping Beauty's castle, after the spirited but careless princess pricked her finger and fairies barricaded the place for a hundred years.

Stooping under an arbor collapsing from the weight of jasmine gone wild, we crossed a brick courtyard slippery with moss and finally confronted an imposing wooden door with a brass-gargoyle knocker. We rapped it to summon the real estate agent.

"Let's do a tour of the gardens first," she suggested, somewhat apologetically. The house was well known in the neighborhood, and the man who had built and owned it was described as unconventional. This was said in a way that implied a flair for the artistic that could go either way, talent put to good use or sliding down a slippery slope toward something dicier. Certainly it was not the sort of place that appealed to the average Kiwi, who prefers clean lines, aluminum-clad windows, and sunlight. Maybe the house on Darch Point Road was too theatrical for them.

Thousands of millennia ago, Mount Aubrey had spit out two great boulders that came to rest on what was now the back lawn. Here, a cock pheasant sashayed and a covey of quail scattered into the hedge. Blue herons would flock in spring to nest in two centuries-old pohutukawa trees that grew on top of one of the rocks, their roots swathing it, seeking purchase.

We slipped between the boulders into a sunny spot where starbursts of tiny white flowers sprouted in the grass like a fairy garden. Past a paddock with a dilapidated pigpen and chook house, we pushed into the bush to a stream that trickled around two sides of the property. It had freshwater crayfish where it pooled and a glowworm cave along its shady bank.

Backtracking through the secret passage between the rocks, we looked down at the house, so snugged into the contours of the hillside that this was the only spot where one might appreciate the layout of the place.

The front door was flanked by stained-glass windows of a texture and opacity that concealed the interior. It was so dim inside that it took time to acclimate and take in the room. A rock-solid, jade slate floor expanded into the open-plan kitchen/lounge. The ceiling sloped from a high, timber-clad wall in near darkness down to a bank of casement windows over the kitchen bench. In the shadowy architrave above, native birds perched in a frieze of vintage tiles from Waipu. The supporting pine poles were exposed, and the pitched ceiling was lined with bundled straw. It felt like a Middle Earth grotto.

The bath down the hall housed a pedestal sink and six-foot, cast-iron, claw-foot tub, which sat in a nook by a sliding window that opened onto complete bush privacy. Imbedded in the wall were two more tile tableaux that depicted scenes from stories by the Brothers Grimm.

The master bedroom was next to the bath on the westerly, bush side that was sheltered by more pohutukawa trees. Its ceiling was draped with pink silk like an upside-down parachute, and the sink recalled a European B and B. The room I claimed as my study had an old church window that framed Mount Aubrey's full height and shared a courtyard with Adrian's study. Both looked onto the back lawn.

The laundry and shower were situated in a shotgun space off the lounge, the toilet farther hidden away in a box of a room with a high, louvered window that backed onto the bush. It felt like an outhouse. A gnarled branch served as the toilet-paper holder, which enhanced the long-drop impression, as did the fact that you had to use the sink in the bath—or the bedroom—to wash your hands. Facing the toilet was a collage of arty black-and-white photos.

From the lounge, the slate floor transitioned to polished kwila in the corner sunroom. Pohutukawa branches pressed in on more church windows, and the panes in the peaks of the arches on the sunny side tossed barbs of ruby light across the room. Mullioned French doors led from the sunroom onto the verandah that ran the northwest length of the house. The kitchen bench overlooked the verandah, which in turn overlooked the swimming pool, fishpond, sleep-out that used to be the old McLeod Bay fire station, and One Tree Point across Whangarei Harbor.

In every way, the house on Darch Point Road was (as Frank Lloyd Wright said it should be) of the hill, not on it. The swimming pool was built around more volcanic boulders. A waterfall that began as a gurgle in a stand of bamboo seeped through a fissure in the rocks into a soaking pool and curtained over more rocks, past fuchsias, and into the deep, indigo basin. Every spot where something intimate was likely to occur was concealed in the bush: the toilet, the bath, the conjugal bed. You could skinny dip unabashedly in the pool. Every window was positioned to take advantage of the landscape, a glimpse of the sun rising over Mount Aubrey, the panoramic sweep of it setting across the harbor, and still maintain privacy. The night we moved in, a fishing moon spilled a glimmering path down the harbor and dotted the pool with its own reflection, an X that marked the spot for all the serendipity that was surely on its way to our new home.

Just like it takes time to see a flower, it takes a long time to really see a house, and usually this doesn't occur until after you have bought it. Then it takes even more time to refashion that house to what you thought you saw before you bought it and really saw it. At some point, it ceases to be a remodeling project and becomes a tug of war—between you and the house—and often between the two people who bought the house.

When the wind picked up, the limbs of the pohutukawa tree banged into the church windows in the sunroom like battering rams. The perimeters of the pool and fishpond were besieged by banana palms, papaya trees, ladder ferns, and a litter of agaves, including one sending forth an awesomely phallic mast of white flowers. Fungus had rotted the slats in the fishpond bridge. My study flooded on a regular basis. Condensation on the church window fogged the view of Mount Aubrey. Mold prospered on the walls. The courtyard caught a smidgen of sun in the morning and what backyard runoff my study didn't get. It smelled like a compost bucket. The house on Darch Point Road was not just of the hill. The hill was trying to reclaim it.

Most of the artificial light came from bare bulbs in sconces or dangling from the ceiling. On noteworthy cloudless days, sunshine did not pour in like it had into my house by Taurikura Bay, the morning sun flooding the bedroom, the afternoon sun in the lounge so luminous it made you want to paint, even if you had never picked up an artist's brush before. Sunlight had to worm its way into the house on Darch Point Road, dispersed through the great pohutukawa trees, diminished by opaque glass, so enfeebled by the time it reached the back wall of the cave of a lounge that we had to leave a lamp on all day. Even the northwestern exposure was tempered by the roof over the wide verandah.

From our vantage by the two big boulders, we should have seen that the house was a hodgepodge of architectural salvage and the visionary had run out of steam on a fair number of his enterprises. Even the ones that had been completed, although imaginative, lacked spit and polish.

There wasn't a closet in the house or a gutter on it. Some of the walls were made from biscuit board so crumbly a baby could have put a fist through it, others from rare and native recycled timbers like matai and kauri, permeated with must and so tough you couldn't drive a nail into them to hang a picture. The carpet in the master bedroom was the color and texture of a furball the cat coughed up, and it wasn't Europe. Why was there a sink in there? When you sat on the toilet, you saw that the photos were mostly of children, including one of schoolboys playing near a warehouse with a sign faintly lettered in French, Deliveries in the Rear. Every Continental or artistic eccentricity looked decidedly seedy once we had to live with it.

But we glossed over it all: the crack in the pedestal sink, the powder coat in the tub flaking away, the leaky pool and fishpond, noncompliant electrical system, ancient wall oven, ceramic cooktop split clean through one of the burners, the omen of the fairy-tale tiles that foretold the changes in store for me as we settled into the house on Darch Point Road.

We gave no more than a passing glance to the state of the rimu woodwork, mildew-stained, weather-beaten, gummy with kitchen grease. We barely registered the invisible tripper of a one-inch discrepancy between the floor in the lounge and the sunroom, or the rise-to-run ratio of the steps from the verandah to the pool deck, a neck breaker unless you were an Orc with size-four shoes. There was a wasp's nest hidden in some cranny of the kitchen skylight, and we never managed to get rid of it.

Adrian and I took none of it to heart. I wasn't worried because I had made certain assumptions, namely that he had all the money in the world and wanted to put some of it into refurbishing our new home. All I had to do was let my creative juices flow and supervise. Wasn't Adrian accustomed to hiring out work that had to be done? "In South Africa, we had people to do those things for us. Monday wash. Tuesday iron. Polish the silver and copper on Wednesday. Do the windows Thursday, unless it rained. Then the people polished more silver and copper instead."

Adrian wasn't worried because he had never rolled up his own sleeves to remodel a house in his life. He was clueless about the extent of the renovations we were signing up for. And he had other agendas.

"The house has been on the market a long time," Adrian said. "He'll be getting desperate. We'll lowball an offer. It'll be a good investment. We can subdivide the sleep-out to pay off the mortgage, peel off the pigpen and chook house for some extra cash. We'll split the down payment—"

Shuck that oyster, this was beginning to sound like a business deal. Adrian saw me hesitate and added, "In the meantime, we'll raise alpacas."

The idea of a herd of alpacas wandering from the fairy garden through the secret passage between the rocks so enthralled me that I didn't even stop to wonder if an alpaca could squeeze through a crevice I had to suck in my stomach to get through.

I tapped the proceeds from the sale of my bungalow in Kansas City for half of the down payment. At this point I should have paused, taken a deep breath, pulled my head out of my ass, and asked why I was forking over NZ$50,000 to go into joint debt with a man who had all the money in the world. But I was too busy skipping across the rocks with confidence like the guide at Upukerora River had told me to do. I was, in fact, so confident that I failed to appreciate that after you take the bait, you often encounter the hook.

AT THE BUTCHER COUNTER OF LIFE

Date: March 19, 2002
To: Jim C.
Subject: Change of Address
Attached: First sunset from the verandah of my new home

Darch Point Road
Whangarei Heads
New Zealand
Still on the Other Side of the World

Date: March 19, 2002
To: Sheryl O.
Subject: Journey to Middle Earth
Attached: Secret passage to the fairy garden

Last week at the pub, Rex told us he knows our property well. "Old man Tiller used to shelter his sheep under the two big rocks in a blow." He thinks we're daft to take it on.

The guys have accepted my changes in stride. All Dick had to say was "Adrian is your friend, girl, and that's good enough for us because you were our friend first."

It seems that Adrian rode into God's Holding Paddock on my coattails, and I have ridden into Middle Earth on his, with a small down payment for the trip.

AT THE BUTCHER COUNTER OF LIFE

Date: March 20, 2002
To: Anne B.
Subject: My Fairy-Tale Home in the Bush
Attached: Cinderella
      The Frog Prince

"Shake shake Hazel tree   "Whats the matter Princess?
Gold & silver over me."   Your howling would melt
                                           a stone!"

    Foibles and fables old as time: the Grimm brothers collected them in Germany from a rich oral tradition (their earlier, darker versions definitely not for the faint of heart). Decades ago in Waipu, a Scottish settlement on the coast about an hour's drive from here, an artist rendered these two in tile. And the fellow who built our place imbedded them in the wall of the house on Darch Point Road. Folklore wears seven league boots.
    Adrian kept an oil lamp burning on the bedside table last night

"in case you have to get up and go to the loo," he said. "I don't want you to lose your way the first sleep in our new home."

I believe I have landed a prince, and know for sure that I now officially own one half of the fairy tales—at least Cinderella and the Frog Prince.

Chapter 14

What fun's the fruit without a worm?

—#28, God's Holding Paddock

We were in bed, and something was hanging over my head. Adrian did "the dismount," which involved a mandatory embrace before I was allowed to get up for afternoon coffee, which is when you have your first cup of the day if you're on a sailor's rhythm. I looked up at the ceiling and noticed that the silk that had looked so exotic before we had bought the place was disintegrating. And where exactly did things stand with the wife? The question had taken on the proportion of an elephant trying to execute a twelve-pose yoga salute to the sun in our lounge.

My divorce was underway, a formality on the lawyers' tables. Jack had relented on annulment, and we were going the traditional route. But Adrian didn't seem to be taking care of his loose ends.

"When will your divorce be final, Adrian?"

"Soon."

"How soon?"

"I don't think you understand. It's more lax in New Zealand."

"Really?"

"Rex and his wife haven't lived together for years, and he's not pushing divorce."

"He can have a hop-on, though."

"Divorce is just an expensive fuss. The point is that I love you now."

"And I'm just obsessed with nitpicky details?"

"I have consulted a lawyer."

"You said you were as good as divorced!"

"You must have misunderstood."

"What the hell!"

"Why are you causing shit?"

"I just bought a home with you!"

"Precisely. You are the Duchess of Darch Point Road. You don't have to work at Bay Audiology anymore. And you have me. This is my business, and I will take care of it in due time."

We pulled the silk off the ceiling that afternoon. It shredded, and a shower of mummified moths, dead blowflies, and the excrement of lively daddy-longlegs rained on our heads.

The next day *the wife* slapped a caveat on our property at Darch Point Road. "Let him who takes an interest in this house beware. Part of it is mine."

When Adrian began negotiations in earnest for financial settlement with her two years later, it came to light that he had taken his portion of the down payment out of their joint marital account. The not-ex-wife wanted her share of our house back. That is how loose ends start to unravel.

Date: April 2, 2002
To: Jim C.
Subject: The Poppet

I just got back from Dargaville. Adrienne moved onto the dairy farm with Peter shortly after my first visit, and she gave birth to a girl the day before we took possession of the house on Darch Point Road. (Told you so two years ago!)

She and Peter are over the moon. It was endearing to see him, eyebrows trimmed, hold the baby as if he had an armful of china teacups and mumble about getting married next.

Mary has been designated honorary grandma, and Nana Mary dubbed little Emily "Poppet," a term that conveys all the warmth of a New Zealand hottie.

I can't pop out poppets anymore but am happy as a clam at high tide with the newest addition to my life, a fairy-tale home in the bush.

JANET PARMELY

Date: July 18, 2002
To: Anne B.
Subject: A Hammockful of Worms

Adrian has invested in a worm scheme. The little moneymakers live in a hammock and are going to turn our garbage into gold.

He ordered the contraption and a pound of Red Wigglers off the Internet. It's a canvas cylinder cinched at the bottom and secured around a hoop that hangs from the ceiling like a hammock, for worms. We toss in our eggshells and melon rinds, and the worms go to work devouring half their weight in a day. What goes in must come out, and they excrete the ultimate compost (vermicastings) and tiptop fertilizer (worm tea).

The tea oozes into a bucket set under the hammock, but it's trickier to harvest the castings because you don't want to throw out your worms with the compost. The information that accompanied the starter wigglers indicated you can sort it all by hand on a drop cloth and "children love to do this." The only kid I know around here is a four-month-old poppet, so that could get messy.

If you want a less personal encounter with the worms, you can scoop everything to one side of the hammock and add new bedding and garbage to the other. The worms migrate on their own. They're sensible down-to-earth worms.

Adrian's not worried about the details of packaging the stuff and selling it to organically minded gardeners. He says it's just another one of those bridges we don't have to cross until we come to it (like divorce). Maybe he's right. Why worry about shit until you actually have some?

He suspended the hammock from the straw ceiling near the oven because he doesn't want his investment catching cold, it being July in the Winterless North. All in all, it's not an operation you want in the middle of your kitchen. I did not set out on this adventure to be a worm farmer. I expected to raise alpacas. But I'm trying to be a good sport and tell myself I'm an entrepreneur now, turning crap into cash. I named a couple of the worms Lily and Willy. Just nine hundred ninety-eight to go.

We were cooing over Lily and Willy in their hammock last night. I looked up at Adrian and said, "I thought you promised me alpacas."

Adrian looked down his patrician snoot and said, "Are you kidding? Do you know how much a stud costs? Or a breeding female? And you can't have just one. They live in herds. You might be able to buy a wether for eight hundred bucks, but what's the point of that? The money in alpacas is in breeding them."

I told him, "You need to trim the hairs in your nose."

Date: July 20, 2002
To: Laura P.
Subject: La Contessa and the Duchess of Darch Point Road
Attached: Home fires burning

The wind shifted into the south today. We had our wood-burning stove, an upscale Contessa model, installed just in time. It's got shiny brass fittings and is covered with tiles the color of Hawke's Bay Pinot Noir. We call her La Contessa, befitting the hearth of our new home, and so I still outrank her as Duchess of Darch Point Road.

We keep a pot of soup simmering on top of it all week long. Every time we ladle out a couple of bowls, we toss in a new ingredient: carrots, potatoes, barley, chuck from the Mad Butcher. Daisy and Colin came for dinner two weekends in a row and never suspected they were eating a work in progress, it had so transformed. "Great, beef and barley tonight! We really enjoyed the chicken noodle last week."

Adrian just poured me a gin. Butter is frizzling in the pan, ready for the oxtails dredged in flour. Abracadabra, he'll turn last night's soup into curry with all the fixings, poppadoms, naan, and sambals. The fire has been banked all day, and he just threw on some tea-tree logs that are snap-crackle-popping as they burst into flame. La Contessa is heating up with a creak and a groan, and the pitchy residue is burning off the window to reveal a cheery glow. The sweet smell of garlic sautéing is in the air and soon, when the flames start to caper, the warmth of it all will creep across the jade slate floor.

You're too far away to share a pot of soup, but otherwise, it's beginning to feel like home.

Chapter 15

If the romance isn't perfect, it damn well better involve confit of duck.

—#39, God's Holding Paddock

The cat died, and the Antarctic Express blew in the day La Contessa was installed in the lounge, and Adrian had already lost interest in remodeling.

Initially he had gone gangbusters and hired handymen to revamp the woodwork, replace the biscuit board, and open up my study with a storybook leadlight window that looked up to the boulders (but not alpacas) on the back lawn. The eight o'clock starts, however, put a crimp in the sailor's rhythm. "I never would have committed to this house if I'd known it meant we couldn't sleep in," he complained.

I pestered him for a closet, and he rigged up a bamboo pole spanning two ladders and secured for extra support to the bedroom ceiling with sailor knots. It took up half the room. Two weeks later, I grabbed my chic, red-wool jacket from Voon off the rack (New Zealand designers had bounded out of the midcentury) and stuck my hand in a crust of muck on the shoulders. The daddy longlegs evicted from the pink parachute had moved to the bare ceiling and were excreting from there.

I told Adrian that closets are not optional when your house shares the bush with creepy-crawlies.

He told me, "We can't do everything at once," and sat down in front of the fire with a mug of tea and his *Wired* magazine.

The tug o' war had begun.

Four years earlier, I had spent a summer holiday with friends who had rented a farmhouse in southwest France. Anne and her husband brought along their two children and invited more friends, who invited other friends, and we ended up with a congenial mix. One of them arrived with hatboxes, the whole affair was that picturesque.

Lolling on picnic blankets, we had watched the sunflowers nod while the irrigators *tchuk-tchuked* and sprinkled the cornfields with rainbow mist. Sipping Côtes de Buzet in the shade of great rolled bales of hay, we passed around A. J. Liebling's epicurean romp, *Between Meals: An Appetite for Paris*, reading impatiently over each other's shoulders. "My turn now!"

We dragged our mattresses under the stars and got up early to shop at the open-air market. Anne and John's kids played *baby-foot* with the locals at the bar while, over blond beer, the grown-ups inventoried their purchases: beady-eyed shrimp, Charentais melons, Bayonne ham, frisée, lemons, garlic, farm-fresh eggs. Alfresco dinner on the farmhouse porch was shaping up nicely. "Let's sauté the shrimp in garlic, make croutons out of that old baguette, throw it all in a salad, and top it off with a poached egg—but we need more wine!"

The visit had culminated in what we fondly called the "The Duck Fest" hosted at a nearby farm. This eight-hour, nine-course meal featured the local specialties: duck, foie gras, and plums in every imaginable gastronomic incarnation, all served up with aperitifs, digestifs, and rivers of wine at trestle tables overlooking the fields and ducks that hadn't made it to the kitchen yet.

Beforehand however, we were obliged to observe the foie-gras process from duckling to tin. (There is no such thing as a free lunch, and even if there were, it would probably taste bad.) The abattoire was lined with shiny white tiles, sterile as an operating room, and a venue for serious work, it was clear, as our guide pointed out the electrocuter, bleeder, plucker, grinder, and canner.

In the old days, a duck whose foie would be gras got fed in Grandma's lap, the hairs in the mole on her chin quivering as she murmured encouragements and worked a funnel down its gullet. This was a modern operation where the funnel slid mechanically along a row of cages, allowing one operator to accomplish in an hour what it used to take Granny a day to do.

When the sun over the terrace had climbed to high-noon position, the pouring of Kir from big earthenware pitchers began to fuzz the edges of a realistic respect for the foundations of our meal. The farmer's daughters mingled through the crowd and offered pâté de foie gras on toasts served in plum-drying baskets even broader than their bosoms. It was all so overwhelming that Anne's husband leaned over for a canapé and almost fell in.

By the time the duck breasts grilled over grapevines were served, we were a handsome lot under the psychedelic glow of the blue awning, cheeks flushed purple and toothy smiles black from all the red wine. The kids skipped rope, and everyone danced and played cards between courses to make room for more. Evidently I did the tango with the postman after dessert and a couple of helpings of *prunes à l'eau de vie*, plums marinated in eighty-proof alcohol.

My friends were returning to the farmhouse and annual Duck Fest, and they invited Adrian and me along. It was a no-brainer: winter in Whanga-rain or summer in the south of France?

We found a babysitter for Lily and Willy, flew coach out of Auckland, and arrived thirty-three hours later, gravely jet-lagged, in Lot-et-Garonne at the grapevine-covered farmhouse where 1839 was carved over the entry in stone. Morning broke to a cock-a-doodle-do. We rolled over in our bed under the eaves and went back to sleep.

Adrian fit right in. That lasted two days. On the third, we all set out at midday to a country restaurant, sat at a table in the stippled shade, and ordered a bottle of wine. Adrian looked at the menu, laid it face down, and said, "I don't like to eat a big lunch."

I knew what I had my heart set on, but no one was compelling Adrian to eat confit of duck with a side of potatoes *Sarladaise*. Simple fare like that—potatoes, garlic, and duck fat—is not for everyone. There were lighter dishes to choose from.

"*Salade Niçoise?*" someone suggested.

"I don't eat fish."

We all finished the wine and went back to the farmhouse for a light, fish-free meal. My friends were polite, or astounded.

Jeez Louise, this man doesn't handle jet lag graciously, I thought. Then I remembered The Duck Fest. Uh-oh, talk about a big lunch. This was a marathon, a nine-course ode to duck, but it rolled out so tranquilly, so lyrically, and surely Adrian's jet lag would be over by then.

It started out fine, with the requisite tour of the abattoir and plentiful Kir. The afternoon progressed from tomato soup Gascon to sunny melons steeped in Monbazillac wine. It slid to a galantine of duck stuffed with foie gras, took on ballast with confit of duck, got lost briefly in a blur of salad, fruit tart, and cheese, and finally revived, fueled by alcohol, with *prunes a l'eau de vie*.

The conga line was forming at dusk, but Adrian refused to join in. Even though we had danced at the ball in Whangarei, he said, "I don't dance, and these shoes are killing me."

He took to bed the day after The Duck Fest.

"Too much duck?" I asked.

"You know I don't like to eat a big meal in the middle of the day," Adrian said, as if he had been surprised with a nine-course meal we had made reservations for two months ago, propped in my lap, and force-fed through a funnel like a duck.

I stayed home with the invalid while our happy-go-lucky companions went on to a brasserie and took in a castle or two. Adrian perked up after they left, *la grippe*, or *crise de foie gras*, or whatever ailed him resolved.

He offered to make mayonnaise for dinner, but it curdled, and he took to bed again. I tried to be sympathetic. It's hard, after all, to be dropped into a circle of someone else's old friends.

Let it go, I told myself. *I'm going to be eating and drinking my way through France on our canal boat soon. I can put up with a man who has a problem with shoes and doesn't want to eat duck all day. No one's perfect.*

The market in Villeneuve-sur-Lot next morning conflicted with the sailor's rhythm, as did the excursion to see Josephine Baker's chateau and banana-leaf belts the day after that.

By this time, my friends were barely speaking to us. Daisy had already made it clear that nothing's more tedious than middle-aged nitwits in love. Obviously we had spoiled the farmhouse mix. But when Adrian declined to go to Lac de Lougratte—"What idiot swims in a lake?"—he was beginning to irritate even me. Who doesn't appreciate that remember-when-I-was-a-kid feel of a summer afternoon, by any body of water?

Leaving Adrian behind at the farmhouse, I swam in the lake and pedaled a boat in circles under the Aquitaine sun with my idiotic friends. We loafed on towels and licked ice cream cones next to the French women sunbathing topless, while the men tried hard to be nonchalant.

Adrian took a nap while we were gone, and the compromise would have been fine, except he didn't speak to me for two days save an outburst in town when I suggested we buy a head of Savoy cabbage to stuff for dinner. "Can't you understand English? I said I don't eat that green shit."

At the end of our stay, Anne told me that I wasn't someone who would dance with the postman anymore. It took her six more years to tell me the rest of the story. Anne was that good a friend. She wasn't going to burst my bubble. She was willing to wait until it popped on its own.

Out of the blue at the farmhouse in France, Adrian had taken Anne aside and asked her what good her children were. (They were ten and twelve at the time.) He wasn't being funny. He wasn't being sarcastic. It was as if he were an alien studying human specimens he couldn't explain, or validate. Didn't they do anything besides read under the fig tree, eat steamed mussels, drink, play on hay bales, and swim, which was pretty much all the adults were doing, except the kids were tippling Orangina, not wine. And wasn't that the point of summer vacation in France?

On our way back to New Zealand, we detoured to visit Adrian's South African friends who now lived in Sallèles-d'Aude, where the Canal de Jonction runs through the middle of town.

"We'll talk to them about the canal-boat scene," he said, and good to his word, we sat under a freckled plane tree on a canal boat tied at the quay while Adrian and his compatriots weighed pros and cons of the layout of the galley.

There was one more tidbit that Adrian had confided to Anne at the farmhouse. She kept that one under her hat for years, as well. He was never going to buy a canal boat. We would never eat and drink our way through France. "That girl's delusional" is what Adrian had said.

Chapter 16

A whistling woman and a clucking hen are neither use to God nor men.

—consensus, all handles, God's Holding Paddock

Spring had sprung when Adrian and I returned from France. Blue herons flew back to nest in the pohutukawa trees, and my furniture arrived in a twenty-foot container after three months at sea.

"Bubbles," who was built like an ox and had an admirable ability to set boundaries around a woman's prerogative to change her mind, offloaded the baby grand piano. Before it was heaved into its appointed spot, he fixed me with a stare and said in no uncertain terms, "Make sure this is exactly where you want it because you only get one chance."

I had thought I would be elated to have my things about me, but amid the mountains of kraft paper, reams of corrugated cardboard, and boxes left to unpack, all I felt was a weight as hefty as a coffin nail. Adrian wanted to cut off the USA plugs on all my lamps and splice in Kiwi. I said I would use adaptors for a while. (This is also something to bear in mind: when you move halfway around the world and let someone talk you into shipping your furniture there, as well, it can be a significant anchor if you ever want to go home again. Dorothy could not even have attempted to climb into the wizard's hot air balloon with a baby grand piano on her back, and we'll never know if her ruby slippers had enough pizzazz to transport chattels, as well as Dorothy, back to Kansas.)

Shortly after my furniture landed, we spent the night at Daisy and Colin's place in town. "Drink driving" is taken seriously in New Zealand.

If the weather doesn't force you to hole up at one friend or another's house, sooner or later, the threat of the Booze Bus will. These heart-sinking roadblocks feature flashing lights, police cars, and a breathalyzer test. They are always set up past a blind corner or rise in the road, and there is never a back way around it. If you fail the breath screen, they take you to the bus, "And if they get you in the bus, you're a goner," the men at God's Holding Paddock had knowingly warned.

When I woke up the next morning, his shoes were by the bed, but Adrian was gone. The Mercedes was gone. He had driven away barefoot. I thought back to the night before. Colin and I had sung a rousing chorus of "Pick a Bale of Cotton"—with air drums—and we thought we were pretty darned good, which is how you feel about most anything after several bottles of wine. But even if we had cackled like hyenas, it wasn't grounds for a runner.

Adrian answered his cell phone on *Jingle Bells* in the Town Basin. When I demanded an explanation, he said, "It's your fault. I love you too much." This was the best he could come up with: he was afraid he might lose me, so he ran away?

For a nanosecond, I was flattered that someone could be that nutso on my account, and had we been pimply teenagers, this line of thinking might have been excused. But really, what grown man deserts a naked woman in the middle of the night? What grown woman takes heart in such behavior? And what was up with the shoes?

Adrian drove back to Daisy and Colin's to get me. "We need to pick up avos" was all he had to say.

I stood outside our house that night looking past Mount Aubrey, but there were no answers in the shooting stars because I didn't even have the right questions yet.

Adrian was in front of the fire reading when I came in, and I had a mind to say good night to the back of his head. He glanced up from *Heretics of Dune*, and we leaned into a kiss instead. His eyes were veiled like the haw-obscured orbs of a Nile crocodile. The dewy sky that was a hallmark of the mild northeasterlies hardened to aniline black, and the wind took one last swing into the south for winter's sake.

Date: November 29, 2002
To: Anne B.
Subject: The Bloody Wetsuit
Attached: Ocean Beach

Adrian has been teaching me to bodyboard at Ocean Beach. Here is how it goes. He chides me past my comfort zone (the shore) until I am in over my head. Either he has no idea where my comfort zone lies, or that is immaterial to the project at hand. We dive under the pounding waves together to get past the break (well beyond my happy place now). Then we bob among the Portuguese men o' war that can sting you with their slimy tentacles, some nearly a foot long. When Adrian judges that the wave thundering down upon me is a good one, he gives me a push, and away I go, with the solace that if I get stung, Adrian will pee on the wound and that will relieve the pain, so he says.

About half the time I catch the wave. The other half, I feel like

Annie Edson Taylor must have felt. She was the sixty-three-year-old schoolteacher who was the first person to successfully go over Niagara Falls in a wooden barrel. The barrel had first been tested on a house cat, then Annie took the plunge in 1901. She was in financial trouble and hoped this stunt might raise some money. Talk about dire straits. She got a gash on her head, but no fame or fortune.

I am not that desperate, so why do I persevere? Why do I let Adrian pack me into the barrel once more, only to tumble over Niagara Falls again? I believe it's for the 50 percent of the time that I get to ride the wave.

But first! First I have to get into a wetsuit. Everyone thinks it's hilarious that I'm wearing a wetsuit in summer. Let them laugh. I know it's under fourteen hundred miles from Bluff to the Antarctic Circle any time of year.

I got a custom wetsuit because nothing ready-made will fit a woman older than eighteen. The fitting started with a team effort at the Kerikeri Dive Shop a month ago. A girl who can buy her wetsuit off the rack wielded the tape measure, and a well-set lad recorded the numbers.

"Front to back waist, please," Surfer Boy called out in a cheerful and efficient manner that was meant to put everyone at ease. I held one end of the tape to the front of my waist and Junior Miss popped her head between my legs, retrieved the dangling bit and slid it, via private parts, to the back. It was a minor chagrin, and might even have been titillating had Surfer Boy been in charge of the tape measure.

I waited four weeks and drove to Kerikeri to pick up my custom-made wetsuit. In the dressing room, I stared at a garment that was so inflexible it stood up on its own and was exactly proportioned like the woman I would like to be in my dreams. I pretended to try it on, called out, "That's great!" paid them NZ$500, and drove back to Whangarei.

Although it's high summer, the temperature of the water at Ocean Beach has only risen to a point where, if someone flushed a baby alligator down a toilet in similar conditions, it would die of frostbite. I put on a modest one-piece "costume," as my mate from South Africa calls it. (Who equates the humiliation of wearing a swimsuit with the fun of playing dress-up?) And then I tried to get the wetsuit over my costume.

I struggled to get my feet through the elfin leg openings. I grappled with the neoprene, five millimeters thick on the body for warmth and three millimeters thick on the arms and legs for flexibility (righty-ho). I got it over my hips. Now the shoulders were at my waist, the crotch at my knees, and the kneepads at my ankles. I was getting claustrophobic. I wrestled my hands through the sleeves, like a cartoon character shoving cats into sacks.

On the bright side, I had expended two thousand calories attempting to get into the thing, and it just might function like a full-body girdle when in place. But let's be realistic. The odds of getting it in place were equivalent to my family of origin becoming a functional unit. And even if I did, it would be like super-sucker panty hose, as Laura says: the skirt might look divine after you zip it up, but you know it's a lie, and it's only a matter of time before someone else finds out.

I succeeded in getting the wetsuit over my shoulders after coercing Adrian to bounce me up and down to settle me in, much like you might do with a toddler in a snowsuit. But I couldn't stand up straight because the neoprene crotch was still at my knees. I looked like the hunchback of Notre Dame. Not Foxy Roxy, or Rip Curl Girl, or Billabong Babe. But Quasimodo, Igor, or a sausage stuffed by a butcher on LSD. And I wasn't even in the damn water yet.

AT THE BUTCHER COUNTER OF LIFE

Date: December 30, 2002
To: Sheryl O.
Subject: Hakuna Matata

We're spending the holiday in the Town Basin Marina on *Jingle Bells*. Boats turn out to be like much of what we sign up for in life. Hop on board for more than a day sail, and you discover that things were more appealing from shore.

Jingle Bells has floated untended for nearly a year. The miasma over the four roomy berths below hovers somewhere between cat piss and walrus breath after a clam feed. Fungi in rainbow colors adorn the saloon window shades. I woke up peppered with mildew and thought maybe I had molded in the night, until I took a close look at the sheets.

Adrian is presently lying under the navigation table in an inch of water near the buzz bars that supply power for the lights and instruments, trying to ascertain why seven hundred liters of drinking water he pumped into the storage tank last night ended up on the saloon floor.

I brought up the possibility of electrocution, but Adrian said, "No problem. It's DC." Then he explained hakuna matata to me. That's basically Swahili for "don't worry; be happy," which has a certain appeal—until you consider the implications of living with a man whose guiding light is a song from *The Lion King*.

The drinking rations cascaded into the bathroom and our bunk below. Since I haven't gotten the knack of flushing the toilet yet, which involves a lever and a lot of pumping, it's always wet down there anyway. The sheets were already mildewed, and there'll be no jolt, DC or AC, because Adrian won't let me use an electric blanket. He says I have his love to keep me warm.

Most of the food stock on board dates back to Adrian's circumnavigation with the family. This makes for pretty old gingerbread mix, and just how long do peanut butter and Vegemite really keep? He tells me I will be happy to eat anything when we start cruising, the odd lemon, a crust of bread. His wife-who-is-not-yet-ex learned to be grateful and how to flush the toilet, and so will I.

Cap'n Adrian has now removed the offending water pump and is standing over it with a tube of Molykote Valve and O-Ring Lubricant, so I must squish on over and see how I can help. If lubrication doesn't do the trick, he'll replace the valve, provided he can find a spare one. It might be with the seasick meds, which might be in one of the V-berths that look like Fibber McGee closets. After Adrian finds the spare pump, he will take a look at the generator, which for some odd reason isn't working either.

Cheers from *Jingle Bells*. We be happy and don't worry here. That's why every day on board's like Christmas.

AT THE BUTCHER COUNTER OF LIFE

Date: January 15, 2003
To: Sheryl O.
Subject: Prisoner of Love
Attached: Poolside, Darch Point Road

What is wrong with me? I'm the Duchess of Darch Point Road. I woke up at noon to a lavender-cream, full-body massage, three new grown-up toys from the House of Fun, and a sex life of crime. Adrian says the parallel universe is full of orgasms that people aren't using, so it doesn't matter if we reach through the quantum fog and steal a few.

We ate toasted cheese and toe-mah-toe on Vogel's bread for twosies on the verandah overlooking Snake Bank, emerging at low tide like a mirage. For dinner, Adrian pierced a leg of lamb, slipped in an entire head of garlic, slivered clove by slivered clove, slow-roasted it in the Römertopf casserole, and then took it all off the bone and roasted it some more until the end bits were sweet and crispy.

But I am beginning to—what? To chafe. I think I've got diaper rash of the soul. Everything on the boat is wet. Everything in the house seems to leak, which wasn't apparent when we signed the purchase agreement. Probably the fact was obscured in a downpour of optimism.

When I told Adrian that the fishpond leaks, he said, "It doesn't leak. The plants just suck up all the water." Hakuna matata.

I don't believe it, and I know because I'm the one topping up the pond so the papyrus and water lilies don't die, or the googly-eyed goldfish, if it doesn't get eaten first by the kingfisher that sits on the telephone wire, portending rain and patiently waiting to dive in for the kill.

"The pool filter leaks, Adrian."

"It still works." Hakuna matata.

"The skylight in the bath leaks."

"It drips right into the tub." Hakuna matata and hip-hip-hooray.

"The verandah roof leaked on my new tablecloth and stained it."

"Move the table." Hakuna matata.

"There's a leak in your study, and it warped the wallboard."

"It's my study, and it doesn't bother me."

Hakuna matata makes me feel like a nag. I know what they would tell me at God's Holding Paddock, but I can't help myself.

"The verandah roof leaks, Adrian." *Ba-gawk! Ba-gawk!*

"No it doesn't."

"It ruined the gramophone and that seventy-eight of Italian love songs. You're the one who took them to the dump. The verandah roof leaks; this I know to be true."

"No you don't."

Hakuna matata makes me feel bullied and gagged. Is it just an East African proverb, a happy Disney song? Or is hakuna matata a more sinister version of the smile-on-face-mouth-zipped rule that makes a woman feel like the leaky walls are closing in on her and she's not a duchess at all but just a waterlogged Prisoner of Love on Darch Point Road?

Chapter 17

Become one with the stumble.

—#39, God's Holding Paddock

While I was coming to terms with my incarceration as Prisoner of Love on Darch Point Road, Dad was having troubles of his own back in Arizona. He had been an academic before his parents put him in long pants, a nitpicker who annotated his Ektachrome slides down to the aperture and exposure at which each was taken. Mom wore a perpetual gravy stain on the generous shelf of her ample bust and misplaced every cap she ever screwed off a ketchup bottle or toothpaste tube. They had been at odds from the get-go.

But women of Mom's era were generally not empowered to take on the single life, nor were their men apt to put them in that position. They stuck it out. As long as Dad had a real office to go to, Mom had been free to star in her own fantasies on the home front. Sticking it out wasn't so bad. Their wartime marriage evolved into a private cold war.

When Dad retired from university life and began alphabetizing Mom's fossilized spices, however, tensions increased. My divorced brother, his three-year-old daughter in tow, moved in with our parents about the same time. Hostilities escalated. Ten years on, the child turned thirteen and promptly started tearing pedal to the metal through adolescence. Conflicts erupted. It was a right hullabaloo.

In an effort to re-create the serene cold-war days, my father must have hit upon the idea of moving his base of operations—and himself—back to "the office," in point of fact a one-bedroom apartment across town. He still had his mail delivered to the family home, an excuse to visit and tip of the hat to respectability from an eighty-year-old gentleman.

Finally Dad had a routine—"which my wife never had"—that he couldn't maintain in a household that included a grown son and audacious teenager. It started at five o'clock in the morning on his Exercycle with a Berlitz tape: "¿Hola, Fernando, qué hora es?" Then he did a hip-replacement shuffle around the mall and returned to the office to read the *New York Times* and *Arizona Daily Star* over breakfast. He shopped at Costco and bought Cheerios in U-Haul-size boxes and Marie Callender multipacks so heavy that passersby had to help him hoist the pot pies out of the freezer and into the cart. "I'm cooking for myself now," he proudly told the cashier.

For the next five years, this arrangement clicked for all concerned. The crew at home ran amuck like anarchists. My father was shielded from the worst of the rumpus and tumult, if not the financial fallout.

When the granddaughter was a junior in high school, about the time that Dad hit eighty-five, things stopped clicking. He still worked crossword puzzles from the Sunday *Times*. He could figure out that "tax due on foreign pottery" (twenty-three letters) was "what is owed on a Grecian urn," and that was more than I could do. The task of setting an alarm clock, however, stumped him, and he was tending bar like a soda jerk mixing a Suicide Coke. If you ordered gin and tonic at the office, you were as likely to get Metamucil, bourbon, and crème de menthe, as well.

Dad's mail began piling up at the family home, and Mom couldn't resist temptation. Employing the time-honored, tea-kettle method, she steamed open the letters one by one: confirmation of his lifetime membership in *Reader's Digest* Country Mouse and City Mouse Adventures Video Club, ten proposals for afterlife care (including an offer to scatter at sea the ashes of a man who had lived happily in the desert for twenty-five years).

After perusing fifteen credit-card statements with balances that totaled over $20,000, Mom made the SOS call to New Zealand. "He bought two new computers in a month! He's your father—do something."

Like what? I flew to Tucson and slyly photocopied Dad's checkbook register. Seemed as good a place as any to start. With that one maneuver, I officially assumed the most low-down role in this particular family drama: snitch.

When I asked my father about the computers, he said, "This modern technology is worthless. The first one deleted my spreadsheets. The second one crashed when I went into DOS. And you can't repair the damned things. I donated them to charity."

"You gave a brand-new Gateway to Goodwill?"

"The Dell, as well, after I dismantled the motherboard."

Mom and I compiled the information from Pandora's mailbox and Dad's records. He was shifting credit-card balances to secure lower interest rates. It was a sound strategy with one catch. He entered each transfer as a deposit in the register. Dad must have thought he was a millionaire because he had donated his entire TIAA-CREF February annuity to the American Civil Liberties Union.

Mom brazenly took a letter opener to the bank statement, and we gasped. Thank goodness he had bounce protection. The snitch confronted her father with the bad news: he was no millionaire. Disappointed but not for long, Dad made a new plan.

"I've come into a windfall," he confided. "Visa is sending me free money."

"Is that so?"

"They send blank checks, and I write in whatever amount I need."

I could see Dad hunched at his desk, gratified with the responsibility of so much money to manage, unaware that the checks were cash-advance vehicles. *What'll it be today? Five hundred? Two thousand? Mustn't be greedy. Let's do a thousand.*

A week later, he tripped over a jumping cholla on his way to meet me for lunch. Picking cactus needles out of his chin over a green-chili burrito, he assured me, "No serious damage. Luckily, I know how to fall."

Dad had a theory that it was counterproductive to break the impact with his hands. Better to just go with it. He had probably bounced off his substantial Teutonic nose and right back up like a Bozo the Clown bop bag. It was a touching meditation on Zen and the acrobatics of life.

"See?" He offered his glasses. "Didn't even break the lenses."

I gingerly removed the nose pads imbedded in his translucent skin. Dad put his glasses back on. "Much better. I can't remember what they call those whatchamacallits, and I know some people find them useful for something, but I think they're no good to anyone really."

How many tumbles, aside from the great hip breaker, does it take to say now is the time? Now is the time to move a parent from his home (or office). Now is the time to start the nasty business of wresting power of attorney from a Harvard graduate. Now is the time to slide my father from the driver's seat to the passenger side of the car.

In two months an eighty-six-year-old man would careen through a farmers' market in Santa Monica and kill ten people when he apparently mistook the gas pedal of his Buick for the brake. The horrific incident would stick in the head of every baby boomer with a creaky parent at the wheel.

Dad's Altima was already dinged on four fenders and missing both side-view mirrors. Should we forbid long voyages but allow him a trip to the grocery? (The California episode would make this tactic indefensible.) Take the coward's way out and anonymously turn him in to the DMV?

Maybe Dad could still work a crossword puzzle and fall like an expert, but the evidence was mounting. He was the Energizer Bunny of dementia, and it was time to rain on the bunny's parade. One evening,

Dad and I were watching the blush from the sunset skip across the craggy Catalinas. An idea came to me at that agreeable moment when the mountains turn pink.

Dad had first seen the Catalina range north of Tucson in 1958, and it was love at first sight. He took the chairmanship of the Political Science Department at the University of Arizona two decades later, and alongside the rattler, roadrunner, and gentle tarantula, made the desert his home. He had hiked the Grand Canyon to celebrate his seventieth birthday and explored the mountains surrounding Tucson until his hips gave out and he put away his tramping boots with much regret but little complaint. (Mom got valley fever a month after they moved in and never made peace with the landscape.)

The world must have seemed so vast for so long, from his Piper L-4 Grasshopper in the war, the ivory towers of academia, and summits of Mount Wrightson and Boboquivari. Now it was shrinking, and except for his ears and nose, Dad was shrinking as well.

The five-foot-five-inch gnome standing next to me said, "Mountains pink, time to drink!" and added, "How could anyone be depressed in a world with beauty like that?"

"Hey, Dad, how about moving to an office with a better view of the Catalinas?"

He liked the idea. The old scout was running out of new territories to explore. If options start to dwindle in midlife, by ripe old age, they go *poof.* The possibility of a fresh vista, if only through the window, was better than nothing, and possibility is hope's first cousin, spring's alter ego, the bloom that puts the canary glitter in the paloverde trees in April.

Dad was also probably ready for a helping hand, although he would never admit it. Along with the struggle to clip toenails, tie shoelaces, and restrain cappelini on the business end of a fork, the world, in general, was becoming trickier for him to negotiate.

And he enjoyed the attention. Invisibility is one of the less-publicized penalties of getting old. My brother took Dad to the barber shop and sporting-goods store where he picked out a new pair of "Dutch shoes." This is what he called the Aqua Socks he had taken to wearing. No one could figure out what Holland had to do with it, but they did solve the shoelace problem.

In search of an office with a better view, the family set out with Dad, smart in his yellow Dutch shoes and trim of what little hair he had. He wasn't worried if it was nearby or far away.

"I drive better than ever. Got seventy years' experience, after all."

Mom sighed.

"And I discovered the secret for driving after dark."

"The secret, John?"

"Sunglasses."

"Sunglasses?"

"Yup. Headlight glare causes night-blindness."

We found an office with mountain views just around the corner from the family home. Palms swayed by the front door, signposted "Retirement Living, Assisted Living, Alzheimer's Care." There was a shuttle-bus timetable at reception in the lobby. Now we just had to work out how to ditch the car.

We moved Dad, along with a gross of Post-it notes, two hundred legal pads, and a million staples. (Office supplies were also purchased at Costco.) He tacked a photo of Mom, fifty and blithe, above his desk, overturning a quart tin of rubber cement in the process, its fumes redolent of the days of galley proofs spread on the dining-room table, when editing really meant cut and paste.

Dad was giddy. He took a dip in the swimming pool under the blue shade of a jacaranda tree. When a 103-year-old woman almost ran him over with her rolling walker—"Out of my way, sonny boy; I'm late for art class!"—Dad congratulated himself on moving his office to an active community.

He could BYOB (the staff mixed the drinks) and invite guests to dinner. I joined him one night while he commiserated with a veteran who'd eaten sausages made from sawdust when he was captured in World War II. Dad told him in turn about the time an officer attached to the 84th Division joined him for K-rations in the Ardennes Forest. The lieutenant colonel complained because Dad's noncom air mechanic was eating in the Officer's Mess.

"Jesus Christ, we were having dinner in a chicken coop!" Dad exclaimed, flushed with the gusto of playing to an audience, and took another bite of Boston cream pie.

Mom visited the new office, and Dad kissed her good-bye twice, a level of affection not demonstrated since Eisenhower was president.

The car and the checkbook got "lost" in the confusion of moving, and it was hoped that Dad would get preoccupied with his new routines. To distract him, my brother loaded up his dirt bike and his father, and they drove to the Patagonia Mountains. While his son rode the Ghost Town Loop, Dad waited in the truck, and the thrill of new adventures filled the air.

Mom reluctantly took over the finances, and I returned to New Zealand, confident my folks were shored up in Tucson and relieved we had contrived to lose the bunny's batteries along the way.

Chapter 18

A full hitch of Clydesdales is nothing compared to what two tits on a woman can do.

—#28, God's Holding Paddock

Rosy Promise doesn't even need tits.

—#39, God's Holding Paddock

Culture shock rolls out like a roller coaster, but you don't have to expatriate to appreciate the dizzy ride. A move across town will do.

Dad spent three pleasant months on the peak, living communally. Then he hit the trough and phoned Mom. "Who put me in this institution? It's full of old women, and they're all Republicans! Where's my checkbook? Where's my car!"

"Talk to your daughter—it was her idea. Better wait a couple of hours. It's four in the morning in New Zealand."

But Dad didn't call me. Instead, probably about the time the war veteran was on his ninetieth repeat of the sawdust-sausage story, he got off the roller coaster—and called Hertz.

AT THE BUTCHER COUNTER OF LIFE

Date: August 8, 2003
To: Jim C.
Subject: Bunny on the Run
Attached: Runaway Bunny

Dad had a rental car delivered to the "institution," drove two miles down the road, signed a lease for another one-bedroom office, and put the deposit on his AARP Visa card. Mom gave him back the Altima.

"Hell's bells, just because he has a little memory problem, your father thinks he can do what he jolly well pleases. I give up."

Mom is slogging along—without the elation of buying in bulk—keeping track of two mortgages and bills for gas, electricity, telephone, security, trash collection, pool maintenance, and cable TV. She pays twenty-two dollars a month for pest control, and pack rats are still eating the insulation under the hood of her car. She is living with an incontinent dog and a granddaughter who will graduate next year and is already demanding eight hundred dollars for a portfolio of airbrushed senior pictures. She's tired of attempting to stretch their retirement income to support her place, his place (wherever that might be), the graduate's glamour shots, and the backlash of a string of financial fiascos from the *Reader's Digest* spree to the free-money caper.

My mother may be flagging, but I think it looks like the old bunny has one last adventure in him, don't you?

AT THE BUTCHER COUNTER OF LIFE

Date: August 8, 2003
To: Jim C.
Subject: Dad's Last Great Adventure

And this is how I choose to believe the adventure went:

My father ran away from the old folks' home in a three-quarter-ton V-10 Chevy Super Sport pickup. He took his AARP Visa card with him and left behind a brochure that featured an octogenarian in safari pants and Aqua Socks. It touted:

- The Active Choice!
- The Intelligent Choice!
- The Long-in-the-Tooth Last Great Adventure

"Simple, dignified, economical," the pamphlet continued. "Twenty thousand dollars is a sensible investment and competitive with the cost of six months in a lifestyle community, or a decent burial. Notification of Social Security included, if necessary." It went on to describe activities in remote places that involved more dexterity than tying shoelaces or eating cappelini: paddling up a Brazilian River by dugout (Amazon for the Aged), mountaineering in cold climes (Everest for the Elderly), and exploring the north rim of the Grand Canyon (Off-Roadsters for Oldsters—We'll deliver the truck and dirt bike to your office).

Dad rang me yesterday. He must have been calling from a pay phone, because he's mystified by the three cell phones he's purchased, each with a three-year contract.

"I don't hold it against you for locking me up," he said. "You probably didn't know the people there were so old. And they were all Republicans. I've never hung around those people before, and I don't intend to start now. I am not going to live in a place that doesn't represent a cross section of the American public. My God, there weren't any babies! And I was hoodwinked by the Boston cream pie. There's more to life than eating in a fancy dining room. I'd rather cook for myself."

"Where are you, Dad?"

"Flagstaff. I'm on my way to the Grand Canyon."

"The Grand Canyon?"

"I'd forgotten how much I love a road trip."

"You're eighty-five-years old!"

Don't worry. I've got sunglasses in case I have to drive at night."

Click. He must have run out of change.

I thought about calling the Highway Patrol but decided against it. He can go three weeks without food, three days without water, three minutes without air, but he won't last one second without hope.

Part III

Seeker in the Shit

Chapter 19

When all else fails, take the next sensible step: the pub.
—#28, God's Holding Paddock

Dad settled into life at the new office in Tucson, although he didn't appreciate getting his allowance from Mom. South of the equator, I had given up on Joseph Campbell and his damn doors. I just wanted to hunker down at someone else's keyhole to see how the rest of the world managed to get things right.

I had lived with Adrian for a year and a half and still couldn't fathom the man. He was poetry in the water but careless on land. He tripped. He chipped dishes. He poked at the fire and sent sparks flying that singed the lambskin rug. He lost tools, left them to rust in the rain, misplaced critical screws, stacked leaded-glass windows against a tree on a windy day—*Crash*! His rudimentary grasp of courtesy recalled what Anne's ten-year-old daughter had said at the farmhouse in France: "Sure I know about good manners. Don't put your feet on the table, and don't poke anyone in the eye."

It took me by surprise to discover Adrian was allergic to bees. (In my defense, I only learned this after I had planted a massive bed of lavender outside our front door.) In full bloom, it was abuzz, but there were always stragglers about. I had coaxed Adrian to help me pull some weeds nearby, and he had fiddled at it all morning. I didn't pay much attention when he went inside, lay down on the sofa, and said, "I don't feel well." I already suspected he was allergic to work. But he started to wheeze, and his face turned splotchy, then an odd shade of puce. He held up his index finger swollen to twice its size. "I got stung."

We rushed to Whangarei Hospital, where epinephrine was administered for anaphylactic shock. Adrian was sent home with an EpiPen in case of another bee sting, and that was the end of his gardening career.

The house on Darch Point Road also continued to reveal itself in discouraging ways. It was built on an anthill. Argentine ants are in the Top 100 of the World Conservation Union's worst invasive species. They hitchhiked into New Zealand around 1990 (probably from a single Australian nest) and made themselves at home. Argentine ants swarm up your legs and bite. They farm aphids for honeydew and protect them from predators. They attack nestlings, and the kiwi, which lays its eggs on the ground and can't fly, is in peril enough already. Most ants jealously guard their territory, but the Argentine ants from Kaitaia in the Far North to Christchurch on the South Island seem to get along well, all part of one big happy mega colony. Green blobs of poison had to be regularly applied across our property on Darch Point Road to keep their chummy population under control. Thank you again, Australia.

A cloud of fruit flies hovered over the worm hammock, and it stunk from an overload of garbage. Adrian was asking the worms to work double time, and they were crawling out of the hammock in protest. He stumbled over a bucket of worm tea, and the foul liquid splashed across the floor. His eyes narrowed. He pursed his lips and did not say a word but retrieved a can from under the sink. With deliberation he sprayed the whole operation with Doom. That was the end of Lily and Willy.

My life savings were commingled with the finances of a man who didn't explode often but whose rage was as chilling as any Rumpelstiltskin ripsnorter when he did. It appeared that besides a marital dilemma and bad manners, Adrian had anger-management issues as well.

Our honeymoon phase had lasted as long as a fresh fig. Adrian was supporting two households now, the wife's in Auckland and this home on an anthill at Whangarei Heads. It was making him cranky.

He tightened the feed into our joint account and sat me down for the budget lecture (money doesn't grow on trees), fool's rebuke (you expected a man to give you orgasms, dinner, *and* mad money), Dutch-treat change in plans (I'm out of cash—let's see what you've got). That's when I went back to work for Bay Audiology and lost my crown as stay-at-home Duchess of Darch Point Road. My Toyota Trueno got totaled. Adrian diverted the insurance money toward plane tickets to South Africa, and that's when I lost my wheels.

I had never seen so much of the back of a man's head: saying good night while he gazed at the fire, trying to strike up conversation while he stared at the computer and scribbled codes for option trading that covered pages in a mind-bending fashion that called Escher to mind. "I am doing this for us. I could make some money at it if you didn't constantly interrupt me with meaningless shit," he said. (I bit my tongue: *How about I find a stray bee in the lavender, trap it between the rim of a glass and stout piece of paper, and deposit it in your study, invisible on the jade slate floor instead?*)

I looked at the back of Adrian's head while he stood barefoot at the kitchen bench, scritch-scratching Bovril on toast, surveying the harbor traffic through binoculars and muttering, "Sailors rot in port."

And then it dawned on me: sailors go barefoot. Birds on wires don't wear shoes!

Certainly I wasn't pleasant company either, with my slew of pending projects and what-the-hells about the wife. Adrian did not feel dangerous, and he was not having fun anymore. The besotted man who had tucked Christmas gnomes in the bookshelf vanished. So did small talk, little kindnesses, and grander generosities. He no longer rhapsodized about murmurations of starlings or "monkey weddings," the sun showers that misted our home. The tug of war escalated to something meaner.

From his study window, Adrian had watched me spend a morning sketching a layout for tiles on the courtyard cement. I asked him to come out and take a look. "What do you think? A café table, couple of chairs. We could watch our blue herons come home to roost in the pohutukawa trees."

He scowled at the chalk marks. "We can't afford this. Is it because it's my money that you're happy to waste it? Did you see a big yacht parked outside Reva's and decide you would go after a millionaire? Well, you were wrong."

The sailor's rhythm that I had so gratefully welcomed was beginning to suffocate me. I stared at the Ben Franklin quote that Laura had given me years ago, decorated with grade-school panache in puff paint and sequins. "Up, sluggard, and waste not life; in the grave will be sleeping enough." It sparkled, the only two-bit aphorism on my bulletin board that still made sense.

Something Adrian had said back at Taurikura popped into my head. I had only paid attention to the first part: "It's easy for me to be a stone. You keep me from going there—"

Golly gee willikers, am I good or what?

Too busy congratulating myself, I had blown off the rest at the time: "—and you need to make sure that I don't."

Like the worms, I was falling down on the job. But it was too hard! Kevin at God's Holding Paddock just wanted his woman to be tidy. Peter the dairy farmer's ideal gal had to be able to dig a post hole, darn socks, turn over a ram, drink Speight's, and clear a pool table, but at least her guidelines were clear.

How was I supposed to keep Adrian from turning into a stone? Keep a smile on my face and my big mouth shut, that's how. Hakuna matata.

To top things off, it was becoming evident that things in Tucson were not shored up at all.

Date: October 23, 2003
To: Jim C.
Subject: Y-fronts in a Tree

Dick says an evening at the pub should make you feel better when you are already well. I think it's a tonic even when you are not.

Pete was in rare form tonight. He'd been away for several days driving his train, and Rex inquired how the trip had gone.

"Sacrebleu!" Pete said. "I had a heavy bout of social imbibing at the Grand Hotel the night before I went to work, and got my jugs mixed up."

"Your jugs mixed up?" I asked.

"It's a proven fact that an ardent Lion drinker cannot switch to DB during a session without explosive results, and to be fair, I must point out that a DB drinker has the same problem in reverse. The drinking population in Northland is split fifty-fifty as to which of the two is preferred, as you may or may not know."

Dick said, "Wait a minute," and went up to the bar for another handle. He could see that Pete was getting ready to spin a yarn.

He continued when Dick returned. "I was well on my way to a what-the-hell state of mind, so my taste buds did not get the message through to my sozzled brain, and I drank the dreaded DB at the Grand Hotel."

"Oh no!" resounded around the table.

"The next morning the alarm brought me back to life, and with a struggle, I made it to the bathroom and showered, shampooed, and shaved, not necessarily in that order, but I am sure I got through all my hygiene duties, albeit on autopilot. Unable to eat or drink anything, I lurched outside to find where I had parked the car.

"On arrival at the depot, I proceeded to ready my locomotive for the day. This was also done in a semiconscious state with my offsider doing all the work that required one's head to be lowered towards the ground.

"I should also point out that my fireman and mate was a Maori from up north. This is significant because of the issue of diet. He had spent a long weekend back home in the Hokianga and consequently had been living on kina, paua, and beer. Needless to say, I began our trip with some trepidation, knowing he had three days of shellfish and carbonated beverage under his belt.

"Everything went along smooth enough for an hour, and then it hit me. It stealthily slid over the floor, crept up the walls, and in one fell swoop permeated the cab. The stench was indescribable, worse than any long drop I ever encountered.

"I choked, spluttered, gagged, and banged my head on the edge of the window as I threw it open to suck in the untainted air that was rushing past the loco. Once I had recovered my composure, I glared at my mate. He was sitting there giggling uncontrollably.

"'You dirty-arsed bastard!' I yelled. [Dick let this one slide. Even God's Holding Paddock has to bow to the momentum of narrative.]

"This accusation seemed to increase his mirth. As no apology seemed forthcoming, I returned my head to the great outdoors.

"Just as normality had returned, I felt a boiling and a bubbling building up in my stomach, and the devil in me said, 'Payback time.' I lifted my left leg towards my mate's direction so as to improve my aim, and let rip.

"My mate noted my movements, glanced over in my direction, and saw the look of horror on my face. With a squeal of delight, he exclaimed, 'Ya shit yaself, ya prick, ha-ha!'

"I grabbed the brake and wacked it on, and the train screamed to a stand in a cutting at Taipuha. Moving very gingerly, I eased out of the seat and, grabbing the classified section of the *Herald*, left the cab and walked back along the train, seeking a bit of privacy.

"I was wearing overalls and tight jeans, and my feet were in lace-up boots. All of these I had to divest, so as to remove my undies, and I have to say this operation was not easy, as there was a light drizzle happening, and I had to stand on loose ballast, which was moving under my feet whenever I shifted my weight. However, I managed to disrobe and proceeded to clean myself up with both my undies and the pages of the *Herald*.

"When I was dressed again, I looked at my new Jockey Y-fronts lying in the ballast, not a pretty sight. In a fit of anger, I picked them up and threw them over the tea trees adjacent to the track. Unfortunately they opened up midflight, and the aerodynamics went wrong. They floated for an eternity, finally snagged on the highest branch, and just hung there, a monument to my embarrassment, and a dire reminder for all never to mix up one's jugs of beer.

"On top of that, now I'll have to look at the bloody things every time I go through Taipuha."

Date: October 25, 2003
To: Sheryl O.
Subject: Vows of Silence

Adrian and I had another tiff, the usual—I gripe and get the back of his head in return—so I borrowed his car and drove to the pub.

Dick was the only one at God's Holding Paddock when I got there. Neither of us mentioned my coming alone. No good would come of airing my problems in this sacred spot that is meant to make you feel better when you are already well.

"I'm going to buy you a beer, girl," he said. "And I brought you that Barry Crump book. But first, I'm going to tell you a story. Get out your notebook."

He returned from the bar and began. "Once upon a time, there was a monk. When this monk entered the monastery, he took a vow of silence. He was only allowed to speak once a year.

"After the first year, the abbot asked him, 'Is there anything you would like?'

"The monk replied, 'Yes, please, I would like some milk in my tea.'

"The monk stayed on, and at the end of his second year of silence, the abbot asked him again if there was anything he wanted.

"The monk replied, 'Yes, please, I would like some sugar in my tea, as well.'

"When the end of the third year rolled around, the monk had had enough of the vow of silence. He told the abbot, 'I can't do it. I want out.'

"And the abbot said, 'Good. All you do is complain.'"

Then Dick handed me the book he had promised to lend: *Bastards I Have Met*.

Date: October 26, 2003
To: Anne B.
Subject: The Demented Leading the Blind

We were packing our bags today, and I asked Adrian, "Where's your EpiPen?"

He said, "You were supposed to put it in a safe place for me."

"Oh." Putting me in charge of Adrian's adrenaline at this point is like asking Madame Defarge to assemble her knitting into a comely garment for Marie Antoinette.

We're going back to the States to rain on the Energizer Bunny of dementia's parade once and for all. The Triple-A incident did it. Dad couldn't get the car going last week, so he called my brother and asked him to get AAA out for a jump start. My brother arrived in the parking lot of the one-bedroom office shortly after the tow-truck driver. The burly guy was in the process of pointing out to my father that his car was jacked up and set on concrete blocks. Someone had stolen the wheels.

I called Dad to let him know we're coming for a visit and couldn't help hinting that all was not well here. I didn't mention that Adrian won't allow me to get out of bed until he's delivered a post-coital lecture on gasoline consumption: "If you paid attention to the rpm's and your shifting behavior, you could get seven more kilometers to the liter." But I did tell him that Adrian makes me feel like an errant sheep, the way he uses the purse strings and cold shoulder to keep me in line. Stop! Get away back! Come in! Walk up!

I wonder what's worse: looking to someone with dementia for guidance or asking for relationship tips from my father, who until he was eighty, never attempted a conversation with me about anything more personal than voting behavior in his home state.

Actually, it can be helpful to bounce ideas off old people's heads. You get to vent, and because they often have short memories, they don't hold it against you for failing to follow their advice and continuing to engage in the same dumb behavior that got you into the predicament you came to them gritching about in the first place. They can be more forgiving than girlfriends in this respect and certainly boyfriends, whom old folks beat by a country mile.

Dad asked me, "Are you afraid?"

I said no, that I supposed I was more frustrated than anything.

And Dad said, "Then you are not paying attention."

Chapter 20

The whole lot was planned out, not one damned thing worked,
and it all turned to custard.

—#21, God's Holding Paddock

When I got to Tucson, Dad filled me in on the Triple-A affair. "At least they only took the wheels. Last month they swiped the car. After the hooligans went for a joyride, they parked in a different spot to throw me off. The damnedest thing is they did it without unlocking the doors. Kids that sharp would have been doing something more productive in my day."

Dad's "day" started with a scholarship to Harvard. A bright but poor boy from a German immigrant family, he used to say he got the award because he was a minority student from a disadvantaged community. (The Cincinnati relatives did not appreciate this comment.)

He served as a liaison pilot in World War II and was discharged after the war as a captain with five battle stars and the Air Medal with two oak leaf clusters. Dad returned to Harvard to complete his doctorate on the GI bill and went on to climb the academic ladder at home and abroad, writing weighty texts on legislative behavior and biopolitics.

Mom decided it was time to consult a gerontologist about the man who used to be a walking encyclopedia and was now doing a hip-replacement shuffle around the corners of his mind.

Mom and I looked on while Dr. P. administered a mental status exam developed at St. Louis University (with the winsome acronym SLUMS).

Dad got an A+ on the initial questions. It was indeed a Wednesday in December 2003 in Tucson, Arizona.

"That's not the point," Mom said under her breath.

"*Shush*," Dad said.

The good doctor then read a list of five objects, "apple, pen, tie, house, car," and advised Dad he would have to repeat them later. When the time came—after a couple of math problems involving a hundred dollars and the purchase of some apples and a tricycle (Dad failed) and an exercise to see how many animals he could name in one minute (seven)—of the five common objects, Dad remembered only "apple."

Dr. P. told Dad a story about Jill, a stockbroker, and Jack, the handsome fellow who married her. Jill stopped working to bring up their three children in Chicago, went back to brokerage when the kids were teenagers, and they all lived happily ever after.

"What state did Jill live in?" asked Dr. P.

Dad flunked the fairy-tale test. (I passed it, at least that fairy-tale test, but I wondered, *What the hell came after "tie"?*)

Mom couldn't hold her tongue any longer. "Tell him, John. Tell him how you bought all those computers."

"I have no idea what you're talking about."

"And tell him how you lost the car at the mall three times last month."

"This is pointless. We are not going to waste the doctor's time like this."

"Tell him, John, about Triple-A."

Dad looked at Dr. P. and told him with a shrug, "She blows everything out of proportion."

Spit and Spat were at it again. The squabble escalated and sidetracked Mom from what she really wanted. She was begging Dr. P. for an answer: What should we do with him?

He gave her a three-month trial of Aricept. "One in his applesauce every night."

On the way out, Dr. P. took me aside and said, "I understand why you moved to New Zealand."

The appointment with Dr. P. confirmed what the AAA episode had already made plain: Dad couldn't live on his own at the office anymore. He couldn't move into the retirement home again because the family budget wouldn't support his impending demotion from independent to assisted living. There was no choice but to move him back home. Oh dear God, a hurricane had hit the bunny's parade.

Date: January 15, 2004
To: Sheryl O.
Subject: Bad Ass Girls Drive Big Ass Toys, and
My Boyfriend Stole My Daddy's Car

We moved Dad back home last week. My brother, his fiancée, Adrian, and I are bunking at the office for a couple of weeks until his lease is up. It's a place to hide the car, red rag to a bull at this point, and the uproar at the house has been stupefying, too much to bear. I need someone to hold me in his arms and just let me bawl.

It won't be Adrian. Last night he clenched his teeth and said, "I didn't fly over here for this. I don't do stress, not mine and certainly not someone else's." Then he stalked off to bed. When I got up this morning, he was gone, and so was Dad's car. No word. No note. He didn't even leave his shoes behind.

On a hunch I called the airport. Because I couldn't think of anything more plausible and less embarrassing, I said my boyfriend had stolen my father's car to catch a flight to New Zealand. (I did not tell them my boyfriend is sixty years old.) Security was incredibly helpful. They located Dad's car in the parking lot and Adrian's name on the passenger list to LA and on to Auckland.

Adrian had abandoned me to the Crazies! And you know what? I almost don't blame him. It's only been a week since Dad put Mom's photo over the desk in his new office, the spare bedroom, and the dogs are already running for cover.

"You took my cane, John!"

"It's not your cane. It's mine!"

The granddaughter's apple-head Chihuahua startles and jumps off Dad's lap. The beagle pees on the carpet and runs to hide under the bed.

"No, it's not! Your cane is the one your daughter sent you from New Zealand. Mine is the one I had to buy for myself at Osco."

"And where do you think you're going at this time of night, young lady?" Mom turns to the granddaughter and asks.

"Up yours, Grandma," she mutters, and slams the door. Spitting gravel in her half-ton, Hemi-powered Ram, "Bad Ass Girls Drive Big Ass Toys" illuminated on the license-plate frame, she screeches—*varoom*—into the night.

Chapter 21

There comes a time to depend on the parachute not the plane.

—#9, God's Holding Paddock

I was appointed trustee for my parents two weeks after Adrian flew the coop. We had enlisted a specialist in elder law, intending to sort out finances without the shameful formality of declaring Dad incompetent. Mom started the hoo-ha.

"Dr. P. feels that John's memory isn't what it used to be."

"I don't recall Dr. P. telling me I have a memory problem."

"Hell's bells, John, then why did he give you memory pills?"

"I don't remember any memory pills!" (To his credit, she was slipping the Aricept into his applesauce.)

They were off and running. The lawyer looked at the figures, which included credit-card debt that was now up to $43,000 and ran the gamut from Victoria's Secret, Guess, and all major gas stations and department stores to twenty-four bank-affiliated Visas and Mastercards. He recommended loan consolidation and suggested obliquely that neither parent was competent to handle fiscal affairs. The best solution would be to appoint me trustee.

Mom said she would rather die first, and I said, "So would I." The lawyer told her to cool down and advised Mom that she couldn't afford to pay a stranger enough to do a job as onerous as the one he was suggesting her daughter take on for free.

In that moment, I hated my mother. I hated the lawyer for guilting me into bondage to my parents until the days they died, and most of all, I hated Adrian for running out and leaving me alone with the mess.

Full of resentment herself, Mom surrendered. "How much do we owe you, please?" She opened her purse. This wasn't what she had wanted the checkbook for. The aim of this visit had been to vindicate her. She got double-crossed instead. Fumbling with the pen with her pianist's fingers, as familiar to me as my own hand, Mom wrote a check to the lawyer for three hours of humiliation.

In that moment, I saw what it meant to be the wife of a prominent, dominant, and now dotty husband, a woman who at seventy-nine still had fire in her belly and was struggling to have a voice. It must have been much like how hakuna matata made me feel.

And in that moment, I also understood that denial is not always the coward's way out. It doesn't have to be some pact with the devil. Seeking shelter from the blinding light of truth might just be a covenant with life to get you through.

The story that was family legend began with Ruth, a beauty with obsidian eyes and a cryptic gaze, an exotic uncommon in Pittsburg, Kansas. Spirited Ruth drove her trap through town so recklessly that shopkeepers ran out and shouted, "Slow down!" She was clever, but girls in those days were not supposed to be clever any more than they were supposed to race around in pony carts. She was also a tad unhinged, maybe because she was so clever.

An affable man of Irish descent, Dale, married Ruth, whose roots were established back to the family of Lady Jane Grey. (She was queen for nine days, and then off with her head!) Did the blueblood pedigree account for Ruth's quirks of mind as well as her regal brow?

Dale was a doting husband, who surprised his wife with lacy underthings from Joplin. He proved to be a loving father, as well, when Ruth bore him two daughters, Joanne, my mother, and two years later, Patricia, my Aunt Pat. What fun "Jody" and "Patty" had, decked out in party dresses, Patty's curls twirled into corkscrews that her naughty sister once cut, every other one. They took tap, ballet, and piano lessons. The stacks of sheet music were three feet high. The red, red robin was always bob, bob bobbin' along at Jody's place when she was a kid.

The background music her sister heard, however, sounded more like "Mood Indigo." Patty remembered the trips to Menninger's in Topeka for nebulous treatment, respite, bouts of hope, insinuations of shock therapy. Patty remembered that they didn't always get to those picnics in the old Ford V-8. Somewhere along the way, Ruth slipped her moorings, and Dale turned the car around and headed back. The girls unloaded the basket on the kitchen table while Dale tended to Ruth, dulcified, coaxed, lost his temper, and started all over again until he anchored his wife to the tangibles of family and home, or it simply ended in a row. Jody dug into the hand-squeezed lemonade, double-fudge brownies, and tuna sandwiches so carefully wrapped in a damp tea towel to keep the bread moist. Patty lost her appetite, wondering if Ruth would be the good mother the next day or the bad one, hiding notes in vases warning that the whispering walls had ears. Would she be standing by their beds smiling good morning or feeling her daughters' faces as if she were reading Braille?

The girls grew up, married, left home. Joanne moved back with her folks in Pittsburg while her husband (John, my father-to-be) served in the army during World War II. She taught in a one-room schoolhouse and had to get there early to light the fire in the potbelly stove. Dale drove her so she wouldn't have to walk to work while it was still dark.

One morning they had a big argument on the way, and it was over Ruth. Dale told his daughter that she needed to be more patient with her mother. She didn't understand that Ruth wasn't well. Joanne didn't want a lecture. She slammed the car door and didn't look back, but her father was right. She was only nineteen, and she didn't understand.

Dale didn't pick up his daughter that night. A neighbor came in his place to tell Joanne that her father was dead. He had lain down while Ruth was fixing dinner and never gotten up. Dale died of a heart attack at forty-nine.

When John returned from the war, he and Joanne went east to Cambridge, Massachusetts, where he resumed studies at Harvard. Ruth was left alone without the prop of a loving husband. She was poorer, and that will certainly make an odd widow odder. There was no insurance money, no pension from the Marion Steam Shovel Company on whose behalf Dale had made sales calls in places like Joplin, where he bought fancy underwear for his wife. Social Security was in its infancy and a pittance when Dale had died.

Eight years after Dale's death, Patricia returned to live with her mother in Pittsburg while her husband fought in the Korean War. Ruth, proud, poor, and unbalanced, had grown ever more reclusive, covering her face with a scarf when she went into town, darting behind laundry on the line to avoid the neighbor's eyes, certainly prying.

April 1953 was an unseasonably cold and stormy month across the country. The night Patricia called Joanne, they had freezing rain in Pittsburg and snow in Cambridge. But she hadn't called her sister to talk about the weather.

"Mother locked herself in the bathroom this afternoon, Jody. She threatened to kill herself. I tried to reason with her, but I couldn't make her open the door. I screamed at her to open the door. I pounded on it. I pounded harder."

"You're just a little thing, Patty. You can't be expected to break down a door."

"Yes, that's what the policeman told me."

The officer who had arrived at the scene later couldn't believe that a woman who was five foot and a bit had been able to break down a door. Patty had screamed and pounded and hurled herself against the door again and again until it splintered off its hinges, but by then, Ruth had downed a bottle of Drano.

My mother left us with Dad (I was four and my brother not yet two) and flew from Massachusetts to Kansas. When she told the man at American Airlines that she had to get home because her mother was dying, he said, "Lady, I hear that story every day. Now step to the back of the line." By the time Jody got to Pittsburg, it was clear that in spite of her superhuman strength, Patty hadn't broken down the door in time.

It might have been full of music and fun, but in the home where my mother was raised, you had to fashion your own guidelines. Joanne settled on romanticism and denial. Patricia kept a smile on her face and her big mouth shut. But their MOs were immaterial because all coping mechanisms eventually fall short when it comes to dealing with a mother who would chug-a-lug lye.

Chapter 22

It's not terrible to want to go back to the way things were. It's just unlikely.

—#6, God's Holding Paddock

I was now trustee for a three-generation family that included a son with a second wife and a granddaughter who Grandma couldn't say no to, all under one twice-mortgaged roof. It was a responsibility no one in her right mind would have assumed for all the hundred-dollar bills, apples, and tricycles in the world.

Mom and I patched things up and attempted later that week to sort out the budget, matching receipts with the credit-card charges. The balances had doubled since Dad's heyday. "It's those darned computers," Mom said.

"From Victoria's Secret?"

"Well no, that particular charge is for some underpants I bought last month."

"Fifteen thongs?" My mother, nearly eighty, stood five-foot even and weighed two hundred pounds at the time.

She looked me straight in the eye and said, "Yes."

"And the iPod on the American Express card?"

"Your father insisted. How could she refuse? No child wants to see her grandfather make a scene at the Apple Store."

So this was how it was going to be.

"I'm too old for this nonsense," Mom said, and opened the freezer to get a bag of corn to sit on. "My hemorrhoids are killing me." *Harrumph, Deanna Durbin never balanced checkbooks.*

In the meantime, Adrian had sent an email. The subject line of the first was "I love you." To say that I found this incongruous would be an understatement akin to describing medieval torture as an uncomfortable way to pass an afternoon.

He went on to elaborate how it was my fault he flew back to New Zealand. I couldn't see that the strain in Tucson was destroying our relationship, and he had to save us. Adrian hadn't abandoned me at all. He was waiting at home with roses. The afternoon on the rack unfolded with a firebrand held to my buttocks while my tormentor leisurely increased the tension on the chains and grunted, "This is hurting me as much as it's hurting you, but I am doing it for your own good."

By this time, I had lived in New Zealand for almost four years. I owned half of what the bank didn't possess on a fairy-tale home in the Kiwi bush. Old folks there didn't make my life difficult. They reminisced.

"'What do you want for breakfast, Dick?' Joan would ask me."

"'Flounder, Joan, I think I'll have flounder,' I would say, and you know what I'd do, girl? I would go down to Parua Bay and catch it. The harbor back then was full of flounder, crayfish, scallops, snapper. You took whatever you needed."

When Adrian got to me, I walked down to Taurikura Bay, where a man might be whistling "Amazing Grace" while he mended a net. He would likely be there an hour later, still whistling, when I headed back up the hill.

Or I climbed Mount Aubrey, with fantails darting for the insects I stirred up. Under a canopy of bush so dense that sunlight penetrated one ray at a time onto epiphytes growing with mutual consent on the bark of the pohutukawa trees, I climbed. Across viridescent liverwort, I tramped through water that seeped from springs deep in the mountain. Over kitchen middens, tree roots, and boulders, I ascended to a glimpse of the Pacific Ocean. And once, only once, I saw a morepork as I set across the ridge through the prickly gorse in the waning sun.

In the States, the TV reminded me at high volume that there were a thousand ways to expire or get bedeviled from death by peanuts to restless leg syndrome. I was greeted with billboards that screamed:
1-877-
Collect calls from your cell phone!
Hotels, hospitals, jails, prison!
Or 1-800-
Reverse that vasectomy!
Or 1-888-
Can you really afford to die?

In the Land of the Long White Cloud, a man could whistle on the beach in peace while he mended a net and watched the tide come in. And I had people there: Dick and Joan, God's Holding Paddock, Mary, Daisy and Colin, Peter, Adrienne, Emily the Poppet, the official at Passport Control in Auckland. I had people to say, "Welcome home, luv."

I could not come up with a better option than returning to my home on Darch Point Road. No one but Dad volunteered to drive me to the airport, so I called a cab. Mom told me I had no family loyalty, and my niece said, "Go back to New Zealand where you belong. Nobody wants you here." My brother had already left town with wife number two to look for land where they could build a ranch called Pie in the Sky.

Dad waited in the garage with me, ready to go. He asked me one last time to help him find his checkbook and car because he would need them in New Zealand. I hugged him and whispered the motto of the Harvard marching band, which he had recalled to me during several hard times of my own: "*Illegitimi non carborundum.*" Don't let the bastards grind you down.

Dad said, "Good-bye, old girl," and I climbed into the taxi with a hole in my heart as big as a supermoon. He waved and called out—I heard him faintly as the cab pulled out of the drive—"*Illegitimi non carborundum.*"

With an elementary knowledge of online banking, my parents'

checkbook, and no idea where else to call home, I returned to New Zealand. Three months later, Dad was in Depends.

Date: March 2, 2004
To: Sheryl O.
Subject: Sad News
Attached: Waxing moon over Manaia, from Mount Aubrey

I got a big "Welcome home, luv" from the guys at God's Holding Paddock tonight. When Dick got up to get a beer, Rex told me that Joan was diagnosed with metastatic ovarian cancer while I was gone.

"She was at the pub last week, and I asked her what she was going to do. She said, 'I'm not going to lie, Rexy—the world is confused enough already—I plan to go down smoking and drinking, but it's going to be hard on my toy boy.'"

I hiked up Mount Aubrey at dusk today. At the summit, a morepork watched me with yellow eyes from a tea tree while I sobbed for all the good-byes we have to say in this wonderful world. Then I headed back home in the dying light.

Chapter 23

I had this starboard/port confusion, no paddle,
no bailer, and was night-blind as well.

—#6, God's Holding Paddock

Adrian was finally dissolved from the wife. Dissolution is the polite name for divorce in New Zealand and an option for partial disengagement (dissolution of the marital union) when you haven't yet succeeded in extricating your money. His finances were still tethered to settlement of the marital property, and the caveat was a real pea under the duchess's mattress.

"Why can't you just pay back the money you took out of your joint account for the down payment, Adrian?"

"I don't have that kind of money, and I have to pay off the credit cards. The caveat will be lifted when we settle. Don't tell me what to do."

Pay off the credit cards? Adrian and I shared a checking account and one credit card. He had several bank accounts in New Zealand and offshore, as well a fistful of his own charge cards, but why would he carry balances on them? I had been on salary or an hourly wage all my life. I earned money, saved it, spent it. The possibility of manipulating money, leveraging debt, and squirreling away assets escaped me.

"This has been dragging on for two years, Adrian!" I was back at the Mouse Crossing, losing patience. Lagging behind the rodent, far behind the two-ton tortoise and crippled inchworm, the snails arguing over marital property hadn't even come straggling into view. "You and your wife made this bed, and I'm tired of sharing it. It's getting a little cramped."

"She's just causing shit to annoy me. Ignore it. I'm divorced. Isn't that what you wanted? All you do is whinge. You do sweet bugger all."

"Excuse me?" This man had casually handed off a two-carat diamond. He had promised me anything short of a Learjet, his very words, so yes, I had assumed that maybe for once in my life, I could do sweet bugger all.

"Why are you picking on me?" he said, and took his lunch onto the verandah to eat alone.

I looked at the mess on the counter and stewed. '*We have people in South Africa to throw away the banana peels for us, put the mayonnaise back in the refrigerator.*'

I headed him off on his way to the study. "You may have had people to pick up after you in South Africa, but here on Darch Point Road—"

"In South Africa, our women know better than to talk to a man like this. I have worked my entire life not to have a boss. You are not my fucking boss. Don't tell me what the fuck to do." Adrian went on to say that he had offered me the sun and stars, and I was neither grateful for nor worthy of his money, his house, his family, his friends. "I've talked to them about you, and they all agree that you must be mentally ill not to be thankful for all I've done. And by the way, I don't appreciate your pocketing the travel allowance when you're driving my car to Kerikeri."

I cried. I yelled. I pummeled Adrian's back as he walked away. I grabbed a dish, but thought about it first—a chipped bowl from The Warehouse—and hurled it off the verandah at the rocks by the pool. It broke with an unsatisfying clunk into three pieces.

Adrian packed up his gear and went windsurfing. When he came home, I was on my hands and knees scrubbing the kitchen floor, trying to be worthier. He looked at the wet floor between him and the jug and said, "How am I supposed to make my tea?"

We put our fairy-tale home up for sale barely two years after moving in. It was hardly market ready. But Adrian was eager to liquidate assets, and the Prisoner of Love had a notion that this might provide her means of escape, if necessary. The property wasn't subdivided yet and had to be sold in its entirety, which put it out of reach for most of the locals. We were in the position of every Kiwi trying to sell a home in an upscale bracket: "seeking an overseas buyer." The house stayed on the market an entire year without one serious inquiry.

We opened a six-figure overdraft account, a line of credit against the house, to proceed with remodeling and subdivision in the meantime. The loan corresponded curiously with the mounting bills from lawyers and forensic accountants for Adrian's financial settlement with the partially-ex-wife. I had cosigned a mortgage and a home-improvement loan. Ye gods, was I hogtied now!

Adrian stopped making sure I took out my earrings at night so they didn't get tangled in the bedclothes. I stopped sleeping until noon. He ate his oyster while he carved the chicken and left mine on the edge of the platter. The relationship itself, so joyously transparent at first, had mutated into a big drooling monster trailing green slime across the jade slate floor.

How had it happened? Was the flaw in Adrian? Was the fault in me? I tried to pin it on Daisy because she had set us up on the damned blind date. But that wasn't gratifying. Daisy and Colin had just moved to Australia. When the blaming thing teams up with the missing thing, there's no fun in being righteous.

I began the long search for some strategy to work around Adrian's erratic ways and volatile temper and stumbled on a magazine article about prisoners of war in Iran. It discussed interrogation and torture training and in a sidebar, outlined the essentials of comportment for POWs. Maybe Hostage Rules would work for me? I had a head start:

1) Obey orders. (Don't tell him what the fuck to do.)
2) Don't speak unless spoken to. (Hakuna matata was probably okay.)
3) Don't whisper to fellow captives. (Since Lily and Willy's demise, I had none.)
4) Don't look captors in the eye. (Mostly I saw the back of his head.)
5) Don't offer suggestions. (Don't tell him what the fuck to do.)
6) Don't argue, threaten, or draw attention to yourself. (Ditto.)
7) Don't make sudden moves—ask first. (But not to put mayo back in the fridge.)

Things ran smoother with the hostage rules, but they were really just a military version of mouth-shut-smile-on-face, and the issue of lobotomy would have to be addressed soon. Focusing on a restricted set of behaviors did, however, slow me down long enough to be still and listen. This is what I heard: *You cannot explain this behavior of Adrian's, but it rattles you at the core, a place that seems to be inhabited by a child sustained by no one in particular and replete, therefore, with longing and dread. You are uninformed about his finances, too, but one thing's for sure. He's got more money than you do, and that's the majority that rules on Darch Point Road.*

My transequatorial life had been built on certain assumptions, namely that I had a vote in it and Adrian had my best interests at heart. And if that weren't the case? What if he refused to fly me back to visit family and friends? What if he wouldn't cooperate to finish remodeling? (I had paid for the new front and back stable doors and copper spouting, but that was the best I could do unless I acquired another car and totaled it.) What if he bailed on the mortgage installments? What about the down payment I had invested? Where did all the money go!

Taking baby steps toward the right questions, I started paying attention and found out that Dad was right. I was sharing a bed with Adrian, his partially-ex-wife, and a slimy green monster. I was alone in the midst of the crowd on Darch Point Road, and afraid.

On my way back from the next Kerikeri clinic, I bought six wine glasses with pin money from work. They were hand-painted with scarlet and emerald pohutukawa sprigs and dots like gilded snow. When I arrived home, Adrian set down his mug of tea, looked up from *The Coming of the Quantum Cats*, and asked, "What's in the box?"

"Wine glasses to cheer us up."

"What part of the word *budget* do you not understand?"

He removed the excelsior with care, informing me as he unpacked each glass, "I bought it. I can break it." He set the glasses one by one on the kitchen bench, save the last. He held this one under my nose and repeated, "I bought it. I can break it." Adrian sauntered onto the verandah with the glass, took careful aim, and threw it off the balcony. It smashed against the volcanic rocks in a bedazzling shower. Weeks later, bits of colored glass still twinkled around the pool.

"You did it, my dear. I can too.

"My tea is getting cold," he added, and strolled back inside.

I did not protest that I had used my own money for the purchase. It didn't matter. Adrian was making a greater point: if it weren't for his generosity, I wouldn't be able to spend my pin money on frivolities, against orders. Hands shaking, in no condition to appreciate the exquisite irony on the labels—"Individually handcrafted by the team at Smashing Gifts Ltd."—I hid the remaining glasses where they would not remind me how easily this man sucker-punched joy.

Is this abuse? I asked myself. Certainly not. The Never-Ending Divorce was just getting to us both. We weren't at our best. Anyway that stuff doesn't go on in the family of a Harvard graduate. It's for the crackpots on Judge Judy. Isn't it?

He says, "She broke my TV."

She says, "He sold my jewelry."

He says, "Maybe I stole her cable box and yelled at her, but I ain't never been charged with no beatin' a woman. I want ten thousand for harassment and pain and sufferin'."

Judge Judy says, "A little hard, sir, when you are the one pleading guilty."

Date: March 31, 2004
To: Daisy S.
Subject: A Man Who Would Hold the Lantern While His Mother Chops Wood

I started painting the roof on the sleep-out this week. The job entails climbing a ladder, and Tom Sawyer says heights make him dizzy.

First I applied rust inhibitor to the corrugated metal, then primer, and just before nightfall yesterday, the first coat of color. We picked a shade that is exactly like Taurikura Bay when cloud shadows skip across the celadon water on an otherwise sunny March day. I call it "Whangarei Heads green."

When I looked out the window this morning to admire my handiwork, I couldn't believe what I saw. The roof was primer gray. Where was the Whangarei Heads green? In a puddle the length of the new wood deck.

I called the paint store, and the clerk discussed the problem in a way that made me feel ashamed to have lived in New Zealand so long, holding, in fact, a residence permit and returning resident's visa, yet be so ignorant about painting metal roofs. "Everyone knows it's temperature dependent. If there is a bit of condensation in the air, the paint will slide right off. It's best not to apply it too late in the day, or too early, or at high noon."

Now I have to apply a second first coat of paint in a window of opportunity about two hours long, but Adrian has promised to hold the ladder for me while I paint the eaves.

AT THE BUTCHER COUNTER OF LIFE

Date: April 7, 2004
To: Sheryl O.
Subject: A Girl like Alice
Attached: Sunset over One Tree Point

One day Adrian makes me feel like a pimple on Tom Thumb's butt, a dandruff speck in a dwarfling's pompadour, a penitent pipsqueak in the Parallel Universe of Adrian.

The next, he draws my bath and throws in a cup of cider vinegar to keep my skin soft, and I grow tall enough to get my head above the pea-soup misery on Darch Point Road. I feel like Alice in Wonderland. The caterpillar asks her what size she wants to be, and she says she's not picky, but no one likes changing so often, you know.

I apologized to Rangi today for all the crap I let loose on Mount Aubrey. He's probably surveying all this from on high, ready to turn me to stone like those other mortal fools on top of Mount Manaia. It's a StairMaster of a climb to the summit. I sweat frustration, pump fury out of my pores, and sometimes just wail when I clear the gloom of the ancient bush and crest into the light on what feels like the top of the world. If the knobbly peaks ever crack and avalanche into the harbor, I know it will be my fault. It feels like the kind of rage that could destroy a mountain.

When I got back to the house, Adrian was putting the finishing touches on a pork-belly casserole, adding flageolets, baby carrots, onions, Italian parsley, fennel root braised in ghee, and a generous splash of Pernod. He'd opened the windows over the kitchen bench to the autumn evening breeze, and sunrays illuminated One Tree Point like an apparition of some long-lost citadel across the harbor from our home on Darch Point Road.

Chapter 24

I was happy just to hear her voice,
like a maiden's sigh or the pop of a champagne cork.
—#6, God's Holding Paddock

Joan was losing weight. Her stomach bloated, which prompted the only complaint she ever made during the course of her illness. Adrian and I were at Sŵn y Môr one night, continuing on continuing on. Joan said, "I thought Dick would go first. I was planning to take a trip around the world on his pension. But what really gets on my wick is this potbelly."

Her wry smile was less toothy than normal because some quack had talked her into having her teeth pulled in case her problems were related to the mercury in her sixty-year-old amalgam fillings.

"Never mind, luv." Dick glanced at Joan with that look that spoke a thousand words. "She can still put in the exclamation points," he assured Adrian and me.

"Exclamation points?" I asked.

"You know, those little touches you women do best, lipstick, perfume, whatever that is you do with your hair."

Dick thumbed through his records and settled on Perry Como, "Hot Diggity (Dog Ziggity Boom)."

Date: May 4, 2004
To: Jim C.
Subject: Gardyloo!

High drama tonight in the women's toilet at Parua Bay Tavern. Note, no euphemisms here. Not powder room. Not bathroom. You go to the toilet or you go to the loo. Or if you are Dick, you call it the cat box, so when I get up from the table, he can call out, "Be sure and put the sand back!" (Joan still sends him to the pub every night, in spite of her illness. I suspect that their roles are now reversed: it might be good for her, but at this point, Joan understands that it's better for Dick.)

Theories abound on the origin of the word *loo*. The fellows at God's Holding Paddock generally agree that it evolved from a bygone pronunciation of leeward, the recommended orientation when urinating over the gunwales. (Don't piss into the wind, mate!)

But I did some research. Perchance seventeenth-century Jesuit priest, Louis Bourdaloue, deserves the credit. Ladies, it was rumored, hid chamber pots under their petticoats to get through his long-winded sermons. Certainly it's an easy jump from Bourdaloue to portaloo to loo, but historians scoff at the idea. What self-respecting Parisian would pee in a pew? I say, "Might do." You never know what a woman under pressure is capable of.

Proponents of an earlier French connection claim the word derived from a warning shouted when slops were tossed out the window in the Middle Ages: "*Guardez l'eau!*" (Look out for the water, essentially, look out below!) Guardez l'eau got anglicized to gardyloo and easily trimmed—voilà—to loo.

At any rate, it had been barely ten minutes since I myself had visited the loo at the pub when a right kerfuffle broke out there.

Cindy, captain of the women's pool team, the Mako Sharks, had been out back having a cigarette, practicing for the smoking ban that is to be enacted this summer, when something tumbled out of the sky and smacked her on the head. Her empty billfold!

Cindy looked up at the women's toilet and saw two girls going through her purse, pitching nonvaluables out the window. She had left it on the table when she went out for a smoke. Cindy ran inside, and the gathering crowd helped her lock the girls in the loo. Dick checked it out when he got up for another beer and reported that the thieves were incensed. They had called the police on Cindy's cell phone and complained that they had been kidnapped. "We're being held in the loo against our will!"

The cops arrived promptly (they were just down the road with the Booze Bus) and hauled the perps into Whangarei PD. Cindy's decided, "Bugger this. I'll smoke inside until the ban well and truly goes into effect." And Dick admitted that he hadn't seen this much excitement at the pub in years.

Date: May 6, 2004
To: Laura P.
Subject: Lenny's Three-Legged Pig

Things have settled down here since the Great Parua Bay Pub Loo Robbery. Now we're back to worrying about Dick. There's an unspoken agreement here to keep the conversation light, so Rex wangled a story out of him. A good yarn cheers up both audience and storyteller.

"Darlin', did you ever hear about Lenny's pig?"

I told Rex no, I hadn't.

"Tell her, Dick. Tell her about Lenny's pig."

"Well, girl, it was an amazing pig, a three-legged pig."

"It saved Len's family twice. Go on, Dick," Pete said.

"Back in the floods of ninety-five, it nosed its way inside and woke up Lenny. The water was lapping at his front door. They'd all be dead if the pig hadn't warned him."

"Bloody wombles and drifting dreamers, that lot." This from Kevin. (Lenny wasn't there to defend himself.)

"The pig raised the alarm when the kitchen caught fire, and it was a good thing because the whole house would have burned down."

It made me think of Ngaere's pig, and we talked about Highway for a while.

"I've never known a country with such awesome pigs." I was on my third beer and feeling sentimental.

"We could tell you a thing or two about sheep," Kevin began.

"There'll be no mention of Velcro gloves with a lady present," Dick reminded him.

I thanked Dick for sparing me and asked him, "So how come the pig only had three legs?"

They all smiled. Dick licked the glue on the paper of the cigarette he was rolling and lit it up leisurely. "Girl," he said, after he blew a wisp of smoke out his nose, "with a pig that useful, you can only afford to eat it a bit at a time."

JANET PARMELY

Date: May 16, 2004
To: Sheryl O.
Subject: "What a Wonderful World"

Joan passed away at home two nights ago. We knew the end was near because the GP had given Dick a bottle of morphine, and when Dick asked him, "How much should I give her?" he said, "You give her whatever she needs."

Joan held on one month longer than the doctors had predicted, just long enough for number-two son to make it back from America, so all four of her boys were in town when she died. She got to see another Mother's Day and even snuck in a farewell at the pub, but no dancing on tables.

Dick was back at God's Holding Paddock tonight, which is exactly what Joan would have wanted. There were so many well-wishers that they had to pull up three big tables in front of the fire. It was a mark of enormous generosity that the publican had a blaze going when we are only on the cusp of winter here in the Winterless North.

I sat at Dick's right hand as usual, just a bit closer, and could tell he was grateful for the anonymity of the racket and crowd. God's Holding Paddock is as tenderhearted a collection of men as you could find, but they are not about to act like sooks.

Dick said that Joan had been in and out of consciousness Friday morning. The hospice nurse helped him pull her bed into the lounge.

"I wanted—" he began. The rims of his cataract-cloudy eyes got redder, and they are red enough already from the sun and wind at sea and smoke and Lion Red in all the pubs of his youth and old age.

"I wanted," he started again, "for her to be able to look over

Sŵn y Môr and see Parua Bay one last time. I set the picture of Kidwelly Castle by her bed and played the dancing dog for a while. Then I put on a record and just held her hand.

"She looked so gray and awful, but do you know, the moment she died, she became beautiful, just like she was relieved and went to sleep. I loved that girl. I really did."

I barely mustered the question, even though I knew the answer. "What song did you play for her, Dick?"

Chapter 25

Life can be easier if you weasel out of things, at least for the weasel.

—#39, God's Holding Paddock

Adrian had been doing more than muttering about rotting in port. In a surprise move, he flew out friends from South Africa to tidy up *Jingle Bells* and crew a blue-water passage to Fiji.

With youthful zeal, the couple organized Fibber McGee's V-berths, scrubbed the decks, and shook out the mildewed sheets. They found the seasick meds, all expired, and the dan buoy. This, a three-meter staff with a weight at the bottom, a float halfway up, and a faded red flag atop, was the only piece of emergency equipment that Adrian considered mandatory. "Monohulls sink. Catamarans float. But a man can fall off either one of them." I was going cruising!

Unfortunately we had overlooked one technicality: you can't leave New Zealand and expect to return at some undetermined time if your passport expires within six months. I would have to make a last-minute trip to the US Consulate in Auckland to renew my passport. Even if they could expedite the process, it meant a two-week delay.

But Adrian was ready to go. He was set to get as far away as he could from home improvement. He was sick of negotiating over his marital settlement. He wanted to sail where the partially-ex-wife couldn't find him. Adrian was preparing to do another runner, in a yacht.

He drove home one night in a squall from the marina where they were making the boat ready and flew helter-skelter through the house, loading up the TV, computers, CDs, sound-surround system, contents of freezer and pantry, and his foul-weather gear. He said the tide was right and they had to leave now! Then he took an hour-long shower.

"You can get a ride into town to pick up the car," he said as he was toweling off, "and there are some Krugerrands in a plastic bag under the futon in my study. You need to take care of them."

"Take care of them?"

"Give them to my lawyer. They have to be divided up."

"You want me to take a taxi into Whangarei with a sack of gold?"

"I don't want to discuss it. I am providing you a holiday in Fiji, that's the point."

"How?"

"When you get your passport organized, I'll fly you in."

Adrian's hair was damp from the shower, and it was raining hard. Slick as a wet weasel, he jumped in the Mercedes and drove away to the rattle of a diesel engine in need of a tuneup—*kapluey-kaboom-chicky-boom*—into the stormy night. I had no idea if I would ever see him again.

On August 17, Adrian set sail for Fiji with the South Africans. He left me behind in the Winterless North, counting gold coins in front of the fire. There were 110 of them, a mere $50,000 worth at the time. Like her share of the house on Darch Point Road, the partially-ex wanted her cut of the stash of gold. I should have taken the money and run.

The following week, I flew to Blenheim on the South Island to cover a clinic. The bed in my motel had flannel sheets and an electric blanket, luxuries that Adrian had denied me because I had his love to keep me warm. It also had a wool duvet, coverlet, and surplus of pillows, one of which I laid next to me to replace Adrian.

It was an improvement. The pillow didn't have issues with flannel sheets. It wasn't jealous of the electric blanket. A pillow would not talk me into putting my life savings into a house and moving my furniture across the world to make sure I stayed there. A pillow wouldn't run off to

Fiji without me. It was a better listener than this man who was so fixated on his sack of Krugerrands and clattering bag of bolts in his head that anyone else was immaterial.

A month later, the South African couple abandoned ship.

Date: August 31, 2004
To: Anne B.
Subject: The Pot of Gold Is Not at the End of the Rainbow

It was under the futon all along. When I delivered the Krugerrands to Adrian's lawyer, he said he thought Adrian was honest even if it didn't appear that way to a number of people. And I am beginning to have my doubts.

"Adrian would make a good pirate, wouldn't he?" the lawyer said, which seemed contradictory to his previous statement. He dumped eight pounds of gold onto his desk, and we sat, like pirates ourselves, counting doubloons.

Everyone loves an adventure, but the esteem that Adrian's irresponsible behavior inspires infuriates me. The guys at God's Holding Paddock aren't impressed, but I can see the cogs spinning as the handyman, lawyer, and GP imagine a dangerous life so jam-packed with fun. *I wish I could tell the world to go to hell and sail away in a fifty-two-foot yacht!* But they aren't the ones left holding the bag of Krugerrands that they have to share with the partially-ex-wife.

Shiver me timbers, yo-ho-ho, and *argh*!

AT THE BUTCHER COUNTER OF LIFE

Date: September 6, 2004
To: Sheryl O.
Subject: Which Man Overboard?

I finally heard from the buccaneer. He made landfall in Niue, a Polynesian island twelve hundred kilometers off course from Suva, Fiji.

"You go where the winds take you," Adrian informed me when he called from Alofi, the tiny capital. "If you don't, you'll get into trouble."

I go where the winds take me; ergo I never get into trouble. This bit of arrogance is a far cry from what J. M. Synge had to say on the matter: "A man who is not afraid of the sea will soon be drownded, for he will be going out on a day he shouldn't. But we do be afraid of the sea, and we do only be drownded now and again."

Do I really want to risk getting drownded for a little R and R in Fiji, which Adrian is providing, I might add, in an exceedingly roundabout way? Now they plan to sail to Tonga and fetch me at the airport.

Niue was hit by Cyclone Heta eight months ago, and Adrian and his crew had already explored the ravaged island. "They had two-hundred-sixty-kilometer-an-hour winds. Most impressive," he said. Two hundred homes were destroyed, and one person was killed in the storm, so I doubt the islanders were particularly impressed.

They had swum in a lagoon, "twenty-seven degrees it was," which is centigrade speak for bathwater. Mind you, the temperature in the surf back here at Ocean Beach is cold enough to precipitate cardiac arrest in a battery-heated wetsuit.

Adrian's going to send me a skipper's letter so I can fly out of Auckland. In addition to a passport with more than six months left on it, you need a skipper's letter to catch a one-way flight if you plan on returning to New Zealand. Wouldn't want it to look like I was doing a runner, now would we?

I know I have hemmed and hawed about joining Adrian in Fiji (Tonga now, it seems). I am spitting angry that he sailed off to the tropics and left me behind in New Zealand—in winter. The best thing that has happened since he left is that I got to stay in a motel room with four layers of warm bedding and a sympathetic pillow.

Adrian emptied the joint account on his way out of town. There is some court date approaching, and his lawyer is getting nervous that Blackbeard may have made a one-way trip to the islands.

My inbox is filling up with advice. Anne is afraid that Adrian is going to push me overboard. Laura got straight to the point: "Mama, there is no happy place you can sail where he won't be a dick."

But here's the problem. I feel like the kid who had to stay in at recess, my nose pressed against the window at Bay Audiology. I don't even like those kids swinging on the monkey bars, but look at them having all that fun without me! Why give up my island holiday just because Adrian's been a creep?

He should be the one worrying about getting the heave-ho, except I don't know the first thing about sailing.

"What if you fell overboard, Adrian?"

"You throw me the dan buoy. If it makes you feel better, I'll teach you how to use the SSB. Radio for help, and they'll talk you through it."

"And if a freighter hits us and takes you out along with the SSB?"

"Most likely it would take you out too, and then all your worries would be over."

Hakuna matata. I'm going for it. Sail ho!

Chapter 26

> There are things to miss wherever you are.
> —#9, God's Holding Paddock

After the holidaymakers sailed, I remained in New Zealand seven weeks waiting for travel documents, wrapping up the Kerikeri clinic for my vacation replacement, and serving as go-between for Blackbeard and his solicitor.

On September 15, my skipper's letter arrived.

On September 17, the South African mutineers phoned from the Kingdom of Tonga. In the breathless fashion of someone with a lot to say trying to negotiate a foreign phone and fearful of getting cut off at any minute, the wife said, "We couldn't take it anymore how do you manage it started out fine but then Adrian stopped talking and then—" We were disconnected.

Adrian called a couple of days later and treated the episode like a nonevent. "Better off without them. She was useless, threw up all the way to Niue, and he didn't understand there is only one captain on a boat."

Fly-in wife is the lowest woman on the cruising totem pole. She's the one who skips the blue-water passage—bumpy seas, electricity finite, water rationed, booze verboten—and heads straight for the mai tais and hair curlers. And I wasn't even a wife. On October 5, I checked in at the Auckland Airport for a one-way flight to Nuku'alofa, the capital of Tonga, and handed over my skipper's letter:

To whom it may concern:

This is to certify that the bearer will be joining the yacht 'Jingle Bells' as crew to sail to Suva, Fiji, from Neiafu, Vava'u in Tonga, and returning to New Zealand from Fiji.

Yours faithfully,
Captain of the sailing yacht 'Jingle Bells'

Date: October 12, 2004
To: Anne B.
Subject: The Friendly Isles of Tonga
Attached: Big Mama's

I flew into Nuku'alofa, the capital of Tonga, a week ago. It was a relief to see Adrian waiting for me at little Fua'amotu International Airport. Since he sailed out of Whangarei, he has managed to drift seven hundred miles off course and precipitate a mutiny. The last I heard, he was in Neiafu on the far side of the Kingdom of Tonga one hundred sixty nautical miles away, hardly a day sail to the airport. He is as dependable as a flower girl.

Jingle Bells is anchored offshore at Big Mama Yacht Club. She looks like a new woman, and Adrian's in higher spirits than I've seen him since he was besotted. He's lost twenty pounds and looks like a Bernard Moitessier wannabe, a happy sailing wraith. He evidently stripped off his clothes, as well as his shoes, and sailed naked from Neiafu.

The boat is crisp white, azure bright, and smells as down-home sweet as sheets on a line. The trade winds have blown life back into her, and the saloon is flooded with Polynesian sunlight, not that hide-and-seek imposter in Whangarei. Adrian may have a point about rotting in port. The islands are definitely where he and *Jingle Bells* belong. We shall see about me. I've shed my shoes. It's a start.

I have slept like I was drugged since I got here. (No, I haven't tried the kava yet.) Adrian says *Jingle Bells* is rocking me to sleep. Personally I think it's the Ikale beer we tip at sundown in the thatch-roofed bar with the other barefoot yachties and Big Mama herself. She is, indeed, very big.

Certainly our routine is not exhausting me. Actually there is no routine. Some afternoons we take the dinghy to Nuku'alofa to get supplies, paddle past the modest Tongans soaking fully clothed in the turbid water, and tie up near a table piled with smelly fish and unrecognizable parts of smelly fish. There's lots of activity, but it's all slo-mo. The connection at the Internet café works sporadically. Tongatapu, where Nuku'alofa is located and the biggest of the Tonga islands, could be explored in a day on a scooter, if you had a death wish. Taxis, buses, dogs, and pigs rule the road here.

It's too soon to tell if Tonga will live up to its amiable reputation. The dogs seem friendly enough. Kids hang around and grin. A lady on the curb deftly fastened a shell bracelet around my wrist, although she did refuse to let go until Adrian gave her a few pa'angas in return for my arm.

When Captain James Cook landed in Tonga in 1777, three things impressed him: the Tongans' propensity for theft, their elegant manners, and their warm reception of strangers, for which he dubbed the archipelago the Friendly Isles. In his chronicles, Will Mariner, a British ship's clerk captured by Tongans in 1806, contended that the friendly islanders had more planned for Cook than a hearty welcome. Murder and plunder, to be precise. But the chiefs quarreled and plans went amiss, the particulars, a vexing loss to history. Mariner's accounts are sprinkled with hearsay and inaccuracies, and his tenure took place three decades after Cook's visit. But he might have had a point. Although Mariner was spared, his privateer, *Port au Prince*, had been seized, burned, and sacked by the locals. In any case, Captain Cook sailed off with his favorable first impression, and Tonga kept its good reputation.

We bought sweet little Tahitian bananas at the Talamahu Market, and I made a batch of banana-bran muffins, ballast for the sail north. It's been nice to cook together again and do the other stuff that people do when they've kissed and made up, well, kissed. We haven't addressed any of the dreary issues that plagued us back home, and I don't plan to force a discussion, an undertaking that would be as successful as the proverbial effort to teach a pig to sing. I'm not going to ruin my island holiday by wasting my time and annoying the pig.

We seem to be getting past our difficulties without words, naked in the island breeze from the little spinnaker Adrian rigged over the hatch above the captain's berth. I am opening up like a hibiscus in the tropical sun.

AT THE BUTCHER COUNTER OF LIFE

Date: October 14, 2004
To: Sheryl O.
Subject: Sailing the South Pacific Isn't All It's Cracked Up to Be

We left Big Mama Yacht Club yesterday headed for Ha'apai, the next island group north, where Captain Cook had lunch with the friendly Tongans.

We set off auspiciously, did not leave for the passage on a Friday, open a brolly, or whistle up the wind. Carefree, I stood by Adrian's side in the cockpit. I was having sex for the first time in two months and looked good in my swimsuit as long as I kept a sarong tied around my waist. There were cat's paws on the water, and a zephyr ruffled my hair. Adrian unfurled the genoa and hoisted the mainsail as Big Mama's evaporated over the horizon.

The zephyr intensified to a light breeze, then moderate, then distinctly fresh. The marshmallow clouds took on rain and congealed into a low ceiling of cold consommé. The swell on the beam picked up. The wind gusted to thirty-eight knots and whipped up spume on the cresting waves. The seas rose to fifteen feet.

Rogue waves crashed into the cockpit and drenched us as poor *Jingle Bells* rode up-up-up the face of the swell and slammed down with a bang. The hull groaned like in the movie *Titanic* right before the ship went down. Two dozen tomatoes, ten banana-bran muffins, all the condiments on top of the fridge, and the gin bottle slid across the saloon floor.

Dramamine wasn't up to this task. I threw up all the way to Kelefesia, eight hours in what felt like a #9 on the Beaufort Scale of Wind Speed, "when circus tents are damaged, chimney pots and slates are removed, and fences and children fall down"—had you been fortunate enough to remain on shore.

Adrian was having so much fun I thought he might sail naked again. Yee haw!

He removed the grate over the drain by the helm so I could throw up while he—who does not suffer from seasickness—advised, "Seasickness is all in the mind."

Then he zipped me into an oilskin that had buckles to harness me to the lifelines on deck so I wouldn't fall overboard. But in case I did, there was reflective tape on the wrists and top of the hood so when the Royal New Zealand Air Force sent out the P-3K Orion on a search-and-rescue mission, they could locate my body in the water.

I threw up in the drain again.

"Catamarans float," Adrian told me.

"Sharks swim," I replied, and threw up once more.

Adrian made me drink some water because it's important to avoid dehydration when you are seasick and ever more pleasant if you have something to throw up. I may as well have been trying to drink a straight-up martini on a Tilt-A-Whirl.

By the time the palm trees swaying along the sandy shore of the islet Kelefesia came into view, the wind was back to a light breeze. I was wobbly but had recuperated enough to help Adrian navigate the reef by kneeling on the bow to look for outcropping coral and give hand signals accordingly (left, no right, no left) while Adrian yelled, "Make up your bloody mind!"

After we had anchored successfully in the Tidy Bowl–blue lagoon, I told Adrian, "You'll have to airlift me out because I am never doing that again."

AT THE BUTCHER COUNTER OF LIFE

Date: October 15, 2004
To: Daisy S.
Subject: The Sorry Case of the Yellow Bikini
Attached: Friday

We are anchored in Kelefesia waiting for a window of calm to day sail to Lifuka in Ha'apai. After going ashore to investigate, we've declared it deserted for the day except for one hungry dog. Low on inspiration, I named him Friday.

Adrian wanted to sail on to Fiji from Tonga, but we changed our plans after I read what *Sailingbird's Guide to the Kingdom of Tonga* has to say about the trip: "Passage between Tonga and Fiji previously won the reputation of being the most hazardous in the South Pacific—many vessels have been lost in this area. Due to the distance involved, it is impossible to pass all the dangers before nightfall, and the 180-nautical-mile route passes through an area riddled with reefs (where only a few dangers are marked by lights) and strong currents."

Adrian thinks I will abandon ship if we have another passage like the last one, although that doesn't seem to be an option unless I hitch a ride with the only other yacht in the lagoon, but I would rather die first.

When we motored in yesterday, the first sign of life was a nymph in a yellow bikini stepping out from a shower at the stern of a monohull already anchored inside the reef. She hailed Adrian for help with an Irish lilt. He had forgotten to reel in the fishing lines we had dragged from Nuku'alofa, and they had tangled around the anchor of her boyfriend's boat.

In the process of getting out of *Jingle Bells* and into the dinghy to help her, Adrian trod on my rose-colored reading glasses, which miraculously had not washed overboard and lay in the cockpit next to my copy of *Moby Dick*, swollen to three times its normal size.

I don't know which rankled me more: the fact that he did not calmly assist the half-naked girl but scrambled over the bench cushions like a hound after a poodle in heat; that he busted my glasses and didn't even apologize; or that I was the worse for wear, still a shade of green, with vomit crusted at the corners of my mouth, wearing foul-weather gear three sizes too big for me, and certainly no match for this welcoming sight emerging like Botticelli's Venus birthed under the fresh-water spray of an outdoor shower.

Or perhaps it was just coming to terms with the sorry truth that, even if it started out as a good day in the sarong department, my own yellow-bikini days are gone forever.

I'm going to swim into shore now to eat sea worms and give my dog, Friday, a bone.

AT THE BUTCHER COUNTER OF LIFE

Date: Oct. 28, 2004
To: Laura P.
Subject: Thank God I Can Keep Down a Cold Lamb Chop Day
Attached: *Jingle Bells*

The wind generator is thrumming, such a comforting sound because it means there will be energy in the house batteries for life's luxuries at sea: lights, fridge, water maker. We set off at first light in a sherbet sunrise and made a smooth day sail, heading farther north to the Vava'u island group. I am getting my sea legs and can keep down a cold lamb chop now.

Four humpback whales entertained us on their way back to Antarctica. They swim to Tonga to mate and calve. The razzmatazz opened with a blow and splash of tail, then a full breach, and for the grand finale, two whales leaped in tandem six meters from the boat. Under sail, we must keep an eye out for freighters, containers lost at sea, and pirates, but there is not much to be done about a forty-ton mammal that decides to surface under the boat, so may as well relax and enjoy the show.

Sailing over the Tonga Trench lends a grand dimension to the age-old worry of not being able to touch bottom in any pool. Six and a half miles down in Horizon Deep, the poor old crust of the

Pacific Plate is sinking under the younger and more buoyant Australian Plate, subducting at a rate of nine inches a year. This might not sound like much, but cripes, they are tectonic plates. There are giant squid in that deep black sea and fish that bioluminesce like ocean liners or miners with lamplights growing out of their heads. (I know because I saw an exhibit at the Museum of New Zealand Te Papa Tongarewa in Wellington.)

The cruising days roll indistinguishably into one another. I have, therefore, taken to naming them in order to keep track. There was, of course, Big Seasick Day, and that was followed by Thank God I Can Keep Down a Cold Lamb Chop Day. We've had It Takes a Day to Fill a Gas Can in Tonga Day, Washing but Not Drying Because It Rained All Day Day, I Practiced My Concertina All Day Long Day, and on its heels, Hell All I Can Play Is a C Scale After Practicing My Concertina All Day Yesterday Day.

We had Snorkeling with Bats Day at Ha'ano and drifted among thousands of neon fish, darting in synchrony as a wahoo and blacktip shark herded them into the shallows. I peered through the shivering shoal into the obscurity, and upon seeing their pelagic silhouettes, sprang out of the water—amazed to find it was only waist deep—just as a black cloud of His Majesty King Taufa'ahau Tupou IV's fruit bats swooped to roost in the coconut palms. The flying foxes are official property of the King of Tonga.

I am learning to do things *faka tonga*, the Tongan way, taking in stride delays, inclement weather, sparse or no supplies at all, saying yes when I mean maybe or possibly not at all. A two o'clock appointment can easily slip to eight. Today may stretch into next week or never ever. As they say here, "We are being just happy all around."

Faka tonga is the island version of hakuna matata, and I can live with it. When you don't have a job to go to or a house to remodel, irresponsibility and perpetual tardiness are quite tolerable. And when you can't keep track of the days, a twelve-on/twelve-off schedule doesn't make you feel like you're wasting however many footsteps are left until you tumble into the grave.

JANET PARMELY

Date: November 11, 2004
To: Anne B.
Subject: Time Out in Paradise
Attached: Starboard view

Reading all day is one of the luxuries of cruising life, but I'm jealously guarding my books. Adrian gives them away to passing sailors or trades them—but that doesn't make him look as generous—and can you really calculate how many bodice rippers a collection of David Sedaris essays is worth? Or he starts reading them before I am done. It's the pinnacle of literary bad manners and really frosts me.

Adrian speaks fondly of all the friends he made cruising. Maybe that's the case if you are circumnavigating for a couple of years, following the same winds, stopping at the same ports of call, but it seems to me that no one remembers anybody's name, just their yacht's—*High Seas, Seven Seas, Sloepmouche, Sprite 2, Freefall*—except for Rick from *Emerald,* who was so cordial that it made me want to weep.

Maybe if someone called me by my name and not the goddamn boat's, I wouldn't feel like the Adrian Talks about Nothing but

Generators and Diesel Fuel if He Talks at All Days are piling up on top of each other.

I miss the easy camaraderie of God's Holding Paddock. I miss stories. *Jingle Bells* and *Freefall* stared at me, pained, while I recapped my Big Seasick Day at a barbeque on the beach at Manimita last week.

"All that worry about sharks, containers, freighters, pirates, and whales, and in the end, seasickness got me, and I wished I would just die."

I read *Freefall*'s mind: *Put it in neutral. No one wants stories with morals in paradise.* "Now tell us, *Jingle Bells*, how do you think the Springboks will do next season?"

Yachting conversations revolve around getting places, fixing things, sports, and vegetables.

"Where can we find lettuce?"

"Go through the first gate past the bakery and ask for Ofa."

Whether it's stories or produce, we yearn for what we do not have. Where starchy breadfruit and taro thrive, we crave the cool-weather crops of a Midwest garden.

I miss lettuce poking out of the loam. I miss autumn's crisp mornings, ripe abundance, sweet decay, the promise of snow, a white Christmas. I miss land, lots of land under starry skies above. Don't fence me in, and don't touch my books.

But then I look up, out, and starboard to this tropical sea shimmering like a gossip of mermaids, sparkling like the crown jewels of the azure kingdom of freedom and boundless opportunities, twinkling and winkling a midcourse correction out of me—until I realize that I'm just a brat with too much on her mind in yet another paradise.

Chapter 27

The man will fail before the boat.

—#9, God's Holding Paddock

Adrian and I had sailed for a month across the Kingdom of Tonga and come full circle back to Big Mama Yacht Club. I was catching a midnight flight out of Nuku'alofa, and any disillusion I might have had with cruising had relented in the face of returning to work and Whanga-rain. Before we paddled over for sundowners, I tucked a note under his pillow:

> Thank you for lunch at the Dancing Rooster where we laughed like old times. Thank you for teaching me how to snorkel underwater, so I could peek at a bashful octopus and then shoot, effervescing, to the surface for air. Thank you for stringing up the hammock where I read in just my sarong. Thank you for making sure I took out my earrings at night. Most of all, thank you for a glimpse of this opalescent world and the sailor soul so fundamental to who you are. This seasick girl from Kansas City and the boy from Port Elizabeth with saltwater magic in his veins are going to make it after all.

Adrian had little interest in deadlines, his or anyone else's, and hadn't worked out the details of how he and *Jingle Bells* would get home. He was reluctantly contemplating crew to help with the blue-water passage back to New Zealand when the yellow-bikini girl showed up at the bar. She and her boyfriend were anchored at Big Mama's too. *Shit.*

She said she would be more than happy to crew for Adrian—his boat was *so* big (certainly bigger than the boyfriend's). She wasn't a dolt. Daisy had already warned me, whether you talk it up or talk it down, "A man's boat is his willy." And, to be honest, I was still bitter about the bikini.

After a polite farewell, Adrian and I took the dinghy back to *Jingle Bells*. He made drinks at the saloon table, and I slid in beside him, but I couldn't let go of the yellow-bikini girl. Sure Adrian had loved the attention she had lavished on his big whatever, but would he really sign her on for a week in close quarters? Even a man on watch can multitask if he's appropriately motivated. My imagination took off. *Ba-gawk! Ba-gawk!* I tried to talk.

Adrian made some disparaging remark about "you and your words," like they were my worthless children, old enough to bring in an income but lying around instead watching TV, snarfing potato chips, and stealing time from him. I started to cry.

Adrian stiffened, his back against the wall.

"I cannot hear you when you cry."

That made me angry.

"I cannot hear you when you are angry."

That enraged me because I knew exactly what he meant: *unless it's hakuna matata, I don't want to hear about it.*

Adrian picked up my piña colada and threw the drink in my face, hesitated, and said, "You made me do it. Someone had to shut you up."

It did the trick. I went below and shredded the note I had hidden, too mortified to bother cleaning up. When the taxi arrived, I plastered myself against the back door, as far as possible from Adrian, and we rode wordlessly to Fua'amotu Airport. I boarded the plane without looking back. Just like that, the easy spontaneity born of trust so joyfully resurrected in the islands croaked. And why was I surprised? A hibiscus bloom only lasts a day.

On the flight back to Auckland, reeking of coconut and rum, I was sandwiched between two Tongan women who overflowed their seats. Their bellies obstructed the armrests, and I could not help but rest my head between their big soft breasts. Smiling like buddhas, they hummed a lullaby, and I returned to New Zealand with my dirty little secret: I was on my way back to Whangarei to continue to live with a man who had now thrown a drink in my face.

Date: November 16, 2004
To: Jim C.
Subject: Every Day On Board's like Christmas

This is my verdict: sailing is camping with a seasick option and risk of getting bored to death. If the containers, freighters, pirates, whales, sharks, or captain of the vessel don't get you first. All the barefoot yachties in the world can say what they want—"She didn't get it"—but they'd be wrong I wanted to purify my days and free them from all those dinky dry-land comforts and piddling pursuits. I was ready to hone myself into a better human being attuned to the rigors and natural rhythm of life at sea. But something changed my mind.

Now I believe that all you get from trimming sails is gaunt. Making do just makes you mean. If you only have the stars to talk to, you forget how to call a man by his first name.

AT THE BUTCHER COUNTER OF LIFE

When the novelty of endless days of fucking, reading, writing (not to be confused with submitting and publishing) wears off, ennui sets in. Zippers start to rust, and the cat-piss stench returns below deck. Your spare time becomes consumed with fixing and drying things or making your way to an anchorage where you might tend to the broken, wet things.

Once you notice the rats scampering across the harbor breakwater, the ports of call start to fray around the edges. When someone turns up the lights, you see the bars for what they are, weirdo magnets with bad rum drinks. Single-handers like Moitessier don't hang out there. The swashbucklers do, and con men, first-class bores, Jimmy Buffets without music, and the guy at The Mermaid in Neiafu who would kiss anything for a beer—anything.

It doesn't matter if they sail a twenty-eight-foot sloop or a seventy-foot yacht with full crew. They all have an itchy patina of enlightened barnacles they think anyone would love to scratch. You could choke on the self-satisfaction: *think of all those dumb landlubbing bastards back home*. I don't think they're so smart. I think they've all done runners of one sort or another. (But then, so have I.)

We met some pleasant enough couples along the way. The wives often wore modest shorts that matched their mate's, made from serviceable material that dries quickly, doesn't breathe, and encourages yeast infection. Several couldn't swim, which shocked me, but Adrian pointed out it doesn't matter. If you fall into Horizon Deep, why prolong the misery?

In most cases, it was my impression that the husband had always dreamed of reliving adolescence (in a soggy environment in constant need of repair), and the wife would rather have stayed at home. But she couldn't run the risk. What if he met some sweet young thing along the way? He'd gather his silver hair into a ponytail, get it beaded, and they'd frolic in the cockpit. What choice did she have but to hop aboard? How did she fare? I wonder.

It probably started out okay, just like it did for Adrian and me. We anchored in a turquoise lagoon. The generator was still supplying power to the freezer, so our meat rations hadn't putrefied. The mold hadn't repopulated yet. Once I got my sea legs and could keep down a cold lamb chop, we had lots of sex.

High on the joy of paring down, I stopped shaving and coloring my hair. Most of the skimpy sundresses I had packed in anticipation of doing some frolicking of my own blew off the wash line. The rest were stolen by a passing Tongan who stuck an arm from his outrigger canoe through the yacht's porthole, conveniently at dressing-table height. I put on five pounds in quarters where one is traditionally supposed to lose weight.

"It's the ginger biscuits," Cap'n Adrian said, the ones I had been gobbling to curb my nausea. "They will also give you gout if you're not careful."

Sitting in the cockpit one sunny afternoon, with my hairy legs and gray roots, developing a second-degree sunburn on my nose where I missed the sunblock, I began to understand that it's impossible for a middle-aged member of the fairer sex to keep the competitive edge at sea. I had a revelation: *Let the girl in the yellow bikini have him. I should have stayed home!*

It dawned on me, as well, that all the old saws about security at sea are simplistic bullshit. *There can only be one captain on board—for safety's sake?* Just a sneaky attempt to return to the days before we got the vote and driving privileges. *A ship in port is safe, but that is not what ships are for?* Depending on who's in the same boat with you, it may not be safe in port.

A boat is not a symbol for paradise or freedom. A fifty-two-foot yacht is a flat-out promise of minimal choice for the crew and maximum control for the captain. Every day on *Jingle Bells* is like Christmas as long as you smile and keep your big mouth shut—which pretty much makes it like one long Sunday in prison for the rest of your life.

Chapter 28

It's a balls-up, God save the queen, but there's no way back.
—#28, God's Holding Paddock

Adrian flew our hale-and-hearty neighbor from Whangarei Heads to Tonga, and he crewed back to New Zealand. The winds took Adrian home. The incident of the drink in my face was behind him, his frustration discharged as surely as a gunshot. He had taken care of the matter, a simple fact on par with the relation between watts, amps, and volts: someone had to shut me up.

Annihilating a tropical reconciliation is certainly not up there with the demise of a world wonder, but for some reason, it made me think of the Pink and White Terraces.

It took Mother Nature at least a thousand years to fashion the terraces that once bespangled the shores of Lake Rotomahana. For centuries, geysers spouted hot water that cascaded down the slopes into the lake, carving out staircases and basins, leaving mineral deposits behind. Layer by layer, the silica accumulated and overlaid it all with a shimmer the delicate tint of eggshells and pearls.

In the mid-nineteenth century, tourists came from near and far to see the Pink and White Terraces. Most arrived via steamer at Tauranga in the Bay of Plenty, then trekked seventy kilometers inland by horseback and coach over corduroy roads. They took lodgings overnight and boarded a whaling boat next morning to head south on Lake Tararewa, stopping along the way to buy cherries and koura, crayfish to steam in the hot-water springs. Southwest of Mount Tarawera, they picked their way on foot across the isthmus joining the swampy shores of Lake Tarawera and Lake Rotomahana. Finally they embarked by canoe to catch a first glimpse of the resplendent White Terraces, suffused with light in the midday sun. Limpid blue water spilled over the tiers, like glazing on a colossal, fairyland wedding cake.

The White Terraces, bleached from the northwest exposure, were more expansive, but bathing was better across the lake in the roseate pools, "like vast open shells, the walls of which are concave and the lips ornamented in a thousand forms," wrote Anthony Trollope, among the Victorians who made their way to the terraces.

Some of the travelers said they would never do it again, and not just on account of the hardship of voyaging bell-toppered, frock-coated, corseted, and crinolined to such a remote spot, but because of the awe. They felt they had looked squarely at something that clearly was not meant for this world.

In the wee-morning dark on June 10, 1886, Mount Tarawera blew its top. There had been disturbances and premonitions beforehand. Steam clouds hovered over Mount Tarawera. Days before the eruption, the level of Lake Tarawera had risen in a matter of minutes and subsided as swiftly. An ancient Maori war canoe appeared briefly on the lake, "glorious in the mist and the sunlight." Close enough to see water glistening on the paddles of the men who rowed it, Maori and European tourists alike attested that the standing members had been wrapped in flax robes, hair plumed for death with huia and white-heron feathers. The lake had borne no such craft in living memory.

In a series of booming eruptions, fireballs and pillars of flame blazed out of Mount Tarawera into a lightning-crazed sky. Fountains of lava roared from a seventeen-kilometer rift that blew out the bed of Lake Rotomahana and uncapped a geothermal system that flashed its waters to steam. The Pink and White Terraces, considered by many to be the Eighth Wonder of the World, vanished overnight into a quagmire of ooze.

Albumen prints and ethereal oils only hint at the splendor, and thus, commensurate loss of the Pink and White Terraces—in much the way a trail of words can only intimate the full extent of what is destroyed when a volcano erupts and takes out a wonder just a few weeks or a thousand years old.

Date: November 29, 2004
To: Anne B.
Subject: Ring of Fire

New Zealand sits on the Pacific Ring of Fire, home to roughly 75 percent of the world's volcanoes and 90 percent of its earthquakes. There is scary stuff going on right under my feet: fractures, fissures, and chambers of magma sticky as toffee and ready to blow.

Nowhere is this more dramatic than in Rotorua, where I'm working this week, eighteen miles from where the Pink and White Terraces used to be. Geysers gush and mineral springs burble into thermal pools. Gas burps shamelessly through mud lagoons, *Bu-lur-rrrp*. The ground smokes, sighs, and moans. Sulfur vents hiss. Fumaroles huff and puff, and it stinks of rotten eggs. Driving into town at dusk was like driving into hell (or what I imagine hell to be).

Outside of town, Kerosene Creek coils in a vapor through the bush. The residue from its sulfurous fumes clings like ghostly lichen to the trees along the shore. It is dammed here and there into pools generous enough to soak in and signposted Don't Put Your

Head Under Water. Some of it's unbearably hot, but once you locate an agreeable spot, you can dig your toes into the sandy bottom and dawdle. As long as you are comfortable in the knowledge that the parasites that cause amoebic meningitis dawdle there too. It is said that they must enter through the nose if they are to migrate to the brain and rapidly kill you. I don't recall a more awe-inspiring immersion of trust, but then maybe the others just weren't signposted. Had it been anywhere but New Zealand, I wouldn't have waded in.

I've offered to help out at more clinics away from home, but I can't escape the Ring of Fire. It can precipitate disaster or make for a happy dalliance, as long as you keep faith and don't get in over your head.

Date: December 4, 2004
To: Laura P.
Subject: Shark!

At the pub tonight, Dick told us that while we were cruising, a pod of dolphins saved the lifeguards at Ocean Beach from a shark attack.

And I told him, "I'm not falling for another three-legged-pig story."

"It's true, girl. Here, I saved the article from the *Herald* for you."

Sure enough, a veteran lifeguard was training three rookies off shore when a pod of bottlenose dolphins joined them. They behaved peculiarly, slapping the water with their tail fins and turning tight circles on the swimmers, as if trying to round them up.

One of the dolphins swam straight at the experienced guard and dived just short of colliding. Watching for the gregarious creature to surface, he spotted a three-meter-long great white shark instead. Seven dolphins ringed the four humans from Whangarei Heads Surf Lifesaving Club and fended off the great white for nearly an hour.

"And you guys told me that sharks weren't a problem at Ocean Beach!"

"They aren't. This proves it."

When Rex got up to get a refill, Dick said, "And while you were gone, Rex packed a sad, stomped out of the pub, and took his handle with him."

"Did they give him a bluey?"

"No, they didn't ban him, but he stayed home and moped for two weeks. Took him that long to realize he was only hurting himself, and by then, he couldn't remember why he stormed off in the first place."

Rex sat back down with a handle of Tui. This surprised me because he's been a Lion Red man as long as I can remember. I asked him what was up.

"Well, darlin', I took a vacation from God's Holding Paddock, and when I came back, I won a fishing rod. Tui sponsored the draw, so I had to switch from Lion Red, at least for a while. I'm a man of principle."

JANET PARMELY

December 22, 2004
To: Sheryl O.
Subject: No Smoking

The smoking ban in pubs has been in effect nearly two weeks now. Opinion has been divided on the issue. In typical Kiwi fashion, there was much heated debate until the day, and then everyone settled down. There were a couple of attempts by the young and dangerous at a clandestine puff, but they were sniffed out by the publican—"Dick, what do you think you're up to?" Now even the head of God's Holding Paddock has resigned himself to quarantine outside when he wants to light up. The powers that be artfully enacted the ban in the stellar month of December. It's hardly punitive to go outside for a smoke this time of year.

Wednesday is Free Beer Spin Night at the pub. You order, spin a wheel, and if the pointer ends up on a winning slice of the cardboard pie, your beer is free. There's been some grizzling about the new publicans. They've been strict about enforcing the smoking ban, and they were stingy with the firewood last winter. There's even some suspicion that they made the free-beer wedges thinner, but no one can remember how big they used to be.

Dick is philosophical: "We've seen publicans come and go. These will be okay once we get them trained." And I'm not bothered because I won a free beer!

There may not be a champion for this lost lamb on Darch Point Road, but I've got shepherds at God's Holding Paddock to look after me. I am not *Jingle Bells* here, but darlin' or luv. I may win a free beer even if someone rigs the spinning wheel of chance. I can take my handle home, be cross for two weeks, forget why I lost my temper in the first place, still be welcomed back, maybe even win a fishing rod.

And somewhere off Ocean Beach, I bet there's a pod of dolphins watching over me.

Chapter 29

Fish the scum line on the outgoing tide.

—#9, God's Holding Paddock

I expanded my commitment to Bay Audiology. I manned the clinic in Kerikeri every other week now and had a standing reservation at Kauri Park in a unit tucked into a subtropical profusion of flowers and palms. Like a traveling chef, I packed my tote with a good sharp knife, pepper grinder, flaky sea salt, and small bottle of olive oil. This was replenished from a five-liter fusti that sat on our kitchen bench. The fusti had been filled, in turn, by Maxi, who cold-pressed the oil from the fruits of her grove along the Pataua Estuary, a twenty-minute drive from Darch Point Road.

The way into Kerikeri is lined with vegetable stands and citrus orchards for which the town is famous. I took home bags of ambrosial oranges for Adrian, but in the motel kitchenette, my menu came straight from his list of taboos. In season I steamed asparagus. I grilled salmon and drizzled the blushing filet with Maxi's oil. As soon as the Marlborough chardonnay was chilled, I drank it while nibbling sesame thins smeared with Kapiti Kikorangi "sky blue" cheese. For dessert, it was chocolate.

I had a system for making myself at home in my home away from home. But the more hours I put in at work, the more stress on me, and the more I was absent, the sulkier Adrian became. The food was great, but overall my system stunk.

AT THE BUTCHER COUNTER OF LIFE

My esophagitis flared up. My dreams got livelier. A rabid Chihuahua chewed its way up my arm. I peed maggots. Atomic bombs exploded over Darch Point Road. In one recurring nightmare, I lived in a cave by the sea. Sunlight never made its way past the entrance into the yawning dimness, and I had to keep a light on all day in the cave. The incoming tide lapped across the floor, and I was going to drown. This was the best my subconscious could do? It didn't take much imagination to figure that one out.

I signed up with a life coach. It seemed like the Kiwi move in a tight spot. Seeing a psychologist in New Zealand would have been a real thumb of the nose at the clean green good life. The life coach emailed me worksheets to reflect upon and called from Auckland to discuss them.

"We've examined the core beliefs upon which you have based your short-term and lifetime goals. Now let's take a look at the assumptions that really drive you. Mmm. There seems to be some discrepancy here."

No kidding? A disparity between the noble sentiments I profess and the crummy little attitudes that power me through the day?

"Let's see what we can do to bring them into harmony."

By all means, let's get my house in order. More cards, please.

"The answer is action! Change is in the doing. We learn from our mistakes."

Change is in the screwing up! That's how we figure out what to do. After lots of mistakes, I will eventually discover by process of elimination what I should have done—if I'm not dead by then.

We discussed my beliefs, actions, or lack thereof. The life coach assured me that I was now empowered to apply the secret of right thinking to enhance my deep insights that when lived fully would make me think right, or something like that.

Laura told me I was paying $150 an hour for a fortune cookie. Daisy sent me an email saying she knew a woman who killed herself because of life coaching. (I didn't request details.)

I wanted answers, not abstractions.

"How are your core beliefs failing to empower you?"

Why is Adrian so mean to me?

"How have you lived your values since we talked last week?"

How do I work with this asshole?

"Are there life experiences you can draw on to establish a new niche?"

What, victim of abuse?

Abuse? It had been an entire year since Adrian had thrown the drink in my face to shut me up. It took this high-priced fortune cookie to force me at long last to seriously entertain the idea.

Searching the Internet, I learned that entitlement and control are the overarching characteristics of abusive men. They use criticism, verbal abuse, financial restraint, cruelty, and isolation to run the show. Prisoner of Love on Darch Point Road! I took the quiz "Are You Just a Loser, or Is He an Abuser?"

1. Does his need to control escalate if you try to become more independent? Check. Things got worse the more I worked for Bay.
2. Does he hold little respect for women, in general, and is your value defined by your usefulness, which usually boils down to sex partner and housekeeper? And roof painter. Check.
3. Does he justify abuse as an expression of his love? "I left you in Tucson to save our relationship." Check.
4. Does he blame you for the abuse? "You made me throw a drink in your face." Double-dog dare you not to mark check.

From abuse, with a run at it from entitlement, over a void of empathy, it was an easy leap to narcissism in all its infantile glory. Back to the Internet again. Narcissists don't have friends or lovers. They have admirers, tools with trifling needs of their own. It takes the fans a while to wise up because Narcissus is often a con artist too. Worse yet, the boy has a nasty streak. When things don't go his way, he may throw his toys out of the cot—at you.

Life coaching might have been a flop, but three other actions I took in 2005 were not. I applied for New Zealand citizenship. I already had permanent residence, the first and biggest step. I didn't have to relinquish my USA passport. They must have scratched their heads back home when I signed up to keep one foot officially in a country where all I did was bitch about the rain. But dual citizen was the most honest reflection of who I had become, essentially half/half, or rah-thah, half/hahf.

Mary said, "Do it. Just do it, you wally-jammer," and I mailed the paperwork to become an official Kiwi.

My second worthwhile effort that year made more sense. I talked to a lawyer. And the third, which seemed inconsequential at the time, involved an incident that occurred at the blind bend in the road, waiting to cross to the pub. Adrian had grabbed my hand and pulled me close.

"Now!" he commanded.

I was sure I heard a car coming and balked.

"I said now!"

I wrenched my hand from Adrian's, and he made the dash without me. I had refused to hurl myself into the path of an oncoming car. It was progress.

JANET PARMELY

Date: September 1, 2005
To: Anne B.
Subject: Mind the Use-By Date

There's a chocolate factory on the road into Kerikeri, but Makana Confections is in no way industrial. It's a boutique operation where white-capped candymakers, like year-round elves, turn out delicacies that include Mochadamia (a fat macadamia nut enveloped in ganache, dipped in dark chocolate, and adorned with white-chocolate ribbons) and Macadamia Butter Toffee Crunch (a concoction of caramelized sugar, butter, and macadamia-nut bits, all coated in milk chocolate and dusted with more nuts that shower in your lap if you tackle a slab in the car).

The goodness of Makana chocolates is most appreciated if you respect the use-by date stamped on each package. Everything is better when it is fresh, isn't it? Love and chocolate. Macadamia Butter Toffee Crunch is meant to be consumed no more than two months after they whip it up. Once I found an expired box in the bottom of my Kerikeri tote bag. The toffee had lost its crunch. The macadamia crumbs were insipid. The chocolate was gray.

I finally figured out my problem: I stayed in New Zealand past my use-by date. It expired while I was living by Taurikura Bay. They should have stamped the termination of the one-year contract on my bum when I flew out of LA. "This overseas experience best enjoyed before March 1, 2001"—now off you go!

Novelty is perishable. Adventures go bad. Overstayers get sidetracked by alpaca promises in a land where beauty is inexhaustible, but chocolate still gets stale, and love dies as surely as dogs that eat poisoned possums.

Date: October 14, 2005
To: Sheryl O.
Subject: Up to My Chin in Ruffles

I spent last night at Dick's. He shifted up the hill because "There were just too many places at Sŵn y Môr where my girl was supposed to be." The house is a few meters closer to the pub with a view of Parua Bay and an old aviary that he'll convert into a barbeque: all his old amenities except for Joan.

Dick had invited us to dinner (and no doubt had the table set five days in advance). Adrian invited his offspring from Auckland for a visit instead. We've been through this before.

"Can't we do it next weekend, Adrian? You know I'm not keen to come home to a houseful of guests after a week in Kerikeri."

"Drop it. I'm done with that conversation. It never goes anywhere. Call Dick and tell him we can't come." The man's milk of human kindness wouldn't top up a thimble.

I went to Dick's by myself, a ballsy move, but I couldn't bear to disappoint him, nor did I think it was fair. We didn't discuss the predicament on Darch Point Road, but near the end of the evening, he said, "You're welcome to stay here, luv. I can make up the guest bed. You shouldn't drive home. The Booze Bus might get you."

He laid out an old nightie of Joan's, size 16 in a blue-flowered print with eyelet ruffles at the neck and cuffs, and a stain I took to be blood that the washing had not gotten out. It was four sizes too big. I was swimming in flannel and haven't felt so safe and sound for a very long time.

JANET PARMELY

Date: December 28, 2005
To: Anne B.
Subject: Kiwi Care
Attached: Delta maritime signal flag

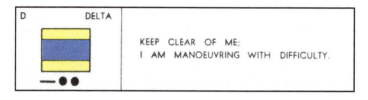

Merry belated Christmas. I hope your holiday was better than mine. Adrian gave me a deck of cards he won tossing a frozen chicken at a grocery-store promotion, a far cry from our first Christmas together. Going from bad to worse, I woke up the next night with chest spasms that I would have rated nine on a scale of ten (ten being childbirth). I've never had problems with my ticker before, so I shook Adrian and said, "I think I'd better go to the hospital."

He said, "You're the only one who can decide that," and rolled over. While I was mulling over this decision of mine, he added, "But you'd better let me know because I will have to get dressed."

We drove to Whangarei Hospital, where they got me right in. Mention chest pain, and they move posthaste in any ER. It wasn't a heart attack. It was nutcracker esophagitis.

Before we left the hospital, a nurse brought Adrian and me hot tea and quartered sandwiches with the crusts cut off. I asked her who I should see about arranging payment for my visit. She looked at me puzzled and then said, "Oh, no worries, luv. It's subsidized."

One of the many things I learned about while cruising was the International Code of Signals, a system of flags and associated meanings that ships use to communicate with each other. There is an A (Alpha) flag, a B (Bravo) flag, and so forth, right on to Z (Zulu). It's a nifty system, concise and universally recognized.

I have taken to flying a tiny signal flag on my desk in hopes that Adrian might respond to a more nautical form of communication. Right after our trip to Tonga, I hoisted the Y (Yankee) flag: "I am dragging my anchor." He did not notice. I lowered the Yankee flag and raised the F (Foxtrot) pennant: "I am disabled; communicate with me." Still no response from Adrian.

After my ER visit, I lowered Foxtrot, gave up altogether on attempting to engage with his ship, and hoisted the D (Delta) flag.

Chapter 30

On the night you need one, any torch will do,
even if it came from the $2 Shop.

—#21, God's Holding Paddock

I gave up on life coaching and talked Adrian into seeing a family counselor. It was a disaster. He folded his arms across his chest and set his face like a wooden puppet with one eyebrow cocked. I yammered on.

"You will never get what you want in this relationship," the dour counselor told me in a private session. *You are a bottomless pit. You will never get what you want in any relationship.*

"Adrian would like you to say thank you more often." *That's all the poor guy wants, you mean old shrew.*

"You are the one complaining, not Adrian. He's okay." *And you are not.*

I gave up on the family counselor.

In spite of all my efforts, I had no insight into this mercurial man who exerted a will so palpable it could have been measured in pounds per square inch. Not one so-called expert had a fix on what it was like to dance a jig on a magic carpet with a whale eye on the genie ready to yank it away on a whim.

Yes, he was abusive—he got 100 percent on the quiz—but he also had an underbelly. I was one of the few people who had seen it. His family in South Africa said so. When he was besotted, he had rolled over and exposed it, and that was the man I had fallen in love with, gentle, I thought, through and through. It took so much work to get to the soft spot now. The way was riddled with mine fields, and it was impossible to relax there, bracing for the next detonation.

Adrian could tend a thousand worms for a year and then off them in a burst of anger without a backward glance. He could grind the coffee for my first cup of the day, wait patiently for the hot water to drip through the filter, decorate it with a whipped cream heart, deliver it with a hug, and explode two minutes later if I asked him to take out the rubbish. "I can only do one fucking thing at a time!"

This man who offered so much would eventually take it all away. Why? Why did Adrian, untroubled by clutter, heedless of mildew and forty-knot winds, have all these bugbears: the glare from the space heater, the scratch of flannel sheets, the offense of green vegetables? Why couldn't a guy smart enough to build boats, circumnavigate the globe, write computer programs, and make enough money to retire before he hit fifty get the difference between an aside and an insult? Why didn't he show some compassion? Why on earth did he smirk when the neighbor's cat died?

I felt like I was losing my mind. Adrian blamed me. The family counselor blamed me. The life coach pushed me to shift my attitudes and examine my core beliefs to find a better way to deal with an asshole. *Cosmopolitan* said, "He doesn't love you anymore." My southern hemisphere friends said, "He's just a man, a South African man." My northern hemisphere friends said, "He's just a jerk."

I lived a little longer with the implication that it was all my fault because I wasn't lovable anymore or wasn't capable of living with a man, let alone one from South Africa, or didn't respect myself enough to terminate a relationship with a jerk.

The dynamics of life with Adrian were a mystery to anyone who tried to poke his nose behind our closed doors. In fact, it took me years to understand that I had bestowed my dearest illusions on the man and bonded to him in that deception. I had imprinted on Adrian like some misguided gosling chasing after Konrad Lorenz.

Adrian rarely left the house except to windsurf or putter or pout on a moored boat, and so proximity and habit made fast the tie that bound us. Except for his runner to the islands, I had never enjoyed the luxury of having my home to myself for more than an afternoon. We never established that balance of dominion that had worked even for my parents until Dad retired: he ruled the office, and Mom ruled the roost. Under the best of circumstances, a man wears out the house if he's home all day. And then he wears out you. But it's a foundation for disaster when the balance of money and power is out of whack and a man doesn't have a job.

And abuse has an intimacy all its own, the hold, even if it is a strangle hold, of the cycle of abuse. Adrian dribbled warm water down my wetsuit before I swam in Taurikura Bay. He rubbed the feeling back into my feet after winter walks on Ocean Beach. He cooked dinner while I watched my favorite soap, *Shortland Street*. Some evenings, still, we sat together in front of La Contessa, and some mornings we had the comfort of familiar sex—when Adrian wasn't thwarted, challenged, annoyed by flannel sheets, aggravated by brussels sprouts, or someone told him what the fuck to do. Adrian's tender gestures made it easier to cling to the myth that he cherished me for who I was. Intermittent reinforcement, as everyone knows, is the most effective schedule.

Adrian's affronts and temper tantrums, his inexorable drive to call the shots were tangled up with beach walks, Kiwi *General Hospital*, Mount Aubrey, Taurikura Bay, leg of lamb, and sex. They were intertwined with Dick and God's Holding Paddock. I worked around the bad bits to get to the good, made my way around it all as surely as the sheep that grooved switchbacks in the hillocks over decades.

It was like bodyboarding, which exhilarated and terrified me. I paddled into the surf and dove under the crashing waves like Adrian had taught me, no easy accomplishment with a flotation device lashed to the wrist. After battling on, two waves forward, one wave back, I made it beyond the break and waited in the eerie calm. It was a spot of immense power and scariness. I felt the chill even through my wetsuit. When I heard it build and roar down upon me, I kicked furiously. If I didn't time it right, I would get creamed by the perfect wave.

But if I did catch it, I rode triumphantly along the crest and glided into the rippling shallows with a momentum that had nothing to do with skill but right-place-right-time happenstance and the birr of the wave. I had no intuitive feel for it, no idea what technique got me properly on top of the wave or victimized by it, but either way I felt alive. It was pretty much how I went about life. At least I was not an orange woman avoiding cracks in the sidewalk in the crabgrass suburbs.

After all the casting about and dead ends, trying to comprehend what was wrong with our relationship, fix my end of it, and understand Adrian's, in the autumn of 2006, I watched an old episode of *Boston Legal*. There was a character with Asperger's syndrome. He had tics and eccentricities and certainly was not square-jawed handsome like Adrian, but something in his stilted manner and disconnect from the subtleties of social interaction struck a chord.

So I got on the Internet again, ordered some books, and bingo! It was the aha moment that is often described by partners of someone on the autism spectrum when they find the missing piece of the puzzle. Now I had something to hang my hat on besides claptrap that did not begin to explain the pandemonium of living with someone bereft of empathy, whose outbursts buried the quiet sweetness that first took my breath away.

But the more I learned, the more I bristled at how small I would have to make myself in order to get this relationship to work, because important chunks of experience eluded Adrian. In fact, the human drama didn't just escape him. It pissed him off.

I could expect no emotional support. My own clattering bag of bolts didn't matter a jot to him, my fantasies, petty resentments, minimum daily requirement for dependable human connection, not a tittle. Adrian was "mind blind." He didn't have any better idea about someone else's feelings than a sightless man to whom you showed a drawing of a family of duckbill platypuses in Bermuda shorts, posing in front of Mount Rushmore, and asked, "What precisely do you see?"

My welfare was not just trivial to Adrian. It never entered his mind. He lacked the neurological equipment to process the messier stuff of life. Adrian wasn't dropped from the Southern Cross. He fell out of the starship *Enterprise*. He was Mister Spock, and I was an earthling with an overdose of attraction to the untidy bits, more rabbity-eared sensitive than a fluffle of bunnies. It was a terrible match.

Adrian's perfect mate would have helped him through the muddle, not back him into murky corners where he exploded. She would have protected him from any overstimulation that might precipitate calamity—heat, shoes, big meals at noon—and she would have been quieter than a moth's poot about it.

I had to accept that my worth to this man I loved even now, past all good sense, was grounded in how I served his needs, like a stool, a handy three-legged stool. I was a willing worker who knew how to use tools (an asset as long I didn't escalate to a frenzy of fix-fix-fix-do-do-do). Adrian tended toward languor and was inept except in the water, which might explain why he spent so much time there. Sailing and windsurfing energized him. His hour-long showers calmed him like Temple Grandin's squeeze machine. I was convenient for sex, which Adrian enjoyed as much as the next guy as long as he didn't have to navigate all those uncomfortable formalities to get to it. And I made social life easier. He was fine with sporty mateship but struggled with the tougher parts of general conversation past how d'ya do.

The past didn't bog Adrian down. Since he didn't empathize, consequences of his behavior—past, present, or future—were irrelevant when it came to anyone else but himself. He was stunted in time, temporally protected, and the easy complacency that implied galled me too. Adrian had spent a lifetime blurting out insults that made perfect sense to him.

"We'd been engaged for a year when my fiancée threw the ring in my face."

"Why?"

"Not a clue. I did tell her father he was a drunken sod. Maybe that was it."

"Adrian!"

"Why should that have worried her? He was."

So what if someone got her knickers in a knot when he asked what good her layabout children were? Her layabout words? Or the hostess sat dumbfounded when she placed in front of him a stalk of broccoli, a salmon filet, or one of the myriad foods that irritated his sensitive palate, and Adrian said, "That looks bloody awful." Why should he sleep on flannel sheets in New Zealand in July when it prickled his touchy skin?

Even if I did everything I was supposed to, shrink-wrapped my spirit and stored it in the deep freeze, quit dancing with the postman, made excuses for his rude behavior ("It's just that dry British humor, *tee-hee*")—even then, there was no guarantee that Adrian wouldn't spontaneously combust when the structure he needed to make the world work for him went awry.

After months of buying into the autism-spectrum theory, I began to wonder just how "bioneurological" it was. Adrian could be engaging when he put his mind to it, just like his headmaster had said. Maybe he was just a narcissistic, abusive crank—or a psychopath. In a country with decent gun control, it's hard to tell them apart. All the variations on a theme seemed to fit.

The implications were dismal, but I took comfort in every one of them because now I had constructs to plug Adrian's wacky behavior into, this unflinching ability to navigate the world with impulse his only guide. In the end, the diagnosis didn't matter. Whatever quadrant it comes from, when a wind like this blows into your life, it's going to be a #12 on the Beaufort Scale, gusting to 260 kilometers an hour, propelling 50-foot waves at sea and uprooting trees and toppling adults on shore.

Date: March 31, 2006
To: Sheryl O.
Subject: 3 + 4 = 7

I sold myself short. Adrian's been in a blue funk over the final settlement of his marital property, and it's forced me to redo the math on the three-legged stool.

The partially-ex apparently cried in a most sympathetic manner in court, and the judge awarded her the spread on the North Shore of Auckland, as well as the holiday home by the sea in South Africa (the appreciating assets—she's no bonehead). Adrian got the boat, poor *Jingle Bells* that no one has tended for nearly two years, a floating palace of memories and mold, a sailor's broken dream.

His holdings were tracked around the world and divvied up along with the Krugerrands. After the lawyers and forensic accountants took their shares, the days of buying anything short of a Learjet were long gone for everyone.

And it's not over yet. The caveat against our home on Darch Point Road expired today. The completely-ex-for-just-one-minute slapped another one back on the property. She's contesting the final settlement.

Adrian is not a happy chappie. He's lost half of what he had to the still-hanging-on-by-a-caveat-ex-wife and half of that half to the handmaidens of divorce. In addition to the house, the boat is now for sale. What man wants to put a price on his dick?

He goes for days without speaking, and when I try to converse, he enunciates as if he were talking to a deaf person or a foreigner, "Can't you fucking understand English? I said I am busy." He did, however, tell me he doesn't know if he wants me to go with him to his niece's wedding in South Africa next year. I am a liability. Having a woman on his arm would increase his chances of getting raped too. "I bloody well don't want AIDS on top of all of this."

Here's how I see it after recalculating. In addition to being handy for sex (except abroad), chitchat, and maintenance of home and garden, I have evolved into a convenient dog to kick. If we take the three useful legs I already knew about and add to them the four belonging to the dog, that's a grand total of seven. I am really a seven-legged stool.

Date: September 30, 2006
To: Laura P.
Subject: Mackerel Sky, Never Long Wet and Never Long Dry
Attached: Officially half/hahf

At ten o'clock yesterday morning, I was sworn in as a New Zealand citizen in front of Mary, Dick, Adrian, the mayor of Whangarei, and somewhere up there, Highway the Snoring Pig. As you know, I have struggled with this decision. But when I raised my hand to take the oath, I basked in a rare moment of smug joy.

Adrian hosted lunch today at Parua Bay Tavern on the new deck overlooking the water, dappled fifteen shades of milky turquoise in the nap-time sun. The pub changed hands last year, and the place is looking quite smart. As long as they don't mess with God's Holding Paddock and we get them trained right, it'll be okay.

September traditionally kicks off spring in New Zealand, but this has nothing to do with the weather. Barometers drop. Daffodils wilt, and lambs freeze to death in cold snaps. But the tide today was high under a mackerel sky, and the flame trees bloomed for my citizenship party at the pub. The guys had just put on their woolly jumpers to take the chill off the late afternoon when Kevin stood up to make a speech.

"As you know, I have a full-time hobby studying women and as a result do not have a great love of the species, which is decidedly feline, dependable as cats. I once knew a woman named Faith, and you couldn't even trust *her*.

"It has also been my observation that ladies, like cats, torture and torment their prey before they kill them, or break their hearts. However, amongst the ladies of the world, there are lighthouses who shine on men and lighten their way. They are thin on the ground, but I believe you are one of them." Kevin raised his handle to me. "So welcome to New Zealand and always God's Holding Paddock. May your greatest problem be an empty glass."

I took this to mean that I am a tidy woman, and for the second time in two days swelled with pride. This is the first thing I've done in a long while that feels right. It's who I am, half/hahf.

Chapter 31

There is no substitute for billable hours.

—#28, God's Holding Paddock

My parents were slipping, and my daughter was getting married. Talk about stress. I returned alone to the States to fulfill my duties as Evil Trustee and Mother of the Bride, bouncing between Arizona and Colorado for the next four months.

The lawyer had been right. Trusteeship had conferred upon me the appeal of a rat snapped in a trap and discovered a week later. Everyone wants to get rid of it, but nobody wants to touch it. My thankless, unpaid job without guidelines had one more drawback. If push ever came to shove, unless I could prove otherwise, I would be assumed guilty of violating my parents' rights and serving my own interests—elder abuse and theft. I kept meticulous records and made only two iffy purchases with the trust money, a bottle of gin and a subscription to *The New Yorker*. But you never know. Three people were very unhappy with me, and Dad was a wild card. Mom had already revoked my power of attorney in a fit of pique.

I had by now an eye-opening understanding of my parents' finances. Except for minimal equity in the house, there were no assets to fall back on. Supporting three generations through the years hadn't been cheap, and we had never been the kind of family that kept a bag of Krugerrands under the bed. Social Security and Dad's TIAA-CREF annuity were deposited into the trust account and covered living expenses, but not my niece's thongs.

Mom was tireless in her efforts to bankroll my bouncing baby brother and his daughter, old enough to vote and still living at home. In an attempt to respect her independence, I drip-fed my mother's checking account. Mom wasn't any happier than Dad had been with someone doling out an allowance from what she considered to be her own money in the first place. But this wily eighty-three-year-old wasn't going to let a little cash-flow problem slow her down.

When Mom had reluctantly agreed to consolidate the credit-card debt, she was required to stop charging on most of her accounts, but there were still a few active cards floating around. Sears, JCPenney, and AARP Visa took a dim view of someone attempting to suspend privileges already granted to family members, let alone curb the primary cardholder's largesse. A man in accounts at American Express asked me what the hell I thought I was doing trying to organize my parents' finances from New Zealand. It was a valid question, except distance wasn't the issue.

Had I been appointed conservator of my charges, I would have had more autonomy, but I possessed neither the bucks nor heart to navigate the tricky legalities required to declare my parents incapacitated. (And let's face it, with my track record, did I have a leg to stand on?) Dad felt perfectly fit and was game for anything—"Reporting for active duty, sir!" Mom was dauntless in her campaign for home rule, as long as she retained the right to complain about it in the moment and regret it all afterward.

My mother was a banker's dream. Interest rates meant nothing to her. She faithfully paid the minimum due on borrowed money. When her son fell behind, she picked up his debts too, including a longstanding loan initiated to buy his daughter's first automobile (an emerald-green tuner car with ground effects, tweaked engine, and carbon-fiber hood) that had been traded up and out long ago. The credit union was always happy to extend her another loan. The second mortgage, a line of credit, had some wiggle room left and was another unprotected flank.

So was grocery money. At first I deposited $1,000 into Mom's account the first of each month, but there wasn't enough moolah to buy a carton of milk by the second week. I set up a tab with a no-cash-out stipulation at a grocery store that also delivered. It seemed like a polite end run to me.

It infuriated Mom. She didn't speak to me for three weeks and told the neighbor, "My daughter is stealing our money and starving us!" Then she borrowed five bucks to buy milk to prove her point.

Mom lost her dental bridge. I put money into her account to replace it. Mom lost the new bridge. When I paid the dentist directly, I discovered that the price Mom had quoted for the first replacement was double the actual cost of the bridge.

She didn't miss a beat. "I don't have any underpants."

"I shifted a hundred dollars last month so you could buy some at Penney's."

"The mall's so busy. I can't park close enough to get in with this bad knee."

"Why don't you order some from the catalogue? They'll mail them to you."

"You'll have to put more money in my account. I spent it on milk."

Two weeks later: "I don't have any underpants."

"Didn't they send any from the catalogue?"

"They were the wrong size. It's too much trouble to return them. You know how long the lines at the post office are."

It was like playing Whac-A-Mole.

When I got to Tucson, Dad was stuck in the couch. Mom had taken to setting one of the bottom cushions on top of another, thereby erecting a sort of rajah's musnud to make it easier for her to sit down and get up. Dad would wander in and invariably plop himself onto the springs where the cushion used to be. When he decided to move on, he concentrated his weight on his cane, heaved himself up, nearly made it, and then—*Whoooah!*—the cane slipped out from under him, and he collapsed, stuck in the couch again. Rural Metro knew the address by heart. "Help! Come quick! My husband is stuck in the couch, and he can't get up!"

Mom had called 911 before I could intercept her, and the fire engine arrived for another lift assist. A hunk, fully booted and spurred, as Dick would say, pulled Dad up with one hand. Mom, proud of her ability to have acted so swiftly in a crisis, turned to me and said with a toothless smile (her bridges were in the dresser drawer), "My, those firemen are handsome, aren't they?"

Whac-A-Mole.

In the family room, Mom had set up command center, outfitted with a commercial-size shredder to destroy any incriminating documents that came to light and might fall into the Evil Trustee's hands. Phone numbers for critical resources had been prominently posted on index cards taped to the wall: a sympathetic neighbor, Southern Arizona Legal Aid, Arizona Adult Protective Services (1-SOS-ADULT).

Mom's Rollator, which she'd nicknamed Red Rover, served as mobile war room, the handlebar basket piled high with manila folders, labeled variously HFC Loan, Power of Attorney, Very Important, and Private—Do Not Let Her See! She kept a copy of the Revocable Living Trust at the ready for her next attempt to fire me as trustee (which wasn't proving as easy as rescinding power of attorney). When Mom tired of pushing Red Rover and the laden basket, she sat on the seat and scuttled backward, propelling it with her feet. You had to give her credit. One way or the other, she kept going.

Trying to organize the house had gotten me nowhere, so I took charge of cooking instead. Mom was thrilled. The task of putting dinner on the table every night for more than sixty years must have been a kind of life sentence for a woman who was no chef at heart and had a fraught relationship with food. The dogs, however, were indignant. *What? No more Salvation Army dinners!*

My folks had been enrolled in the meals-on-wheels program for a year, but Dad, like an impish eight-year-old hiding peas, often sneaked his portion under the table when Mom wasn't looking. Food was his last arena of control. Bessie, the beagle, waddled like a hippo. Bella, the granddaughter's Chihuahua, wasn't going to fit in anyone's purse, and Molly, the Lhasapoo I had left behind when I went to New Zealand, had swelled up like an Alabama watermelon tick. *Oh boy—mashed potatoes, meatloaf, and a Parker House roll—woof!*

I had no strategy to deal with it all except play Whac-a-Mole and bake, roast, and fricassee my way through. But I was doing the right thing. Right? Always I consoled myself with this:

It was the right thing to do.

Really? Sign on for a high-wire act across the equator that didn't involve just two old comedians, but a family circus, as well? They didn't want your help.

Except for Dad.

Except your father. You're probably right.

I wanted to bail. It was disgraceful. I had none of the benefits but got stuck with all the hard work at the end. That's why I bought that fifth of Tanqueray—to even the score.

Forty-three thousand in credit-card debt versus a twenty-five-dollar bottle of gin?

It was the principle.

And The New Yorker*?*

I wrote a thank-you note for all my hard work as trustee and signed it 'Love, Mom and Dad.' The New Yorker *sent it to me in New Zealand with notification of my international gift subscription.*

Well done.

No daughter should have been asked to do what I did. I was just a bur in my mother's lap blanket. Do you know what she told me? She said I was a difficult baby.

You? I bet you didn't even cry when the doctor swatted you on the hiney.

She said, "When I woke up out of the ether, they told me you wanted to be fed. Fed! I was exhausted. I said, 'Take her away.'"

Ouch.

I battled to maintain her dignity and keep up with her shenanigans, and that was my thanks? "Even when you were a baby, you were a daughter no mother could love."

Yet she parted with her mother's cameo.

It about broke my heart when she brought out that old shoebox and unrolled the cotton wool. "Here. I want you to have it. Laura can wear it on her wedding day."

Remind you of someone?

It's beginning to dawn on me, thank you. They give. They take away. They abandon me.

And what did you think was going to happen if you didn't step in?

I don't know. The neighbor had already called in the middle of Kerikeri clinic screaming on my cell phone, "They don't have any milk! Stealing their money when you have a millionaire boyfriend, you should be ashamed of yourself, missy!"

Sounds like another ventriloquist act to me.

Maybe the neighbor would have turned us all in. Certainly they would have lost the house at the rate they were going. They could have been sent to the poorhouse.

This isn't Charles Dickens.

Maybe Arizona would have made them wards of the state.

Maybe Arizona was better equipped to look after them than you were.

Nothing prepares you for this. You think your parents will just keel over

and die one day, or at the very least cooperate. I thought they'd go gentle into that good night.
You'd better reread the poem.
I had no battle plan.
You had no comrade in arms.
I was trapped in a cave by the sea, and the tide was coming in. I was drowning.
And what does it say about you that you were willing to drown in your efforts that were resented by everyone except one old man?
It was the right thing to do, and there were mushroom clouds over Darch Point Road. Tucson was the only place my American half had to call home.

Date: June 28, 2007
To: Laura P.
Subject: Company for Dinner

There are twenty-four pairs of Vanity Fair XL cotton Lollipop briefs hanging on a drying rack next to the dining-room table. Looks like Grandma had plenty of underpants all along.

Whatta mess. Laundry's in heaps. Dirty dishes are scattered on the floor for the dogs to prewash. Someone's peeing on the carpet, but I'm not pointing fingers. The kitchen table looks like an archaeological dig: a sepia photo of your great-great-great-grandfather Parker Rose Gray, frozen austerely in time; a yellowed program from Aunt Pat's first piano recital; five years' worth of Christmas cards, half addressed and never mailed.

When I shook out Grandma's lap blanket, it was like breaking a piñata. Out fell a crackling shower of Cheez-Its, *Remedy Magazine*s,

Frappuccino bottle tops, dog biscuits, pens, blood-glucose lancets, loose change, the water bill, five Xanax, animal crackers—a lion, a tiger, a bear, oh my.

I straightened up some more, but when I started to fold the Lollipops, Grandma drew the line. Her candor astonished me. As you know, candor's not her strong suit. "My underpants are there because that's where I want them. I knew where everything was until you went and put it away." I had pushed her too far.

"If I put this house in order, it means that I am putting my life in order. That means I am getting ready to die, and I won't do it. You can't make me. I'm not going to die, and I won't have you badgering me about picking up around here anymore. It's my home, not yours. Leave my underwear alone."

Fair enough. I've given up on housekeeping, and we'll dine with the underpants.

Date: June 29, 2007
To: Laura P.
Subject: Grandma's Taint

Grandma called me into the bedroom tonight and informed me, "Your father isn't the only one who's got bedsores, you know."

"You do too?"

"Look." She lay down on the bed, hiked up her nightie, and mooned me.

"I really don't see anything, Mom."

"Well, of course not. You have to spread my cheeks."

I need a gin.

JANET PARMELY

Date: June 30, 2007
To: Daisy S.
Subject: War of the Depends

I just arrived in Tucson for a tour of duty. Evil Trustee checking in. We hired a home-health-care nurse to visit three times a week, and Dad has been put on hospice, which is surprising, considering his blood pressure is lower than mine. But his Alzheimer's has progressed, so he qualifies for palliative care in the home.

A lovely aide bathes Dad once a week. She steers him to the dresser—"Let's go, you adorable little man"—and lets him pick out clean socks, shirt, pants, Depends. He follows her like a sheep to the shower, where he strips, sudses up, and probably lets Bo Peep hit any critical spots he missed, all without a whimper.

The hospice nurse catheterized Dad last week due to his incontinence, and we all hoped it might bring an end to the War of the Depends. She inserted a tube into his you-know-what that drained into a flexible bag strapped to his leg by day. At night he had to be connected to a bigger bag, so big in fact, that it had to sit in a bucket by the side of his bed. It seems my father is a prodigious nocturnal outputter of urine.

Mom dreamed up a system where he would ring an old school bell when he woke up and was ready to get unhitched. Ha! He can't even remember where the bran muffin rolled that she threw at him for breakfast.

I was awakened last night by a noise that sounded like Peg-Leg Pete stumping on deck, and got up to investigate. I found my father dragging the bucket down the hall with his dick, muttering, "I'm going to find the woman who did this to me and give her a piece of my mind."

The nurse returned this afternoon, removed the catheter, and it was back to the War of the Depends:

"Did you remember to change your Depends, John?"

"Yes, Joanne."

"No, you didn't!"

"Yes, I did!"

"No, you didn't!"

"Yes, I did!"

"No!"

"Yes!"

"No!"

Chapter 32

To get two versions of truth, put a man and woman under one roof for six decades. If you want more renditions, add offspring.

—#39, God's Holding Paddock

Life teetered along in Tucson under the jaundiced eye of the Evil Trustee. Mom sat atop her musnud. Dad got stuck in the couch.

When I returned from shopping one afternoon, my mother was snoozing, a fruitcake tin of prescription bottles sliding off her lap. She had a full-time job sorting pills, stewing over refills, and prioritizing the Xanax. It was wearing her out. She roused. "Did you get bananas? I think I'm low on potassium."

"Yes, I got bananas, but where's Dad? He's not in the couch."

"Maybe he's in the bathroom. I wish someone would give *me* a raised toilet seat."

"No, he's not there."

"I watch your father like a hawk. He'd never get past me."

"There was mail all over the driveway."

"Well, he has been expressly forbidden to get the mail. I never know where he's going to put it when he brings it in."

I located Dad lying motionless under an acacia tree twenty feet off the drive. It was a hundred and eight degrees on a windy day. He may as well have been in a convection oven.

He's dead, I thought, and it stunned me: all I felt was relief. There would be no more mornings when the early riser slept in, and even Mom stood at his bedroom door checking for a sign of life from his diminishing figure, as wizened as a bog body. There would be no more stage III pressure sores persisting in the face of the hospice nurse's assiduous care, no more Depends blowouts, no more dragging a bucket down the hall with his dick. The appeals were over: *Don't let him die while I'm in New Zealand, but if he has to go, please let it be in his sleep.*

"Call 911!" I poked my head in the door and yelled to Mom.

"He's fine. It's not that hot out there," she protested, but phoned.

I knelt beside my father, and it scared the daylights out of me when he opened his eyes. I asked him his name, and he said, miffed, "I know who I am."

Mom came out, and when she saw Dad stretched in the sand, she opened her mouth in a mute *O*—like she had just pushed Red Rover into a drive-in movie of her life.

She probably saw the lieutenant she had met when he was at flight school in her hometown, and maybe she saw him standing with her in front of the Justice of the Peace. Did she see Uncle Sam shipping her new husband to the European front? They wouldn't see each other again for three years, and by then it would be plain that all they had in common besides youth was geography. They happened to be at a dance in Pittsburg, Kansas, at a time when people did a lot of crazy things. Surely she saw the miscarried boy whose eyes never opened on this world, a daughter coming out the chute, and after that, another son—

And then a shadow crossed Mom's face. Maybe she was back in Pittsburg. Possibly they were putting Ruth in the ground. Jody's father had already slipped out of the world without her apology. She'd lost one son. Now she had let her sister and eccentric, fun-loving mother down.

After Ruth died, Mom's world must not have seemed like a very safe place, and her son was just beginning to toddle into harm's way. As I saw it, he became the focus of our mother's efforts to keep her world intact.

If he ever barred the door, by golly she would be there to break it down in time.

If my brother fell, she picked him up. When he began to lie at five, as boys do, she covered for him. When he had been warned not to play with the bell jars under which the neighbor's tender radishes were sprouting and shattered one, nearly slicing his finger off, he told a whopper: "Her dog bit me!" Mom let it pass, and the neighbor brought him Hostess CupCakes and Grape Nehi to atone for something her mutt didn't do.

Over the years he quit jobs, deserted posts. Mom phoned his bosses and made excuses. She hired lawyers to intervene. She bailed him out of a fix he got himself into with one mighty big boss, but that required a congressman's help.

Mom ramrodded her son's divorce from his first wife and custody for him of their child. She ripped a three-year-old out of her mother's arms and moved her son and granddaughter in, against Dad's better judgment. By the time she was done, the ex had been dumped in the Lone Star State with a suitcase, not much more than she had come to the marriage with. The letters and phone calls to her daughter were intercepted for nineteen years. Mom upended the life of a kid from the wrong side of Tyler, Texas, who knew how to tell someone to kiss her mammy-shakin' white ass but was no match for this woman's chicanery, her son's complicity, and Dad's capitalization.

Mom cut a swath to make her son's way secure, and because she had done all the work, it only doubled back and led him home. It divided loyalties in the family where no lines should have been drawn. It empowered unhealthy behavior, which she nurtured, and her son grew adept at holding the monstrous threat of his own suicide over her head. Together they spun the cocoon that swaddled and trussed them both.

Ever late to the Revelation Ball, I did not understand until years after I was appointed trustee how entrenched the foundation for resentment was. I did not appreciate how firmly my father and I, and later Laura, had been relegated to the enemy's side.

After Dad moved to the office, he had a space of his own in which to reflect and build tentative bonds with his children based on exchange of information more intimate than how he organized his slides. He had never been a *Knows Best* kind of father. He had no pet names for us, no terms of endearment like Princess or Kitten or Bud. Our interior lives had been exclusively the domain of his wife, who had no pet names for us either. Nor could she tell you what we wanted to be when we grew up or what our favorite ice cream was. Was that chocolate, now, strawberry, or rocky road?

She trafficked in confidentialities. They were the coin of her realm. We unburdened ourselves of our worst doubts and fears, and she stirred up the heebie-jeebies. We were the steam vents for our mother's own angst. She got relief, but our precarious lots loomed larger than ever, untempered by perspective or reassurance. We went back for more like Harlow's monkeys.

Mom's manipulation of family relationships had been a force to reckon with even for a Harvard graduate, or maybe especially for a Harvard graduate. It's unclear if Dad ever grasped the ramifications of his support in the more expensive rescue missions, but it was an astonishing effort, if as usual a little late, to attempt at eighty to make sense of it all.

Most remarkably, he enlisted the help of a therapist and held her opinions in high regard. Had the progression of his dementia and untimely death of the psychologist not dovetailed, one can only wonder where his new insights might have led.

"After Ruth died," he told me, "your mother seemed to forget about you and me. She became obsessed with your brother. I called the pediatrician for advice." This was, you must understand, unusual behavior for Dad to get that involved back then.

"Completely normal. He's the youngest and a son" was the breezy verdict of the doctor who looked after little baby boomers.

"What did you do then, Dad?"

"What could I do? I had my work, and the doctor seemed to think it was okay."

But what about me! I wanted to holler like a four-year-old child.

Leaning on Red Rover, Mom must have seen it all beginning to crumble. After her single-minded efforts to cast Dad, admittedly a pedantic debater and certainly not the last of the red-hot lovers, as the villain, she might lose him. What kind of life would it be without this bedrock of disappointment in a union that spanned more than half a century, this man who was now just a plain old demented pain in the ass?

Her son had finally left home for good with wife number three. His daughter was about to crawl out the marriage escape hatch as well. Dust, it was turning to desert dust, this ditty bag of diversions spun with razzle-dazzle like gold from straw, and only big enough for three. It had been fashioned from dreams without grit to keep the scary world at bay and was so formidable that until now not one pupa had metamorphosed. No imago had emerged, hardened its wings, and taken flight from the comfort of its endless possibilities.

But try as I might, I could not get inside the marvelous cocoon. There wasn't a key under the mat. Dad certainly didn't have one. He just paid the mortgage. The sign out front, as explicit as REMOVE YOUR MUDDY GUMBOOTS PLEASE, warned us both: CHECK YOUR REALITY CHECK AT THE DOOR.

The ambulance pulled into the drive. I rode with Dad to the hospital where, except for a jaunt to radiology, his bony body lay for ten hours on a cart in an exam room the temperature of an icebox.

He could still carry on polite conversation and was the only one in the household who could tell you the phase of the moon, but once Alzheimer's was mentioned, no one spoke directly to him. "What's his name? When did he fall?" Dad may as well have been a dehydrated jackrabbit.

EKG, CAT scan, and X-rays were normal. The man really did know how to fall! On our way out, I asked an orderly if he could take Dad to the bathroom—you could smell his Depends were soaked—and spare him the indignity of his daughter doing it. The orderly said no. "It's against hospital policy, a liability issue, you know."

As we left Northwest Hospital, I thought back to the tea and sandwiches that they had given Adrian and me at Whangarei Hospital, and I begged once more, *Please, in his sleep—and not here.*

Sent: July 12, 2007
To: Laura P.
Subject: Grace
Attached: Mom and Dad at Camp Otterbrook, 1947
          Mom and four-year-old me, Fort Devens, 1952

After Grandpa's mad dash to the ER, the darnedest thing happened: a truce in the War of the Depends.

Grandma sat at the side of Grandpa's bed tonight, gave him his Aricept, and reminded him what it was: "Your memory pill, John." She didn't accuse him of putting the dirty dishes in the cabinet on purpose, nor harp at him for the plumbing crisis he precipitated when he flushed one of his Depends down the toilet. She did not reiterate how she resents looking after him: "If you fumble with the tabs on those Depends one more time, John, you can just lie down on the bed, and I will diaper you like a baby."

Consequently Grandpa did not snap at her and threaten to leave (and go where?). They sat quietly together for a few minutes, and Grandma asked Grandpa if he had put his soiled Depends in the plastic bag, and he said yes. They bid each other good night. She turned off the light and looked over her shoulder as she left the room. For just one night, Grandma left Grandpa his scrap of pride that Alzheimer's hasn't taken away yet, and that is good enough for all of us.

Before she turned in, Grandma shuffled through her stack of memorabilia on the kitchen table, and I found these two snapshots on top.

AT THE BUTCHER COUNTER OF LIFE

Date: August 1, 2007
To: Daisy S.
Subject: Meanest Little Underwear Shop in the Whole USA

I'm in Colorado for Laura's wedding. Then it's back to Tucson, and finally, home to New Zealand where Adrian is talking about a trip to Hawaii, which he has been doing since we met. Just in case he's serious this time, I thought I'd look for a new bathing suit.

I found a retro polka-dot number at a shop in town. It had pretty much everything you could want in swimwear at this age. The halter, if cinched up snugly, provided a nice uplift. The spandex blend was shirred forgivingly across the tummy and further concealed a particular of the nether anatomy that I didn't know the slang for until my twenty-seven-year-old daughter enlightened me.

I pulled a size 10 from the rack, and a postmenopausal woman rushed over like an alpha dog having a bad fur day. "What are you doing with that size 10?" she growled.

Where was that lovely college student who had offered me a size 8 just the week before? I hated myself for it but spontaneously regressed to Underwear Dog. I blushed. I babbled, "I'm sorry. I tried on an eight last week. It was little snug. I was running late. I came back to try on a ten. I'm sure it will be just right. Oh please."

"A ten? Really, a ten? Why, you are at least a twelve, probably a fourteen."

Where was this hostility coming from? I had no idea but held on to the size 10 and took the size 8, as well, just for spite. I was determined to buy one of these two swimsuits even if I couldn't fit my supposed-size-14 ass into either one of them.

"You know," she said, pointing to the cardboard Esther Williams above the rack, "our mannequins take an eight and they aren't even three-dimensional like you." She said this as if it were a character flaw.

I headed to the dressing room with the bathing suits, and alpha dog snarled, "You may try them on over your own panties, but be careful you don't stretch out that size 8."

After trying them on, I handed her the size 10 and said haughtily, "It fits just fine."

She peeked into the dressing room to make sure that the size 8 was hanging there and I had not shoplifted it—because it fit a two-dimensional mannequin, I could have sneaked it into my pocket—then grudgingly took my purchase. "Are you sure the polka dots don't distort across your backside?"

Hell, the polka dots were as flat as pancakes, but isn't that the kind of support we look to spandex for?

Laura sparked with the moral conviction of a bride-to-be when I told her the story. "You bought it? You should have told her off and thrown the suit in her face."

She's too young to understand. Maybe I held my tongue, but I also held my ground. I hiked up my big-girl panties and tried on the damned suit over them. I wanted it, and Underwear Dog won in the end.

Anyway, for a three-dimensional person to squeeze into a size 10 bathing suit that hides her big fat camel toe, that alone is sweet revenge.

AT THE BUTCHER COUNTER OF LIFE

Date: October 29, 2007
To: Laura P.
Subject: Happy Birthday, Grandpa
Attached: Testimony to the staying power of the Salvation Army Diet

I head back to New Zealand next week. It's been a long old haul, but Grandpa's party here in Tucson was a great success. I put ninety-one candles on the cake (one to grow on). We invited the neighbors, some old colleagues, and even recruited a couple of babies, so there would be a representative cross section of the American public.

Molly sat on Grandpa's lap, the two of them looking stouthearted and content. Grandpa had three glasses of champagne and fell asleep while petting the dog. Before he dozed off, he said, "Thank you, old girl," which made me feel pretty content myself.

Part IV

The Tide Comes in at the Speed of a Galloping Horse

Chapter 33

Sure he's a decent bloke at the pub, but who is he at home?
—#9, God's Holding Paddock

While I was trying on swimsuits in Colorado, Adrian went to Hawaii without me. Tit for tat. He also hired a contractor, the neighbor who had crewed from Tonga, to renovate the sleep-out. Paul had resurfaced the concrete floor with polished macrocarpa and taken a reciprocating saw to the dreary wall that blocked the view onto the harbor, a stone's throw away. Afternoon sun spilled through new casement windows, cranked open to the salty breeze. The dilapidated old fire station gleamed, finally transformed into the guest cottage of my dreams.

Money had obviously been pumped into our operation while I was away. Adrian had put the proceeds from the sale of *Jingle Bells* into his Forex account, charged thousands of dollars in trading programs, and based on these, invented his own, which he claimed virtually guaranteed 18 percent gain. The boat money had originally been earmarked to settle our debt, but he decided this was a shrewder investment: "I would be a fool to pay off the mortgages when I can make that kind of return on my money," he crowed.

I was, of course, the real fool—as opposed to what, a make-believe fool, a fool who'd been studying for six years and still hadn't gotten a PhD in Folly? Maybe he did think the money was better leveraged in his private accounts, but it was also an effective way to keep a liquidated asset out of my hands and ensure that I shouldered the debt.

If you are looking for a simple investment, forget about messing with property in a country that values its indigenous resources. The nebulous regulations and endless inspections involved in subdividing the sleep-out (Adrian's first get-rich-quick scheme) had begun in costly fits and starts five years earlier. Water and power supply to both properties had to be scrutinized, ecological effects on the little stream that ran past the glowworm cave evaluated. Boundaries had to be surveyed and redrawn. A geologist bored core samples to make sure the property wasn't going to slide into the harbor and take the hill with it. An engineer determined we had to relocate seepage fields to the tune of $20,000, even though installation of a reticulated sewer system was imminent.

When Whangarei Heads was finally hooked up to a sewerage treatment facility, the issue of seepage fields promptly became irrelevant. Adrian crossed the last palm necessary to acquire separate title to the sleep-out, so we could offer it for sale independent of the main house. Our sensible, new real estate agent determined that Adrian would be forced to settle up with the hanging-on-by-a-caveat-ex-wife in order to transfer the property when it sold.

We bought thirty olive trees to replace the dying pittosporum hedge along the drive. Adrian supervised the excavator who planted them. Olive trees and a lavender bed: it was starting to look like Provence. If I was never going to eat and drink my way through France on a canal boat, at least I could approximate the experience at home. By the pool, we set up a gazebo with Aladdin lanterns and a mock-Persian carpet, a sultan's tent in my little corner of France. The whimsy and progress energized me. Adrian was acting like he felt dangerous again. Maybe things were turning around.

A month later, when I swung up the drive, I noticed that the leaves on the olive trees were withering.

"I think they're dying, Adrian."

"That's absurd."

"They're planted right up to the bottom branches. Maybe that's the problem?"

"There is no problem. The trees are fine—" Hakuna matata.

"I think they're dying—"

"Shut up. I had three hundred olive trees in Auckland. I know what I'm doing."

It took another month for the trees to indisputably die. (The nursery replaced them, but suggested planting them this time no deeper than they had been in the growing field.)

After the sun had set on our dead olive trees, we went to the pub. Adrian played the quiet South African gentleman. Rex's caretaker flirted and asked him to dance. A lifetime of cigarettes and diesel fumes had finally caught up with Rex. His emphysema had gotten worse, and he had regressed from tucking an inhaler in his pocket to hauling an oxygen tank to God's Holding Paddock.

As part of his sickness benefit in a kinder, gentler country, Work and Income had provided Rex with a caretaker, a good-time girl who could drink everyone under the table. She cost him a fortune in beer and might not have helped Sexy Rexy's emphysema, but her attentions gave him a new lease on life.

Home from the pub, Adrian sat down in the dark in the lounge.

"You never smile anymore, Adrian," I said to the back of his head.

"That's your fault." He didn't bother to turn around.

"Why did you kiss Rex's caretaker on the dance floor?"

"She made me do it," he said.

Uncommonly dispirited by the loss of a few olive trees so easily replaced, I barely heard him, went into my study, closed the door, and pulled out the little plastic Saint Joseph I had bought in Tucson.

JANET PARMELY

Date: November 10, 2007
To: Anne B.
Subject: Saint Joseph

Can't believe it took me this long to discover that there are saints to look after everyone. Ice skaters, hemorrhoid sufferers, champagne makers, fishmongers, jugglers, and people who want to sell their homes. Saint Joseph oversees the latter because he is the patron saint of family and home, and most home sellers need a miracle.

The notes accompanying Saint Joseph said I might have heard all sorts of rumors about how to most effectively bury him to bring about a speedy and auspicious sale. He should go upside down, no, right side up, in the front yard, no, the back, facing the house or was it facing away? (I hadn't heard any rumors because I only just found Saint Joseph in the nuts-and-bolts aisle of the Ace hardware store when I was back in the States.) But really, what is most important is this: no matter which way I flip the saint, I must ask, believe, and trust. That's the main thing.

I briefly entertained the idea of also adopting Saint Eustace (difficult situations), Saint Eugene de Mazenod (dysfunctional families), and Saint Jude Thaddeus (lost causes), but who wants an overworked saint? I settled on Saint Adelaide of Burgundy, the patron saint of prisoners and victims of abuse. Between her and Saint Joseph, I figure my home team is covered.

Adrian refuses to weigh in on the option of selling our house in addition to the sleep-out. One day he says it's killing him. He can't afford it. It's too much work. The next day it was all my idea. He never wanted to sell our home. I'm going with my old fallback, change of venue, because this strategy worked out so well in 2000, and now it's even blessed by a saint.

Adrian wants to build a log cabin at the Heads if we get rid of the house. He'll order a kit from South Africa and have Paul build it for him. We can live there, and it will also function as a model home. When the Kiwis see it, they'll all want one, and then Adrian will have a lucrative import business selling them kits from Knysna to build their own log cabins.

I buried Saint Joseph upside down facing the front door, and it was a relief to know it didn't matter what I did with him, as long as I ask, believe, and trust. Since we have no idea what we'll do if our home sells, I'll ask Saint Nick to give me the specifics for Christmas.

Date: December 31, 2007
To: Jim C.
Subject: Days of Auld Lang Syne
Attached: Farewell to the bonfire

There's a two-kilometer-long sandbank that emerges from McLeod Bay at low tide. Now and then, when the tide and weather are right, you can ring in the New Year under the Southern Cross on McDonald Bank.

Our neighbors organized the party, and this evening the bush telegraph hummed. There was no time to waste. The forerunners landed as soon as a snippet of land big enough to build a bonfire rose from the bay. The rest of us paddled or motored over in kayaks, fishing dinghies, and rubber ducks. We had three hours to imbibe and get sprightly enough to send the old year out and welcome in the new with style before McDonald Bank was underwater again. (Dick told me once about a place in England where the tidewater flows at the speed of a galloping horse. "The tide didn't go out. It buggered off.")

Waves lapped at the beached boats, and the kids did barefoot cartwheels in the rivulets made by the incoming tide. We hauled the boats to the middle of the sandbank. We rolled up our pants, and the cuffs got wet. Champagne corks rocketed, and there were more toasts. A couple of coolers almost floated away. The mood got merrier. The tide pushed against the bonfire, and finally it was released and drifted off, an island unto itself, sticks flaming and embers aglow, like a puddle of lava under the winking Milky Way.

We hopped in our boats and abandoned the speck of land. Adrian paddled his leaky rubber duck while I bailed. Our friends' laughing murmurs sprinkled the velvety darkness, and an invisible Scot piped "Auld Lang Syne" as we approached the shore of McLeod Bay. In with the new year, off with the old.

Date: January 1, 2008
To: Sheryl O.
Subject: Intertidal Zones
Attached: Southern Cross over Mount Aubrey

Kiwis will tell you that if you pick up a rock while you're poking around intertidal zones, you must always put it back where you found it. If you don't, those creatures that cling to it—and are accustomed to the ebb and flow of the tide in their permanent abode—will die.

And what if you uprooted yourself while poking around the intertidal recesses of your life, and there is no one to put you back? What then? Where do you go when you're somewhere in the middle, pulled between some defunct memory of home and a sullen skipper paddling a leaky boat to the shore of McLeod Bay?

Is the Southern Cross showing the way? Or is it just another charlatan? Not a constellation with a message at all but only random astronomy, a beguiling handful of stars pointing to another wrong turn on the long road home.

Chapter 34

You'd be amazed how fast the tide comes in once it makes up its mind to.
—#6, God's Holding Paddock

In February 2008, the sleep-out sold. Our new real estate agent was an auctioneer as well. "... lovely coastal section ... water on your doorstep ... stash your mother-in-law ... wander down and launch your boat ... I'm looking for the opening bid ... no, sir, it's not a good time to blow your nose ... away we go ... bid's here at one-fifty ... right back at you ... you've come all the way with me ... sir, do you want to come again? ... all finished? ... selling ... done!"

Reserve wasn't met on the house, so that took care of that. It was what we had planned all along, peel off the sleep-out for a profit, except remodeling and subdivision costs had swallowed much of the gain. And I had grown fond of the sunlit space that doubled as guest quarters and writing retreat. The caveat had to be lifted yet, and it would be months before any return was realized from the sale.

Money seemed to be a problem again, or not? There was no transparency to Adrian's finances, although his disposition appeared to be a dependable gauge. Really, isn't everyone happier when his coffers are full? Out of curiosity one day, I looked up the astrological profile for Adrian's birthdate. He shared "the day of precarious balance" with daredevils like Evel Knievel and gamblers. *Gamblers? What if all those hours in front of the computer were about speculation, not investment?*

Charges had come through our joint credit card under "Las Vegas

This" and "Casino That," but I had discounted them as pastimes of the idle rich. Adrian routinely topped up our checking account to cover substantial payments to his own credit cards, but there were no material purchases to explain the transactions. When someone had contacted him about the legality of his trading activities, he had boasted, "They can't stand that I figured how to beat the odds."

I might not have been the wizard that Adrian professed to be, but I did recognize that what went up by 18 percent in the markets—and life—was just as likely to go down by an equal or greater measure. Clearly the richer a man is, the more ruinously he can amass debt. And liquidating assets might or might not be the first step on the road to ruin.

It was all supposition anyway and wearing me out. I was knackered. Where there is no transparency, there is no trust, and where there is no trust, it takes a lot of effort to enjoy the ebb and flow of life. So much concentration is required to live defensively in the face of the galloping tide.

In March, that old prankster of a month, full of sideshow tricks and overblown anticipation, the mess in Tucson finally crashed. Mom called the Rural Metro hunks one last time, but not to get Dad out of the couch.

"I'm short of breath. My heart is racing. My hand is numb. Could I be low on potassium? Maybe I just need to eat a banana? Maybe I should take another Xanax—" They were on their way.

The results at the hospital were inconclusive. Maybe Mom did just need to eat a banana, but I had my own theory. My brother had married for a third time and moved twelve hundred miles away. His daughter had just decamped with Sturm und Drang and a husband hidden in the wings. There was no one left at home to bar the door. Mom no longer had a reason to be there to break it down.

While I made arrangements to travel to Tucson, Mom was detained in a rehab facility, and hospice organized a placement for Dad in a private home. It was called Oh-Be-Joyful. If my father had known he was on his way to a place named after Psalm 100, they couldn't have dragged him there.

When Dad was eight, his grandfather had walked into the kitchen on a Sunday morning to find him all dressed up. "What's this, Clara?" he asked his daughter in his sternest German-immigrant voice.

"We're going to church."

"Church!" the grandpa bellowed. "Isn't the boy a little old for that crap?" It set the tone for Dad's lifelong attitude toward organized religion.

I called Dad after the move to Oh-Be-Joyful, and he asked, "What in God's name is this place in the middle of nowhere they've put me?"

I said, "I think it's called Obi-Wan Kenobi."

My Kerikeri clinic was full tilt. The granny-flat settlement was pending, and I had complicated matters by forcing separate dispersal of the profits because I was convinced they were headed right into the black hole of Adrian's investment schemes. By the time I got things organized in New Zealand and arrived in Tucson, Mom had been transferred to The Court, an assisted living complex. She had refused to go to Oh-Be-Joyful—not on any religious grounds—she just wasn't going to be stuck in the same facility "as that man," incidentally her husband of sixty-five years.

Great, just great. Bible-averse Dad was at Oh-Be-Joyful, and Mom, already too empowered in my opinion, was in a joint called The Court. As trustee, I had to figure out how to absorb a $6,000 increase in monthly expenses and predict whether my parents could ever return to the family home.

Oh-Be-Joyful wasn't in the middle of nowhere. It was a fifteen-minute drive from the family home. Dad was dining *en famille* with the three other residents, all women (the usual ratio at his age) when I arrived, but I knew the place was top-notch before I walked in the door. Prior to his admission, I had signed and faxed a three-page policy agreement and four more pages requesting information on Dad's medical directive (Do Not Resuscitate), daily needs (Depends and Polident), important accomplishments (Dad would have said hiked Grand Canyon), favorite foods (he used to assure Mom it was burned toast), and hobbies (still crossword puzzles). Dorothy, the owner, had told me on the phone, "Don't worry, we'll look after your father until you get here."

Across town, Mom was ringing the bell. Each of her ninety-odd fellow residents had a lanyard with a call button that sounded in the nurse's station. One of the thirty pages of contractual agreements required by The Court indicated there would be a one-hundred-dollar penalty for losing the button. Otherwise the guidelines for its appropriate use were vague, but the staff definitely felt Mom was abusing her privileges. Bell ringing was reserved for falling off the toilet. Mom was first and foremost lonely, of course, and the bell brought her company, not merely someone to screw off a stubborn Frappuccino bottle cap or to warn that she thought she might fall off the toilet.

The Court trolled extended-care establishments for customers, and they probably thought they had found a live one, the wife of a distinguished professor emeritus with no children in sight. The headhunters got to her before I did, and contrary to what Mom had told the neighbor—his third wife did not have cancer—my brother simply chose not to return from Peculiar, Missouri (town motto: where the odds are with you).

They had already shifted a few of her belongings from home: a small couch that matched the larger one in which Dad had spent so much time, a couple of Mom's favorite paintings, TV, and a hamper's worth of clothes. This essentially reduced her from a familiar if disorderly nest full of memories and freedom to ring whatever damned bell she pleased to a dorm room with a hospital bed and nearly a hundred neighbors in her residence hall.

The head nurse called me into her office first thing, like a principal keen to set a parent straight about her unruly child. (Laura's high-school band director had summoned me routinely, but my daughter was a percussionist, so it was to be expected.) It was intimated that they might have to expel Mom if she didn't shape up and quit ringing the bell.

"Fine, I'll ground her, and she can't march in the drum line at the homecoming game" is what I wanted to say, but that might have provoked Nurse Ratched. Corporate was unlikely to forfeit Mom's considerable monthly tuition, although I was threatened with a more expensive level of vigilance if the bell ringing was not brought under control.

Between my suspicion that *Jingle Bells* had been converted into a gambling stake and the troubles with Mom's call button, my hear-the-bell metaphor appeared to be in the crapper.

I had just paid a $5,000 nonrefundable "move-in fee" from the trust account to get Mom into The Court. I couldn't see how they could justify five grand to move in an old lady, two pictures, and a four-foot couch, but I had assumed, with that kind of upfront money, they could deal with a little bell ringing. Opting out of the move-in fee would incur a $500 increase in monthly costs.

It was a dirty rotten lottery. In the midst of life-changing turmoil, I was coerced to weigh up the benefit of prorated monthly fees and lay a wager on my mother's death date. Ten months was the break-even point. If Mom made it past that, the advance money would be absorbed and the reduced monthly costs assured. I put the money on longevity.

I had saved up enough in the trust account that we could afford two more months at this pace, and that was it. At Wells Fargo, where the account was held, I explained the situation. You can imagine how well that went over. I had been virtually invisible in the States for eight years, no car insurance, no gainful employment, not even enough overseas income to qualify for tax liability. Here I was requesting a loan on the basis of someone else's income, even if I was his trustee and needed the money to keep my parents in their now-separate corners until the home got sold. But this was before the big collapse at the end of the year, and they sent my appeal to the Escalation Team.

"It's only money," I told myself, except there was no spare change. You can say "It's only money" if you have enough to pay the bills. If you don't, there is no comfort at all in saying "It's only money."

On April 10—the day before my Wells Fargo advisor called triumphantly to tell me that the unconventional loan application had been approved—Dad died. Talk about a buzzkill. The phone rang at eight o'clock, and Dorothy told me, "Your father ate a big dinner tonight—you know he usually doesn't eat much—and then he lay down and died in his sleep. I've called the university, but there's time for you to come and say good-bye."

Dad had years earlier sifted through his stack of proposals for afterlife care and arranged his donation to the Willed Body Program at the University of Arizona. This relieved me the burden of those details upon Dad's death. (And the larger generosity would be later confirmed at a memorial service and tree planting honoring Dad and the others who had committed themselves to the respectful use of first-year medical students.)

I drove under the merest sliver of a moon to Oh-Be-Joyful. Dorothy showed me into Dad's homey bedroom where he had been laid out with such deference that he looked like he was carved out of alabaster. All the years had sloughed off. He hardly had a wrinkle, and even though his prominent nose came from a long line of German peasants, he looked as noble as the effigy of a Roman emperor on a tomb.

Dorothy had put Dad's few belongings on the antique dresser: comb, handkerchief, billfold with original Social Security card and expired driver's license. She had laid his glasses on top of a newspaper so it looked like everything was ready for him to get up in the morning, read, and do a crossword puzzle like he always did.

I told Dorothy I didn't want any of it, and Dorothy said, "You take some time. You might want to come back and get it. It will be here." And it was when I did.

Dorothy left me with Dad, and I felt shy and then silly for feeling shy. Who was watching us? (Existentially, it was a reasonable question, but certainly not one I was prepared to tackle at that moment.) This was uncharted territory and such a momentous event that it seemed like I had one shot at getting it right. I kissed Dad's cheek and stroked the number-two fuzz on top of his head, things I would never have done when he was alive. He smelled of Irish Spring. I held his hand—he was cool, but not cold—and all I could think to say was "I love you."

I peeked through the window on my way to the car just to make sure that he wasn't kidding, that there wasn't a little smile on his face. Dad had told me just a week before that he could live to be a hundred if he wanted to, and I had braced myself for this juncture so long, I couldn't believe it had finally arrived. He looked so peaceful and, well, undead.

I returned to the house and sat with Molly in my lap under the scanty stars, trying to make sense of it all. Dad had barely lasted a month after he was moved out of his home into Oh-Be-Joyful. I realized that he was just waiting for me to get back to Tucson. In some sensible spot that Alzheimer's can't touch, Dad had already decided, *Jesus Christ, this is ridiculous. All this to-do for someone who is ninety years old. I have had a good life. I am going to enjoy a big meal, and then I am going to go in my sleep, and not in that goddamn hospital.*

I knew that's what he thought because the chime out back rang just when the idea popped into my head, and there wasn't any wind.

Chapter 35

There is one solitary order you cannot dodge,
no matter how many underpants you refuse to fold up and put away.

—#39, God's Holding Paddock

She had never been the kind of woman who slept on a satin pillow to keep her hair nice, but I thought Mom would enjoy the pampering of a weekly shampoo and set. The second-best thing about The Court was the stylist who ran the salon and worked magic with thinning hair of every hue.

Three months to the day after Dad died, I was sitting with Mom, in curlers, waiting for her turn under the dryer. Suddenly she started chattering like a bad cassette tape, going faster and faster until it tangled itself into knots. Mom knew "*Beebledy-doo-da-mupp-mupp-mupp*" sounded all wrong, but she couldn't make it come out right. It was a TIA—transient ischemic attack—a neurological dysfunction caused by disruption of cerebral blood flow. Mom had blown a circuit between her brain and her mouth.

The first TIA resolved long enough for Mom to tell me, "Hell's bells, I'm pregnant. Now what am I going to do?" She had another TIA, and with each successive one, the pain got worse, so she was put on morphine and didn't worry about being pregnant anymore. It looked like the beginning of the end, so Molly and I started sleeping in Mom's room at The Court.

The best thing I had to say about the place was that they allowed small pets. Molly was my mainstay. Adrian was decidedly not. This was a humdinger on the Stress-o-Meter, one of the strongman's best shots at the high-anxiety striker: both parents dying within three months of each other. Ring that bell? No thanks. "Life is for the living," he had told me on the phone when I finally reached him after Dad died. "It's no place for old people."

Mom was now eligible for palliative care, and the hospice nurses visited her on a regular basis. They asked if there might be anything she was waiting for, some loose end to tie up. Like someone else I knew, Mom had never been interested in loose ends. Both granddaughters had called, but there was one person who hadn't checked in, a person so conspicuously absent that it was, if nothing else, a story in itself.

I surreptitiously picked up the phone in Mom's room and called my brother in Peculiar. I told him that if he wanted to say good-bye to his mother, this was probably his last chance. Then I handed Mom the receiver and said, "Guess who called!"

That evening, a spectacular storm cracked thunder and spit lightning over the length of the Catalina Mountains. Mom looked past the foot of her bed and said, "They're coming."

"Who?"

"The Rangerfangers."

"The Rangerfangers?"

I had no idea who the Rangerfangers were, but Mom was happy to see them. There seemed to be quite a few. Mom fingered the binding of her blanket and reached out for them with a smile that was undeniably beatific.

She said, "John's there too," and she said it with no ill will or mention of Depends. Then she called me "darling daughter" and drifted into a morphine haze. Under the circumstances, I decided to treat it as a deathbed confession.

I went back to the house to get Molly for another sleepover at The

Court. When I returned, the aides told me that all the lights had flickered and the fire alarm by my mother's door had gone off. "She was ringing the bell tonight!"

Molly and I scrunched on the little couch. We had been sleeping there for two weeks now, but soon it would be over. The next morning Mom was frothing at the mouth and rattling from somewhere deep in her chest. It sounded like she was trying to breathe underwater.

The hospice nurse administered an anticholinergic to control the secretions and assured me that the noise was far more distressing to the living than to a woman this close to the finish. It was a mammoth act of kindness: to silence that awful harbinger of death. Mom's breathing became so soft and easy that it was hard to tell if she was still alive.

It was Court policy that you had twenty-four hours to remove the resident's belongings after they checked out, one way or the other. After that, fees would be charged at "normal occupancy rates," precisely, ninety-four dollars per day (if you had opted for the move-in fee). I had no interest in returning to The Court the next day or ever again and so was forced into the most wretched multitasking imaginable.

While my mother lay dying, I packed up her belongings. Mom would never walk another step in her ankle socks and favorite ratty sandals; put on her glasses to read the next *People* magazine; run a brush one more time through her uncommonly coiffed hair; or sneak out again with purse in hand to charge thongs at Victoria's Secret. She would not polish off one more Frappuccino or dig into another box of animal crackers with the delight of a two-hundred-pound toddler—but it was an abomination to load it all up before she was dead.

Toward sunset, I sat on the bed and held my mother's hand while she took her last breath. I told her I loved her, and I said, "I am sorry I tried to make you wear a bra. I didn't know what else to do."

The man from the mortuary came back to help me after he had transferred Mom's body from the gurney into the hearse. We tied the little couch on top of my car with jumper cables. Mom, her belongings, and I left The Court in the dark before our twenty-fours were up.

It doesn't matter how much Fibber McGee junk you cram into your V-berths, how many underpants you refuse to fold up and put away, or how long you snub the orange woman, the final order will catch up with you eventually.

Dad slipped over easily, but that is how he had lived, no muss, no fuss. Share K-rations with your men, regardless of rank, in a chicken coop. Use your brain if you were lucky enough to have one. Hike a big canyon because the ability to appreciate beauty is one of the gifts of being human, and it would be ungrateful not to do so. Before his dementia progressed, Dad had packed up his professional library and sent it to a colleague at Bilgi University in Istanbul. By the time he died, other than joint property, he was living pretty lightly on this earth.

Mom's passage was more problematic. She was eighty-four when she rode out on a thunderstorm, ringing the bell—for one more lamb chop, a pork knuckle, she didn't care—because she wasn't done placing orders at the butcher counter of life. She wasn't done causing shit, which is just another name for proving you are alive.

Of all that was asked of me and I agreed to do in the name of looking after my aging parents, some was done well, some poorly, and some I wished I hadn't even tackled. With nothing to guide me, I snitched, finagled, drip fed bank accounts, gave up, jumped in headfirst again, and did my best to respect the integrity of the two human beings I had known longest on this earth, resolute, imperfect, and valued to the end. I probably erred in favor of possibility and hope.

It could have been accomplished in more congenial surroundings, but I was comfortable with how I handled that one last thing. I took my mother's hand like she must have taken mine when she came out of the ether and said her first hello (before I demanded to be fed), like I had held my own daughter's—count them!—five perfect newborn fingers before I put her to my breast. I tended to my mother's crossing. I was there to let Mom go, and Dad and the Rangerfangers were waiting for her on the Other Side, wherever that may be.

When my time comes, I hope that my daughter also errs on the sunny side. And when that is no longer feasible, Laura should move me to the Retirement Home of a Thousand Steps into a room on the top floor, give me three double martinis, and a push. I want to become one with the fall.

Date: July 26, 2008
To: Anne B.
Subject: Transcending the Bra

Mom died yesterday. During her last weeks, we hit an impasse over the brassiere. It's been my observation that the elderly are treated kinder when they're kempt, and I had this idea that my mother would also feel better if she were in good nick. Her double Ds were free ranging under a housedress, but I couldn't convince her to wear a bra.

I wasn't sure if Mom was being obstinate or couldn't manage the hooks on a Maidenform model dating back to the fifties. Giving her the benefit of the doubt, I shopped for front-closing "leisure styles" and took them back for her to try on. She picked one, wore it until she went to bed, and never put it back on. Several times my mother went through the motions of selecting a bra she never intended to wear again, and I failed to discern it as a sign she was on her way out. Otherwise she would have said to mind my own business.

Mom had transcended the bra. She had already moved into some liminal space where she was concerned with greater things than 44DD support, a vantage point from which big brassieres must have appeared very small and a threshold from which even I, scurrying around, preoccupied with the underpinnings of this world, must have been shrinking from view.

Still, it was hard for her to let go. She couldn't help ringing the bell one last time on her way out. Old habits die hard.

JANET PARMELY

Date: July 26, 2008
To: Jim C.
Subject: Safe Sex

Someone called me this morning regarding my dead mother's tissue donation. I don't even know who it was. It's all been such a blur. Who'd have thought? After all those years of what—macrimony?—Mom lasted barely three months without her husband.

Even when Dad ran away from home, he carted a photo of his wife from bulletin board to bulletin board. It makes me wonder what love really is. Certainly not diamonds and roses. (When I told Adrian that Mom had just died, he said, "That's a coincidence. So did Rex.")

I'm not sure it was love, but my folks had sixty-five years of something. Maybe it started out as love. Maybe it drifted in and out of love, and they held on at arm's length. I was privy to none of their intimacies during the fifty-nine years that I was part of the enterprise.

When they got married, Laura and her husband announced that they were going to do it right, implying, like all wise twenty-seven-year-olds, that they were not going to screw it up like I did, like these grandparents did. But somehow they will.

The hubris will be knocked off them as it is off every sentient human being. Some get a thwack, others just a tap, and I don't see that it matters who deserves a bigger kick in the pants. They will grow in the most astounding and unpredictable ways to understand—together, apart, or at arm's length—that it's not about doing it right. It starts and it will end with connection, and there will be a world of something in-between.

The tissue solicitor wanted to know:
"When did she last have sex?

"Did she have safe sex?

"Sex with drug users?

"With homosexuals?"

"My eighty-four-year-old mother?"

There are obviously more worrisome things to consider than love when it comes to Mom and Dad.

Chapter 36

What kind of parents order a bologna sundae for their kid at the butcher counter of life?

—#39, God's Holding Paddock

The dead may pass on to the final order, but the living are left with anything but. Practical hassles pale compared to the cosmic shift. I had just lost the two people I'd known longest on earth and been promoted forthwith to head of the line waiting to exit.

I ordered twenty copies of Dad's death certificate from the health department. (You can't make a move on behalf of a dead person without one.) With its decorative border and seal, it looked like a graduate diploma, and in a way, I suppose it was. I took his cause of death, "dysphasia as a consequence of end-stage dementia," as neat clerical confirmation that Dad had still had the presence of mind to starve himself to death.

For Mom, "respiratory arrest as a result of cardiovascular accident and congestive heart failure," was a whiff of what went on July 25, a transition so monumental for the individual (I assumed) and the family (I knew) that no synopsis was adequate.

Unlike Dad, Mom had refused to weigh in on the delicate issue of what to do with the body, preferring the Scarlett O'Hara approach: "I'll think about that tomorrow." This left the ticklish decision to me, who, based solely on expediency, had purchased a prepaid cremation policy after my mother's first TIA.

I collected Mom's ashes from the mortuary and said no thanks to the sterling-silver locket, pavé-diamond bracelet, pocketknife, lighter, money clip, key fob, and cuff links, all with secret compartments for cremation remains. (Dad's ashes would arrive by certified mail ten months after his death. I went to the post office to sign for the parcel and explained to the clerk, taken aback, "My father came in the mail while I was out. I'm here to pick him up.")

In one of my most overoptimistic, ill-timed decisions ever, I bought out my brother's share of the equity in our parents' house. I needed a base to deal with the backwash of death and wasn't willing to float him while I did all the work. Dad had borrowed against his life insurance, and when Mom died, retirement and social security income had ceased. Someone had to keep up the mortgage payments until the house got sold, and that was me with my proceeds from the sale of the sleep-out on Darch Point Road.

Demanding separate dispersal had been a stand that was even less popular than refusing to run in front of a car. In New Zealand, if you have lived together three years, you are as good or as bad as married, and this gambit was definitely an affront to connubial bliss. Adrian had retaliated. Two months after Mom died, in a foxy, double-dipping maneuver, he tried to finagle the money to settle the caveat out of my share of the profits. My lawyer, Mr. Fairley, stepped in. (Yes, Fairley. Who else would you expect in New Zealand?) Adrian withdrew his spreadsheets and said his lawyer had made a mistake.

In October 2008, I assumed both mortgages on the Tucson home, all the outstanding loans my parents had cosigned for my brother, twenty-five pack-rat nests, and sixty-five years' worth of accumulated crap. I threw out Mom's fruitcake tin of pills (all right, I kept the Xanax). Out went twenty-five incomplete decks of cards, three Cootie games that didn't have a head among them, a Monopoly set missing the deeds to Boardwalk and Park Place. And just what's up with old folks and all those rubber bands?

I went through the contents of twelve filing cabinets. Folder by folder, I winnowed the records of Dad's academic career and voluminous, gracious correspondence, including this benevolent response to a bulk mailing from American Express:

Dear Sirs:

Thank you for extending your generous offer of trip insurance. Although my wife and I have many pleasant memories of touring here and abroad, we have regretfully reached the age when it's time to curtail our travels. We certainly intend to maintain the long association we have enjoyed with your company through the years and continue to take full advantage of the fine services offered by your credit-card department.

I wallowed through Mom's interests in genealogy, art, volunteer activities for the Democratic Party from Estes Kefauver to Jimmy Carter, and more ignoble pursuits. One envelope contained copies of all the birthday checks she had written to Laura (three) to substantiate a written declaration that she had not played favorites with the granddaughters.

Like most women, Mom had a closet of clothes in a range of hopeful sizes. I donated them all to Goodwill, as well as the contents of her dresser drawers, every last hanky and sanitary napkin belt. (Why had this woman who stopped menstruating three decades earlier kept this reminder of what a long way we have come?)

Befitting a true academic, my father's wardrobe was too shabby to give away, but parting with his yellow Dutch shoes and Mom's well-worn sandals broke my heart. It was simple enough but hit me hard. My parents didn't need their shoes anymore. Shod or unshod, they would not be putting one foot in front of the other, forging on. It had been such a basic fact of their lives right to the end.

An estate-sale enthusiast I met later tented her fingers and tapped them together avariciously at the thought of all the treasures that must have been hidden in the house of the globetrotting professor and his wife. If only she had met me sooner!

"You checked the pockets before you gave the clothes to Goodwill, didn't you? You didn't give away the clothes without checking the pockets! Old ladies forget they put rings in their aprons. Old men stash cash in their pants."

No, I didn't check the pockets. I was overwhelmed by a lifetime of stuff, up to my ears in minutia: safety pins, clothespins, thumbtacks, paper clips, bits of string, keys to locks long gone, a buttload of corn plasters, Band-Aids fused to the wrapper, pencil stubs with mummified erasers, restaurant sugar packets, and those damned desiccated rubber bands—all encrusted in drawers with what looked like toe jam. Daily I was confronted with some revolting twist on nostalgia or hoarding to keep death at bay: a toy chest full of balding stuffed animals and pack-rat turds, a cereal box with one Grape-Nut and a roach left in it.

I had to make decisions about the finer effects my parents had accumulated after the first tenured position came along, the middle-echelon belongings that were such a part of their up-and-coming world: museum reproductions and art books whose faded illustrations now looked forlorn, sable paint brushes, oil-color tubes, reel-to-reel recordings, and jazz-band LPs. What about the address book? Half their friends and relations around the world were already dead, and I would never keep up with rest. No one would buy the grand piano because, I was told at each preloved-furniture shop, "times have changed."

A drawer in Dad's tool organizer was labeled "Sewing Needs" and contained a spare pocket. Imagine, a pocket. He must have belonged to the last generation who thought about replacing a pocket. Yes, I forgot to check the pockets. I didn't uncover any jewelry or cash, but I was a pocket ahead for my efforts.

The donations to Salvation Army filled two box trucks. A family from Nogales bought some sturdy if dated occasional tables at a garage sale. They strapped them on top of a pickup already piled six feet high, and that is how Ethan Allen went to Mexico. (Another bit of advice: do not burden your children upon your death with the responsibility of getting rid of things that are sticky with memories. They don't want your keepsakes but know how much they meant to you. Do not put your daughter in the position of being the one to send her eighty-four-year-old mother's bronzed baby shoes to Mexico with Ethan Allen.)

I sold a few pieces of midcentury modern furniture and some bric-a-brac to a secondhand dealer who made the ragpicker mulling over Scrooge's deathbed curtains look downright philanthropic. I overheard him talking to someone else who had laid her own dead mother's riches on his counter for a bid.

"Art doesn't sell unless it's Picasso, but I'll give twenty bucks for the Limoges."

"My mother would roll in her grave if she knew what I was selling her china for."

"Lady, they're all rolling in their graves."

I went through the house in a frenzy. I wanted to get this over and reclaim my life in New Zealand. I didn't even worry about the implications of going back to a man who had just tried to rob me to pay his ex. Animated in the work, I was finally able to put my mark on this turbulent home where I had felt like nothing more than an unattractive duck.

I was driven to let the desert sun shine into every peed-upon corner of carpet, every Do Not Let Her See file of nefarious deeds and dastardly debts, but some were too vile to shine a light on. Those I would have to carry to my own grave. I was on intimate terms with the fragility of all the players, dead and alive, and that put me smack in the middle of a moral dilemma. This steamed me more than anything: it wasn't over. My obligations lived on. I was nothing more than the clean-up crew, a street sweeper who had seen too much, stuck with someone else's trash and secrets.

I faltered only once. One afternoon I shut myself in the garage closet and sat on the floor sobbing while I sorted every single washer, tack, nail, screw, nut, and bolt that Dad had collected through the years—like a kid dutifully trying to finish off a bologna sundae some thoughtless parent had ordered for her.

I should have filled a roll-off blindfolded, sold up, and moved on, but instead, in a wink, I traded the burden of looking after aging parents for the headaches of home ownership in a plummeting market as startling as any seen in eighty years. The exchange rate dropped below 50 percent. I pulled out my New Zealand cash at a loss to pay off Household Finance Corporation (granddaughter's tuner car), Sears (kitchen appliances for my brother's marital home in Peculiar), and Hughes Credit Union (pocket money for someone).

Adrian and I had planned a respite for me in New Zealand. We would recreate the Thanksgiving that we had hosted the year before. I had handed out recipes and fixings to the members of God's Holding Paddock, and they got right into the holiday spirit. Pete baked a pumpkin pie from scratch. Dick made cranberry sauce, and Kevin fell asleep on the sofa after dinner.

Kiwi turkeys are scrawny, dear, and scarce. An eleven-pounder, if we found one, would have set us back NZ$75 at the time. (Smart shoppers in the States were picking up twenty-two-pound Butterballs for twenty-two bucks.) We bought the biggest chicken at hand and tried to pass it off as turkey, but the guys caught on. "That's no Thanksgiving turkey. That's a chook!" Everything had been perfect and complete, it had.

I bought all the trimmings at Williams-Sonoma, regaling them with tales of our Kiwi Thanksgiving. I hadn't felt so buoyant in months. The Year of Death was almost over.

And then Adrian sent an email: "I am pissed off that you spent all that money on Thanksgiving shit. All I see is money going out on a house I have no financial interest in. I am not going to finance any more . . ."

Adrian was not, in fact, financing the Tucson debacle. I was. But I had charged the "Thanksgiving shit" on our credit card. I returned to Williams-Sonoma and stood by the cash register, near tears and stinging with humiliation, as they pulled the merchandise out of the bags and rang up the credits one by one for turkey brine, gravy base, pumpkin butter, pie filling, pie plates, bread pans, relish molds, gobbler-adorned tea towels—testimony to my out-of-bounds enthusiasm and slaphappy sentimentality.

A week later, Adrian sent an "I love you" email, business as usual, but this time he stopped me in my tracks. The Year of Death had definitely slowed me down, but it was his simple, resilient genius that finally did me in. Adrian had an uncanny ability to tap into my innermost myths and shape them for his own gain. The moment he ceased to benefit, *bang*, he got point-blank pissed off, threw an island holiday or Thanksgiving celebration back in my face, and started all over again. Adrian was a man who would hold the lantern for his wood-chopping mother, make no mistake, precisely as long as those logs fueled his fire too. I was no match for this.

I didn't speak to Adrian for four months. I tailspinned and crashed. I was hemorrhaging Kiwi dollars into a house whose value was dropping at a faster rate than I could offset with a lick of paint. I was hopping mad that these parents of mine had not even managed in death to look after me. I was stuck in the desert where I didn't know a soul. If Ruth hadn't already left her black mark on four generations, if Molly could have opened a can of dog food on her own, if I didn't have Laura, I would have killed myself. I had lost hope and had no option but to forge it in the smithy of solitude, sweat, and fear.

Like Ngaere said, "You have to keep going. That's all you can do, luv, just keep going." As long as you can put one foot in front of the other, shamble on.

Chapter 37

Many things that couldn't ever happen have.

—#6, God's Holding Paddock

Eleven and a half months after I had left for the Year of Death, still a homeowner in Tucson, I showed up unannounced on the doorstep of the house on Darch Point Road. With or without Adrian, I was determined to make New Zealand work. (Also the return leg of my plane ticket was about to expire.) I nodded to an elderly couple who stooped in the lavender bed, lopping off flower heads. One leg of my useful stool had evidently been braced up in my absence.

I rapped the brass gargoyle, and Adrian came to the door. "I thought you'd show up," he said, and greeted me as if I had just come back from the grocery store. He pointed out the gardeners' handiwork. They had hacked back the oleanders that once graced the path to the front door, and consequently the impatiens, baby tears, and silver ferns that had luxuriated in their shadow had dried up and died.

"You planted them in the wrong place," the gardeners stood there like trolls and told me. Adrian agreed. It felt like a conspiracy, but I knew it was just the penalty for not being there, for returning like an outsider to my own home that had been entrusted to Adrian—and trolls—in my absence. I told myself, *Yes, it's my fault. I wasn't here to look after my own garden.* But really, you can only tend to dying things on one side of the equator at a time.

It didn't feel like Provence anymore, and down by the pool, it looked like a little corner of the apocalypse. Passion-vine leaf hoppers swarmed the banana palms, and Argentine ants marched in columns across the fishpond bridge. Aphids encrusted tomato plants that struggled up a web of string that Adrian has festooned across the deck. The sultan's tent had blown away, and under its metal skeleton, the magic carpet had disintegrated in the pernicious sun.

At God's Holding Paddock that night, I easily resumed my position at the right hand of Dick. (Adrian was still a regular at the pub. That took care of one more leg of the stool.) The fellows filled me in on a plan to ship Whangarei's refuse on a scow to Auckland instead of disposing of it in the tip by the harbor. I would miss driving by the extravaganza of bulldozers overturning the city's detritus, squabbles of seagulls plunging for spoils. That's how much I loved New Zealand. I had bonded to its trash.

Dick leaned over and whispered, "I've got something for you in the car."

"What have you gone and done, Dick?" I knew full well, and we went out to retrieve the trifle.

"I put extra sherry in the sponge—"

"My favorite part—"

"And that peach on top is from the last jar that Joan canned."

"Oh, Dick—"

"Welcome home, luv."

We shifted the trifle into Adrian's car and returned conspiratorially to the pub. I always knew what the surprise was. Adrian said he didn't care one way or the other because he didn't eat pudding. The guys at God's Holding Paddock left Dick and me to our little sacrament of friendship, a calorie bomb of custard and cream.

When a homecoming is treated as if you stepped out to go shopping, although you were, in fact, gone for a year, there is a peculiar upside. It's easy to slide back into the intimacies of sex. Adrian made me coffee topped with a whipped cream heart the following afternoon, and then I set about reclaiming the house as my own. Accustomed now to the arid desert, I turned on the dehumidifier first. Adrian's office chair squeaked as he got up from his computers.

He barged into the bedroom and turned it off. "Is it because it's my money that you think you can waste it like this? Someone needs to teach you Americans how to run a dehumidifier, and it's not every day." Adrian retrieved the hygrometer from the kitchen—it had amused us in happier times to check out the subtropical humidity—and pointed to the mark at which I was allowed to dehumidify. Satisfied he had made his point, he returned to his study.

Adrian made me a gin before dinner and said we were having leg of lamb, but I had time for a bath. Could he draw it for me? I was six years old again, on my way to White Gloves and Party Manners Class. Mom was already in the department store, but I was trapped in the revolving door at Cain-Sloan, running in circles, trying not to get hit from behind or stumble into the glass in front, afraid to step out for fear of getting mashed. Faster! Slower! Faster! Slower! Love you . . . love you not . . . love you . . . love you not.

We were struggling to reestablish domestic hierarchy, but it wasn't working out too well. Adrian had lived alone for a year as if he had been on a boat, parsimoniously, embracing must and mold. My insubordinate dehumidification infuriated him.

And what about me? I had lived alone for a year as well, if you could call a Year of Death living. I was back in the hemispheric crack. My geriatric parents were gone. Now I had a geriatric dog and a house in the States. I wanted to pull the crack in over me. I wanted routine. I wanted oblivion. I drank too much. I wanted to sell up in Tucson and microchip the dog and have her rabies titer drawn so Molly could begin the voyage and quarantine to become half/hahf just like me. I wanted this cheapskate to be nice to me so I had a safe, known place to come back to.

HIC SVNT DRACONES. Here be dragons, not prowling some unexplored territory off the map, but in no-man's-land between two familiar worlds, becalmed, not a wind on the planet to blow you back to anything you know.

Adrian carried a bucket of garbage to the verandah and slopped it over the railing, "I am not fucking going to pay Council to haul my rubbish to Auckland."

What are you doing? You'll attract possums and rats! I wanted to roar, but I had come full circle in the revolving door back to Hostage Rules.

I got the gasoline-consumption lecture again. I violated the guideline for minimum number of articles to be washed in a laundry load. Adrian took the offending wet items out of the machine and threw them on the floor after I went to bed—in what amounted to a behind-the-back drink in the face. It wasn't easier now that my parents were gone. It was, in fact, worse. I had been out from under Adrian's daily sway for a year. You know how that goes. Once a burden has been lifted, that load will feel like it tips the scales at sixteen tons when you shoulder it again.

The house in Tucson still had to be sold, and that meant more absences. During this one, Adrian had let our plants die and the sultan's tent blow off in the wind. He had given away my Christmas dishes and sewing machine. He had tried to rob me to pay his ex. He had let me go through the Year of Death alone, without charity or tenderness. He had demonstrated that at least two legs of my stool were replaceable. I wondered about the third, but was pretty sure I still had the four that belonged to the dog. Rats were gnawing in the straw ceiling.

By now, I suspected that Adrian's wife had had no idea he had left for good when he sailed from Auckland to Whangarei in 2000. (No wonder she had slapped a caveat on our home.) How would I ever know which of his runners would be the last one for me?

Adrian's whammies had staggered me for a very long time. Had the two-carat diamond been no more than a happier face of his whims? I was getting better at righting myself after the uglier blows, but it wasn't a skill I wanted to cultivate.

No Prisoner of Love anymore, I was merely a hostage in Adrian's unrelenting battle to control a world he didn't understand but sure as hell thought he did. Life had been handed to him in black and white. Forget Technicolor. Adrian couldn't or wouldn't (I still didn't know) make out shades of ashen, bloodless, pearly, flannel, tattletale, grizzled, venerable gray. I was nothing more than a will-o'-the-wisp as disappointing and bewildering as all the rest, forever leading him across the marsh into a mire of quicksilver and soot.

I racked my brain for a way to separate the house from the man, but I couldn't absorb the debt against the property until the place in Tucson sold. We talked about auctioning the house without a plan for what to do next. Adrian assumed his customary stance under duress: "It's a waste of time to worry about shit before you have some." He suggested that, when the time came, I put the proceeds from the Tucson sale into his hands. He gave me the 18 percent spiel, with the added incentive that it worked better the more money we put into it. Although, as far as I could intuit, there wasn't much left of the boat proceeds in the fund. Adrian alluded to the log-cabin ploy. He mentioned visiting his family back home, and that sounded great. I liked them, and it was sunny in South Africa.

We toyed with the idea of shipping my furniture back to the States. The house in Tucson would show better furnished, and it would expedite the sale. "Besides," said Adrian, "who needs a house full of furniture on a French canal boat?" I almost believed him. Can you beat that? Adrian half believed it himself. We were doing CPR on hope.

I had better questions now, but hakuna matata was still Adrian's pat response. I wanted relief. Relief from the solitary burden of questions without answers. Relief from the days of nothing more than a scowl at home and an amicable mask at the pub. Relief from my dogged determination to find a way to integrate the life, death, and rebirth of trust, make something whole of this again.

I had a clearer idea of what I wanted at the butcher counter of life, and this wasn't it. Even when you have the whole picture-book kit and caboodle, if you have no voice, it's only fairy-tale belonging. The only magic beans we get are knowledge of who we are and due respect for it.

We couldn't get a pulse on hope. The house on Darch Point Road sold at auction on April 19. Saint Joseph's work was done. Adrian paid to send the furniture to Tucson, no doubt making my baby grand piano the first to make a round trip between the USA and Whangarei, an insanity of which I was not proud.

We relinquished possession of our fairy-tale home in the bush to its new owners on May 29 and shifted up the hill to an apartment next to the fish 'n' chips dairy, which had expanded into a café. A snatch of McLeod Bay could be seen from the place, but not enough to read the tide. Seagulls perched on our balcony, squawked, and stole fish guts out of the restaurant garbage. Adrian called the move "transitional." It was the most honest answer I ever got from him.

We flew out of Auckland on June 16, 2009. At the gate, we held on to each other like we were going down with a shipwreck, and in that good-bye was more truth than either of us could express, not in Adrian's two-tone vocabulary and not with any of my shadowy words. Adrian boarded Emirates Airline bound for the holiday he had scheduled for himself in South Africa.

I returned on United to the USA, a displaced person, once again taking the long way home—and the even longer journey to make sense of this man in whom I had invested a lifetime of longing, a whirling Janus of beginnings and ends, so painstakingly larding a leg of lamb with garlic slivers that it could have been done out of nothing but love one minute and throwing a drink in my face the next.

For one pyrotechnic moment, my high hopes had exploded in the southern hemisphere, and under the flickering fountain, "I believe in you" writ in the sky, I had seen Adrian, and he was as full of passion as a teenager, content as a fellow who feels he is good enough, shot with whimsy and grace. He had risen to my vision, we were off on our merry chase, and that's not stock-market leverage. That's the leverage of love.

Date: May 3, 2009
To: Sheryl O.
Subject: A Welsh Lullaby
Attached: Dick and I

They've been carving sun-damaged bits off Dick, and he has to keep his legs up for this round of skin grafts, so he can't go to the pub. Some nights Adrian and I take dinner over, and some nights I ring up Dick and ask him, "Will you buy a girl a gin?"

He always says, "Come on over!" By the time I drive to Parua Bay, he has pulled the gas heater in front of my spot on the sofa and set Joan's old crocheted slippers on the hassock. Sometimes his cat curls up at my feet, and Dick says, "That damned worthless cat." Then he fills Bluey's bowl with jellied chunks of fish, chicken, or beef, depending on which tins of Whiskas were on sale at the grocery this week.

We sit and talk, as easy as rolling off a log, gossip about our mates at the pub, who's doing who, and who isn't doing anyone, but no specifics. Dick is a gentleman. We listen to his LPs. When the Welsh Men's Choir sings "All Through the Night" at Cardiff Arms Park, we stop talking because it is so moving. He brings out the cigars and puts on Louis Armstrong. At "What a Wonderful World," I lose it and cry into my Canterbury Cream. Dick says, "I wish you were a little older, girl," and I say, "So do I."

AT THE BUTCHER COUNTER OF LIFE

Date: May 28, 2009
To: Anne B.
Subject: The Long Way Home
Attached: My fairy-tale home in the bush

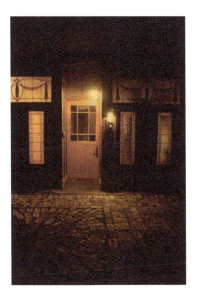

Mary called to say, "It'll be okay, luv." Pete stopped by with a yarn to cheer me up. Our new neighbor in the sleep-out brought over pink rosebuds with a note from someone I've never met. "Every woman who's given up a cherished home knows how you feel today." Paul promised, "You'll be back. You are a part of Whangarei Heads as much as Mount Aubrey."

Pete's ex-wife, Nita, of go-go boots renown, helped me pack and clean while Adrian moved his computer kingdom up the hill. At seven o'clock, we started on the champagne, she with the abandon of exhaustion and me with the recklessness of someone who has nothing left to lose. Adrian headed out with the last keyboard after dark, and Nita took a bypass through the olive trees on her way out, possibly denting, by the sound of it, something important on the undercarriage of her Holden. She ended up safely at Pete's place. (It was an amicable divorce.) I don't know about the car.

The night was clear with a crescent moon. Mount Aubrey was outlined against the incandescence of the Milky Way, and the two pointer stars clearly indicated the Southern Cross—exactly as it had been when Adrian and I moved in seven years ago and sat on the verandah side by side, looking out to the harbor at the shining path of luck and love spilled our way from the yellow ladle moon.

I did one last walk-through and worried about the waxeyes. Now that we are on the verge of winter, they will be expecting that block of lard we used to hang on the verandah in an old onion bag. I remembered how the late afternoon light in summer dances over the moss that covers the big rock under the bedroom window. I tried not to dwell on how the blue herons will come back in spring to nest in the pohutukawa trees, and I won't be here to see them.

I said farewell to my bathtub in the bush and to the birds in the Waipu frieze over the kitchen bench where so many meals were prepared genially and then in stony silence, but always savored. I bowed to La Contessa.

It's been almost a decade since I embarked on this particular journey from darkness into light. When I set out, I believed that a single quest would answer it all. Now I know this is only one trek of many from ignorance to illumination, a birth-to-grave endeavor. We soar out of darkness or take ratchety little steps, backward, forward toward the light, then plunge again and continue on, seeking in ever-widening circles.

This is the hardest thing I have done in these nearly ten years, more difficult even than the Year of Death: heading out the door of my fairy-tale home in the bush for the last time and making my way alone into the teeming darkness.

Epilogue

> Hope, gratitude, and underpants: that's what it's all about.
>
> —#39, God's Holding Paddock

I arrived in New Zealand in March 2000 with a sarong, a jar of sea salt, and an unabridged English dictionary. What the hell was I thinking? New Zealand is an island nation, part of the British Commonwealth. It was likely to have reference books in my native tongue and sea salt, and there aren't enough sweltering days in God's Own to justify a sarong. I had packed for the conceits that mattered most to me at the time and was unprepared for anything else. That's probably why I didn't bob or weave when it got thrown at me.

I don't know a lot more now than I did then, but I have a greater respect for the horsepower of hope, whether it percolates in friendship, you hammer it out, or you pull it from thin air. It makes people do crazy things. They marry in wartime. They jump over the equator with an eight-pound dictionary. Their better visions of themselves collide at spring tide, and they cosign a mortgage in a foreign land with someone they have known for nine months. Looking on the bright side and feeling dangerous, a bunch of the best men ever assembled in one place on earth wait for roundup day. An academic old-timer meanders his jolly way on the quest for a new, improved office. An octogenarian causes shit with a toothless grin. Eyes on the horizon, a selkie plots return to the sea, and some people persist long after they know better in hearing bells.

No ugly duckling, I understand now that I am my mother and

father's child. The willful optimism that kept the old bunny marching flows though my veins too. The slippery negotiations that my mother conducted with reality allowed her to survive two mothers in one, and I have made a few bargains with the devil of denial myself.

Dick remained optimistically engaged in life to the very end. He made sure he had something to look forward to, another night at God's Holding Paddock, the next birdcage barbie, a holiday in Fiji, where he died on June 18, 2010. I am sure he had staked out his pub. He was seventy-nine years old. He had a very good life. And he made life good for a lot of other people.

Hope is the harness we buckle to the lifeline on the pitching boat. It lets us hang on a little longer until we sail over the equator or find something more orderly on the Other Side. I've worked with it, and I've worked without it. Even if it's based on supersize expectations, rosy promises, and blind faith, I'll still take hope. I would go back and live in my fool's paradise again just for that dazzling instant that didn't last longer than two shakes of a lamb's tail, when I felt cherished and safe and the magic carpet rolled into forever.

But I can't, Heraclitus and all. When I left Kansas City in 2000, a friend told me he thought my decision to go to New Zealand was heroic. He was wrong. It might have been heroic to leave New Zealand, but I had no choice. If you hakuna matata a woman too far, she will eventually settle into herself and try to discover who she is at the bone. She will give up her fairy-tale home in the bush if she has to. She will get a one-way ticket back to the country she ran away from in the first place if she must, and that is far more difficult than to bolt on a lark with a song in her heart.

I think I've got the sunny-side angle sussed, but I'm not sure what's up the underpants. There seem to be an awful lot of them around: Pete's in the tea tree, the lacy pairs that Dale gave his unbalanced wife, underpants bearing the names of the days of the week, ill-gotten thongs from Victoria's Secret, dancing thongs in a TV commercial, great big cotton Lollipops, the Underwear Dog's panties under the swimsuit in the dispiriting glare of the dressing-room mirror. What is the meaning of all these underpants, flung out of necessity, bestowed in love, bestowed for no good reason, flaunted to turn heads and sell merchandise no one remembers, hoarded on a drying rack, or worn just long enough to get your way? Mmm.

No, I haven't figured that one out, but that's okay. Life needs hope, and it needs mysteries. Anyway, here's to them. Here's to the underpants, yours and mine, the pair we wear on our way out the door when opportunity knocks—wherever we kick them off after that in the name of love, in the name of life, or thumbing our noses at death.

To: The team at Bay Audiology, in the day
Subject: Safety Net

The work ran me ragged, but without it I would not have had workmates like family, nor seen as much of New Zealand as I did. Without your unstinting flexibility, I would not have been able to tend my aging parents (whether or not I did the right thing), and certainly I would never have had the opportunity to hear all those stories.

Thank you, especially, Peter and Anya.

To: Jack B.
Subject: The Paradoxical Virtue of Bridges

If I had had more than a fairy-story notion of who I was, I wouldn't have dragged you through a box of Q-tips for naught. But without your support, I might have bailed that first difficult year. I might never have gotten to sit at God's Holding Paddock all those nights. I might never have come to love a country where snoring pigs comfort you; widows remarry, die, and are resurrected; you can buy an Optimist; mail finds you without your name on it; and your Internet server promises that tomorrow will be fine. For that gift, and for our brief, terrific time together in New Zealand, I am so very grateful.

To: Mary L.
Subject: Serendipity

You circled the ad in *The Northern Advocate* for the house in the shadow of Mount Manaia by Taurikura Bay. You tried in vain to teach me proper English. Your affection for your country from Invercargill to the Mangonui Fish Shop rubbed off on me. Thank you for prodding me to make my commitment to New Zealand official. And thank the universe that you were waiting on the other side of the world when I leaped.

To: Anne B.; Sheryl O.
Subject: The Candlepower of Girlfriends

Nine years is a long time to stick by someone who moved seven and a half thousand miles from home. You respected my lousy decisions. When you tried to avert disaster and I didn't listen, you were still there for me. Thank you (and your dear husbands) for throwing open the doors every time I was Stateside. Anne, you have been my lamp in the window when the trail of breadcrumbs disappeared, Sheryl, the campfire back home. Thank you doesn't begin to cover it.

To: Jim C.
Subject: Write is a Verb and Finish is the Name of the Game

What would I have done without that crazy-ass man who sent

stacks of snail mail (with my name on it) to New Zealand for nearly a decade and held my feet to the fire? Thank you for reminding me—constantly—what we paid all that money to learn in writing school.

To: Laura P.
Subject: Just Who's the Parent and Who's the Kid?

When I jumped off the last-chance summit and was ready to crawl home, you said, "No, Mama, jump again! I'll be waiting for you at the bottom, which is really the top." You were right. Thank you for refusing to let me freak out in paradise.

You set the example long ago, with your wit and intrepid efforts to take life seriously and still get out there to milk it for all the fun it has to offer, even if you had to bust out the window and shimmy down the drainpipe. May there never be enough nails in the world to keep your bedroom window shut.

To: Adrian J.
Subject: Diamonds Are a Girl's Second-Best Friend

Over the years, Lake Rotomahana filled up with water again. In February 2011, a research team mapping its floor discovered the lower two tiers of the Pink Terraces buried in sediment. Four months later it was announced that part of the White Terraces had also been discovered in their original location. The Pink and White Terraces were not blown to bits after all. Catastrophe, given time, can disclose wonders, not the least of which might be the abiding bond between two determined, flawed, and fragile spirits.

You introduced me to the bone-idle, noodling, and fertile hours so fundamental to any creative effort. I never got my alpacas, but you gave me my adventure, and for that I thank you. I didn't anticipate that the antithesis of an orange woman dodging cracks in the sidewalk is chaos. However, if I hadn't felt so trapped by your oceanic control, I wouldn't have struggled all the more to follow my own sparkling shaft of bubbles to fresh air and speak.

To: God's Holding Paddock, those who have been rounded up and
    those few who remain
Subject: Waiting to Go to Heaven or Sitting Right on Top of It?
Attached: View to Home Point, from the Base of Mount Aubrey
    track

Remember that summer afternoon we sat outside at the pub so Dick could have a drink and a smoke at the table? I bet you thought I didn't notice how you took turns standing up to shield me from the setting sun until it dipped below the wilding pines, protected in your shadows from the relentless glare.

I cannot believe my good fortune at having stumbled into God's Holding Paddock all those years ago. Thank you for making me feel welcome every time I blew in with the gale, better when I was already well, and when I wasn't. You know, I've had a good life.

Glossary

A list of curious Kiwi terms and more.

angel's trumpet: a woody tree or shrub closely related to datura, another deliriant. It has pendulous, trumpet-shaped flowers. All parts of the plant are toxic and can be lethal. It causes vivid hallucinations that may initially involve insects, then move on to zombies clawing at windows and blood dripping from ceilings as the dosage is increased. All in all, not a recreational experience.

Anzac Day: frequently commemorated with a service at dawn on April 25. It marks the anniversary of the first major military action fought by antipodean forces during the First World War. The Australian and New Zealand Army Corps landed at Gallipoli on April 25, 1915, intending to capture the peninsula and open the Dardanelles to the allied navies. Their ultimate objective was to take Constantinople (now Istanbul), the capital of the Ottoman Empire, an ally of Germany. They met with fierce resistance from the Ottoman Turks, and the battle dragged on for eight months. By the time the allied forces were evacuated from Gallipoli at the end of 1915, more than 130,000 men all told had died, including nearly 9,000 Australians and 3,000 New Zealanders. Although the Gallipoli offensive failed to achieve its military objectives, the losses and valiant actions of the Australian and New Zealand soldiers left a powerful impression, and the "Anzac legend" became an important part of the identity of both nations. In 1997, at age 101, veteran Alfred Douglas Dibley died, the Kiwis' last living link to the Anzac campaign. A fortnight before his death, he told the president of his Returned Services' Association, "I've had a great life."

GLOSSARY

atua: (Māori) an ancestor with continuing influence, demon, supernatural being, deity, ghost, object of superstitious regard. May be translated as "god."

avo: avocado.

baby-foot: (French) table soccer.

balls-up: a bungled situation, disaster, clusterfuck. Origin obscure, but apparently not testicular. The term may date from the era of wooden sailing ships. Disasters on board were communicated by hoisting brightly colored balls up the rigging. Each color represented a different disaster, plague, starvation, mutiny, for example, thus serving as requests for assistance or warnings to steer clear.

barbie: barbeque.

bell-topper: high top hat worn by men from the later eighteenth to mid-twentieth century. Usually made of silk and associated with the upper class.

biscuits: in New Zealand, cookies or crackers.

blue cod: an inquisitive bottom dweller found exclusively in New Zealand in shallow waters around the rocky coasts of the South Island, most commonly south of Cook Strait. Caught mainly in winter (April to September). Superb battered and warm from the fryer, or cold for second breakfast.

bluey: (possibly from Australia, late nineteenth century, when it was a summons issued on a blue piece of paper) A bluey from the pub was a warning letter from the owners informing the recipient that if he didn't smarten up his dress and stop swearing and cursing, he would be banned. In Kevin's young and dangerous days, Parua Bay Tavern issued fourteen of these letters that he can recall. It barred eight other patrons directly by order of the court. "Then the females stormed the place, and the pub was never the same again."

Bluff oyster: a dredge oyster that premiers in restaurants and grocery stores in March, a rite of austral autumn. Stays in season until August. The seaside town of Bluff, South Island, is home to the strictly regulated fleet of oyster boats. O, delicate bivalve, plump and sweet, for you there is no match, from a half-shell cradle with a lemon squirt, slip-sliding down the hatch!

GLOSSARY

bollocks: literally, testicles. "Bollocks!" is an expression of contempt, annoyance, or defiance.

brolly: umbrella.

bully beef: corned beef.

cabbage tree: a palmlike tree growing up to twenty meters high, characteristic feature of the New Zealand landscape. To some, its tufted heads of sword-shaped leaves resemble a prickly cabbage, but that's a stretch. Maybe after a few wines. Its fruit is a favorite of the fat, iridescent wood pigeon, which nested in the Waipu-tile frieze of native New Zealand birds in the kitchen of the house on Darch Point Road.

cardie: cardigan, a sweater that buttons up the front.

cheese cutter: a flat cap, rounded, with a small, stiff brim in front.

chilly bin: cooler.

chockablock: (also chocka) crammed full, jam packed.

chook: chicken. *Ba-gawk! Ba-gawk!*

cot: baby's crib.

cuppa: cuppa coffee, cuppa tea.

dag: literally, a clot of fecal matter clinging to the tail end of a sheep. This has given rise to a number of expressions, including "What a dag!" one of a plethora of affectionate insults of which Kiwis are so fond. This dag tends to be a zany, likeable person, maybe a joker or hard case. "Rattle your dags" is pretty much self-explanatory: "Get a move on!"

dairy: corner or general store.

Dali: an immigrant from Dalmatia, an ancient region on the Adriatic coast in what is now southwest Croatia. It was part of the Austro-Hungarian Empire from 1867 to the end of World War I. Between 1897 and 1919, more than five thousand Dalis immigrated to New Zealand. Most were single young men in search of work. Two thirds did not stay. The majority that did became gumdiggers, and some of them saved up enough money to

GLOSSARY

buy land to farm. Other Dalis planted vineyards, and today you'll find their names on wine labels like Babich, Nobilo, and Delegat.

fantail: a restless, insectivorous, and friendly bird. Also New Zealand's little grim reaper. In Māori mythology, it is a messenger that brings death or tidings of death from the gods.

Fibber McGee: *Fibber McGee and Molly* was a classic, old-time radio show that premiered in 1935 and ran for twenty-four years. Its most memorable running gag involved hubby Fibber opening the hall closet door, an avalanche of stuff tumbling out in a racket, usually falling on his head or Molly's. The catchphrase is synonymous with household clutter, if one is old enough to remember this or heard about it from someone even older.

flax bush: The endemic New Zealand flax bush is closely related to daylilies. It has swordlike evergreen leaves that grow up to three meters long and rigid flower stalks that produce red blooms at maturity and can be twice the height of the foliage. The nectar-loving tui can often be seen in a flowering flax bush.

fools beech: shrub native to New Zealand, with serrated foliage like miniature holly leaves. It bears delicate, bell-shaped flowers, followed by white to red berries that ripen late summer to autumn.

gobsmacked: astounded. From *gob* + *smack*, clapping a hand to one's mouth in astonishment.

goolie: (British) testicle, usually plural.

gumboots: (also gummies) rubber boots, usually calf-high, favored by farmers and anyone else slogging around the great outdoors in New Zealand in the mud and rain. Gumdiggers wore them, but the name more likely derived from the gum rubber they were made of.

gumdiggers: mostly men, a few women and children, who dug for kauri gum, fossilized resin, up north in New Zealand at the end of the nineteenth and early twentieth centuries. It had been preserved, mostly in swamps, and examples have been radiocarbon dated to fifty thousand years ago. The resin was also bled from living trees. At the peak of the industry in 1899, there were reputed to be twenty thousand full- and part-time gumdiggers,

GLOSSARY

the majority Dalmatian, but also Māori, British, Chinese, Malaysian, and Northland settlers looking to subsidize a meager income from unbroken farmland. Kauri gum was the key ingredient for varnish and later linoleum. (By the 1930s, with the advent of synthetic alternatives, the market for gum dropped, but there remained niche uses including high-grade varnish for violins.) Kauri gum was Auckland's main export in the second half of the nineteenth century, sustaining much of the early growth of the city. The gumdiggers themselves lived rough and worked hard, scrabbling in damp earth with axes, spears, and spades, digging holes by hand several meters deep. Even a gum buyer realized, "The life of a gum-digger is wretched, and one of the last a man would take to."

hangi: (Māori) a pit oven in which food is steam-cooked on heated stones; the gathering at which that food is served; or the food itself, which is tender and scrummy if properly prepared—no small feat when fire, hot rocks, wet hessian sacking, many cooks, and plenty of beer are involved.

hoki: Not a looker, this bug-eyed marine fish lives in inky darkness about a half mile deep in waters off the southern coasts of Australia and New Zealand. It used to figure prominently in McDonald's Filet-O-Fish sandwiches. But with increasing concern about its wide commercial use and consequent diminishing population in the past decades, the folks under the Golden Arches have switched to more local and sustainable sources.

homekill: slaughtering and butchering your own animal, either DIY or by a listed homekill service provider. Only permitted to owners who have been actively engaged in the daily care of an animal for at least twenty-eight days immediately preceding the homekilling. Homekill meat is reserved for close family but may be served to visitors as long as it is not in exchange for other goods or services. Hefty fines if the guidelines aren't observed.

hop-on: a sexual encounter. Implies a brief liaison, rarely involves roses, and never diamonds or mortgages. Similar to the ubiquitous "bonk" (a bonk in the bush). As with wally-jammer, the author could find no reliable reference to this one, so we'll have to hang it on one of the members of God's Holding Paddock.

GLOSSARY

hottie: hot water bottle.

huia: an extinct New Zealand wattlebird (last seen in 1907). The tail feathers were prized by Māoris and used ceremonially.

jandals: plastic or rubber sandals retained by a thong between the big and second toe (i.e., flip-flops). Winterless North dress-up when barefoot just won't do.

John Dory: another ugly saltwater fish, flat and bony with delicate, white flesh and a slightly sweet flavor. If you like sole and turbot, you'll like John Dory.

jumper: knitted pullover or sweater.

karamu: a large, bushy shrub endemic to New Zealand. It is normally hardy and can adapt to infertile soil and poorly drained and exposed lands.

kauri: a coniferous tree found north of 38°S in the northern districts of New Zealand's North Island. Kauri forests are among the most ancient in the world. In Waipoua Forest near Dargaville, Te Matua Ngahere (Father of the Forest) was a sapling during the bronze age some 2,500 to 3,000 years ago. Tane Mahuta (Lord of the Forest), at almost 14 meters in girth and 51.5 meters high, dominates the forest canopy. When Captain James Cook first laid eyes on the great kauri forests of Northland in 1769, he recorded, "The banks of the river were completely clothed with the finest timber my eyes have ever seen." By the time the heyday of kauri logging (1870s to 1920s) was over, three quarters of those forests had been decimated, the great trees felled to make masts and spars for sailing ships and milled for knothole-free, broad planks of timber. The trees were hand cut with ax and saw and maneuvered with timber jacks. To get the logs out of the bush to the coastal mills, they were guided and pushed along "rolling roads" made of kauri logs, hauled over tramways on viaducts and down inclines, dragged by bullock teams spurred in the right direction with a cracking whip, slid down water chutes with the aid of mutton fat, and propelled downstream on floods created by driving dams. Steam haulers (a stationary engine driving a winch), bush locomotives, lorries, and tractors with internal combustion engines helped later on. But ultimately, the success of the kauri timber industry came down to the engineering

GLOSSARY

finesse, Kiwi ingenuity, and sheer grit of men like gentle Jack Murray, Champion Axman of Northland.

kava: a narcotic drink popular in many South Pacific cultures. It is prepared by grinding or pounding the roots of the kava plant. Or chewing them. George Forster, a naturalist on Captain James Cook's 1777 voyage in the Pacific islands, described the process: "[Kava] is made in the most disgustful manner that can be imagined, from the juice contained in the roots of a species of pepper-tree. This root is cut small, and the pieces chewed by several people, who spit the macerated mass into a bowl, where some water (milk) of coconuts is poured upon it. They then strain it through a quantity of fibers of coconuts, squeezing the chips, till all their juices mix with the coconut-milk; and the whole liquor is decanted into another bowl. They swallow this nauseous stuff as fast as possible; and some old topers value themselves on being able to empty a great number of bowls." Kava has a sedating effect and is primarily consumed to relax with minimal disruption of mental clarity. Not that the author would know.

kerfuffle: a commotion or fuss.

kia ora: (Māori) a traditional greeting that has entered New Zealand English. It literally means "Be well/healthy," and is translated as an informal hello.

kikuyu: a hardy, creeping, perennial grass native to the uplands of East Africa. Considered an aggressive weed by some, it is cultivated by others for lawns with high wear resistance (but limited aesthetic appeal).

kina: an edible sea urchin.

knackered: exhausted, also broken or damaged. The knacker man disposes of dead or unwanted animals, especially those whose flesh is unfit for human consumption. In all its variations, never implies pleasant circumstances.

knickers: underpants, of the female persuasion.

koura: (Māori) a genus of freshwater crayfish found only in New Zealand. Confusingly, koura also refers to the distantly related, marine rock lobster. Both are delicious.

kowhai: native to New Zealand, a little tree of the pea family, which bears

GLOSSARY

charming, hanging clusters of yellow flowers, harbingers of spring. Cutting one down, even accidentally, may be considered a serious breach of tapu. Its blossoms, as well as the pohutukawa's, are the unofficial national flowers of New Zealand.

kunekune pig: a small (by swine standards) breed of domestic New Zealand pig, thought to be descended from an Asian strain introduced to New Zealand in the early nineteenth century by whalers or traders. The name derives from the Māori *kunekune*, meaning fat and round. They are people friendly, docile, loyal, intelligent, and easy to train. No wonder Ngaere and the author loved that pig.

kwila: a slow-growing, coniferous tree that occurs in low densities even in healthy rainforests. Its rot-resistant timber is highly prized for high-end flooring and furniture. When left untreated, kwila weathers to a silver-gray patina. It varnishes to an auburn sheen, as on the floor of the sunroom at the fairy-tale house on Darch Point Road. Kwila has been depleted across most of its original range (East Africa, Southeast Asia, and Oceania) and is now a target for illegal logging.

lady-of-the-night: (the plant, not the dame) a flowering, tropical shrub with glossy, dark-green foliage. It becomes wildly fragrant just after sundown, like true jasmine with undertones of five-spice powder, complex, and almost too much for a nose not used to such exoticism.

lollies: short for lollipop in Britain, in New Zealand, all sweets, candy.

long drop: outhouse.

macrocarpa: also known as Monterey cypress, a fast-growing evergreen and common sight in rural New Zealand. Imported in the 1860s and planted for shelter, it is still sought after as a decorative and building timber.

mana: (Māori) prestige, authority, control, power, influence, status, spiritual power. Mana is a supernatural force in a person, place, or object and goes hand in hand with tapu, one affecting the other. The more prestigious the event, person, or object, the more it is surrounded by tapu and mana. Mana is enduring and indestructible.

GLOSSARY

matai: an endemic New Zealand conifer. Historically, along with rimu, kauri, and totara, one of New Zealand's main sources of wood for furniture and house construction, and flooring timber of choice for over a hundred years.

metal (road): gravel.

moko: (Māori) permanent marking of the face and body. Tā moko refers to the procedure and to the cultural tradition that surrounds it. It is distinct from tattooing in that the skin is not punctured but rather carved with chisels that were traditionally made from sharks' teeth, bones, usually albatross, and stones. Inks were derived from natural products like burnt wood, kauri gum, and caterpillars infected (essentially mummified) with an entomopathogenic fungus. The pigments were tamped into the cuts, leaving the skin grooved after it healed. Tā moko is ritualized, and historically, the tattooing process was lengthy and painful. Both the tattooist and person undergoing tattooing were considered to be in a state of tapu. Moko was a sign of rank, mark of aesthetic appeal, and often a rite of passage. It was and is a cultural affirmation, and the facial tattoo may represent mana, role, prestige, accomplishments, marital status, ancestry, and often served as a man's signature. No two moko patterns are alike. Other parts of the body may be tattooed, but the focal point is usually the face (the head being considered the most sacred part of the body). Men customarily had full facial moko, while women had primarily their chins, lips, and nostrils tattooed. By the mid-nineteenth century, the prevalence of full facial moko for men had declined, but women persisted with their traditional facial moko into the early twentieth century. Since the 1990s, there has been a resurgence of Māori tattooing, often using more modern techniques.

morepork: New Zealand's only surviving native owl, a speckled, brown one, small at 175 grams, about six ounces. Bird of the bush and the night. Soft fringes at the ends of its feathers allow it to fly noiselessly. Named for its double hoot, which, given an active imagination, sounds like "more-pork." If you are lucky enough to see one at dusk in the forest, peering with yellow eyes or gliding silently by, you will understand why the *ruru* is associated in Māori tradition with the spirit world, a watchful guardian, herald of good or bad news, depending on its call.

GLOSSARY

musnud: a cushioned seat used as a throne by princes of India.

natter: also "have a natter," to chat.

nick: as in "in good nick," in good condition.

Ozzie: Aussie, an Australian.

pa: (Māori) fortified village or stockade, often a hill fort.

paua: a large, edible abalone with a very pretty shell.

pittosporum: a flowering evergreen shrub or small tree native to Australasia.

pohutukawa tree: New Zealand's iconic Christmas tree, a coastal evergreen of the myrtle family. It blooms from November to January, peaking in mid to late December, each crimson flower a mass of stamens. Pohutukawas thrive perched on cliffs and wade in salt water, oysters clinging to their roots at low tide. An eight-hundred-year-old pohutukawa tree grows at Cape Reinga, on a windswept clifftop that overlooks the turbulent waters where the Tasman Sea and Pacific Ocean collide. This northwesternmost spot in New Zealand is considered in Māori mythology to be the leaping-off place for the spirits of the dead on their journey back to their legendary homeland, deeply associated with the cycles of birth, life, and death. They jump off the headland and slide down the roots of the venerable pohutukawa into the sea and underworld below. At Three Kings Islands, they climb out of the water, take one last look back at Cape Reinga, bid the land farewell, and continue on to Hawaiki.

Pommy: (also Pommie and Pom) a British person. The origins of this term are cloudy. Possibly it derived from pomegranate, a fruit whose color matched the stereotypically florid British complexion. At God's Holding Paddock, it was generally taken as an approximate acronym for Prisoners of Mother England.

postie: postman (or woman).

pottle: a small plastic or cardboard container for foods like yogurt, Bluff oysters, and the like.

prezzie: or pressie, a present.

GLOSSARY

pudding: in New Zealand, any dessert.

pukeko: an Australasian swamphen. Deep blue/violet with black back and wings. Bright-red bill. Struts on orange legs and feet as if walking across hot coals, will fly short distances, but takeoffs and landings clumsy: consequently clownish. They forage for food beside motorways and in roadside ditches, collecting grit, and never look both ways before crossing. Hence many end up as roadkill. Here is Dick's recipe for pukeko soup (serves 6): Fill a great big pot with water and bring it to a boil. Pluck, dress, and generously salt one pukeko. Add six smooth, round stones, each about four inches in diameter. Simmer covered on low heat for one week. Remove the pot from the flame. Remove the pukeko from the pot. Put one stone in each of six bowls. Ladle the broth over them. Throw out the pukeko, and serve the stones.

quid: Until July 10, 1967, New Zealand had the same incomprehensible monetary system as Mother England. A quid was one pound sterling, so at the current exchange rates in 2000, Ngaere was just about right in her estimate of the traffic fine in the author's envelope.

rimu: also called red pine, a tall, coniferous tree, the chief native softwood tree of New Zealand. The timber is used for furniture and interior fittings.

sammies: sandwiches.

scrubber: a woman of flexible morals who knows just how to make men feel young and dangerous. They run the gamut from round-heeled party girl to tramp who would satisfy the needs of any willing man at the pub with an after-hours bonk on the pool table.

scrummy: scrumptious + yummy. Scrummy is in the same category as moreish, causing a desire for more. "Never drink anything moreish." That was Pete the Train Driver's advice. "Blackberry Nip is the worst." It goes down too easily, and you will have a very sore head the next morning.

shag: (besides the cormorant and dreadful carpet) British vulgar, to have sex, to screw.

silver fern: a medium-sized tree fern endemic to New Zealand. (The koru motif found in Māori art reflects the shape of its frond unfurling.) Along with the

GLOSSARY

kiwi bird, the silver fern is an unofficial national emblem. Its image adorns the jersey over the left ripped pec of every All Black. Sigh.

snarler: sausage. The word first appeared in print in 1941 as World War II Australasian military slang. The soldiers' sausages contained so much fat that when cooked, they hissed, spat, and snarled. The men complained that their sausages were probably made from cats and dogs. (The worst of the lot were called growlers and barkers.)

sod: an unpleasant or obnoxious person. In the imperative, "Sod off!" means get lost.

sodium monofluoroacetate: a synthetic pesticide that goes by the name 1080. Fluoroacetate is a naturally occurring plant toxin that appears to have evolved as a defense mechanism against browsing animals. 1080 targets mainly lungs, heart, and brain, precipitating breathing difficulties, heart failure, central nervous system dysfunction, convulsions, and death. It has been used since the 1950s to keep New Zealand's brushtail possum population in check. (Once thought to be leaf eaters only, possums are, in fact, opportunistic consumers of any high-energy, high-protein foods, including flowers, leaf buds, fruit, eggs, birds, insects, and snails. And they carry bovine TB.) 1080 is usually added to cereal, carrot, or gel baits and dropped from helicopters in areas of high possum infestation or where terrain is too difficult for trapping and laying poison by hand. It is not selective and can be lethal to all mammals, birds, amphibians, and insects. Death is painful, tortuous, and slow. It's understandable that the use of 1080 is a controversial topic in New Zealand. There is no antidote. The best hope for pets and working dogs is to induce vomiting and seek veterinary intervention—immediately. Peter's window of opportunity to save Tommy and Meg was over before he knew it.

sook: a crybaby, timid or cowardly person, also a hand-reared calf.

spouting: gutters and downspouts.

sprats and sprogs: kids, rug rats. A sprat is a small marine fish. A sprog is human offspring, an infant or child. The verb *sprog* means to give birth. "I'm sprogged" means "I'm pregnant."

GLOSSARY

Steptoe: *Steptoe and Son* was a 1960s and 70s British comedy featuring Albert Steptoe, a narrow-minded, foul-mouthed, normally unshaven secondhand dealer with very old and incomplete false teeth.

suss: to figure out, usually with intuition playing a role.

swan plant: species of milkweed and popular food for the caterpillars that metamorphose into monarch butterflies.

sweet as: the phrase that keeps every newbie to New Zealand on the edge of her seat. Sweet as . . . what? More than okay, better than good. Awesome! Choice! A box of fluffy ducks! ("As" may be appended to any adjective to intensify it, *big as*, *cold as*, etc.)

tapu: (Māori) sacred, prohibited, restricted, set apart, forbidden, under atua protection.

tarakihi: More handsome than hoki or John Dory, this fish can be caught off New Zealand coasts. It compares favorably to the more popular snapper in terms of good looks, flavor (somewhat sweet), and texture (firm with medium flake).

tender: a dinghy or other boat used to ferry people and supplies to and from a ship.

toad in the hole: a traditional British/Kiwi dish with several variations. One involves removing a two-inch-or-so hole from a piece of white bread. (Eat the circle you cut out or give it to the dog.) Melt butter and place the bread in a small skillet. Crack an egg into the hole. Fry on both sides until the bread is lightly browned and egg yolk almost set. The toad in the hole that Peter referred to, however, calls for link sausages baked in a roasting pan with Yorkshire pudding batter. Both are good wholesome food for bachelors and children alike.

toetoe: (pronounced "toi-toi") New Zealand's largest native grass. It grows in clumps up to three meters high and should not be confused with pampas grass, an intruder originally from South America and considered to be a weed.

tomokanga: (Māori) entrance, opening, gateway, portal.

GLOSSARY

torch: flashlight.

totara: a majestic, forest-canopy tree, coniferous and endemic to New Zealand. Totara timber is durable, straight-grained, and resistant to rot, so it is often used for fence posts, floor pilings, and railway sleepers. This was the primary wood used in traditional Māori carving. After the kauri, the totara may be the longest living tree of the New Zealand forest, attaining a ripe old age of one thousand or more years.

tui: a nectar-eating bird indigenous to New Zealand. It is also called a parson bird because its iridescent plumage, at first glance black, with white tufts of feathers at the throat, makes it look quite clerical. Its two voice boxes enable it to cackle, click, creak like timber, groan like a bellows, whistle, wheeze, squeak, trill, and chirp. Like parrots, they can mimic human speech, and the author once engaged in lively conversation with a tui that was perched in a red beech tree near Taupo.

ute: utility vehicle, pickup truck.

Voon: a label created in 1996 by Sophie Voon, a Wellington-based fashion designer, who also maintains a boutique there. Favored by the author, along with Karen Walker and . . . but really, there are too many clever ones now to call out favorites. When New Zealand fashion week was first launched in 2001, skepticism was rife. One of its most memorable moments occurred during designer Kingan-Jones's RJC show. Dressed as Russian czarinas, the models teetered out on high heels across fake and soapy snow. One by one, they wobbled, skidded, and crashed to the catwalk (without a broken bone). New Zealand Fashion Week may have had a slippery start, but today they fight for a spot in the photographers' pit, and the media center is crammed with reporters.

wahoo: a large predatory, tropical marine fish, prized as a game fish. Can weigh close to two hundred pounds.

wally-jammer: A wally is a fool, at best, someone who is very intelligent in some areas but unbelievably stupid in others. In British slang, it is also a pickled gherkin. The only reference the author could find to wally-jammer was Australian, "farewell and beat the dingo with a wally-jammer." Really I think we should hang this embellishment on Mary.

GLOSSARY

waxeye: (also silvereye) A lightweight, at around ten grams, this omnivorous, perching bird has an arresting ring of white feathers around its eye, with a fine black line around the outer edge. Native to the southwest Pacific. It arrived in New Zealand in great numbers in 1856, evidently when a migrating flock was swept in by a storm. As an apparently self-introduced bird, it is protected as a native species—a stellar example of Kiwi benevolence.

Weet-Bix: a high-fiber, low-sugar, breakfast-cereal biscuit manufactured in Australia and New Zealand by the Sanitarium Health and Wellbeing Company. Beloved by Kiwis who grew up with it. For the rest of us, a brand as aged and a texture as dessicated as Shredded Wheat. Hard to say which one is less moreish.

whinger: a whining complainer. Never welcome at God's Holding Paddock.

CPSIA information can be obtained
at www.ICGtesting.com
Printed in the USA
BVHW06s0709280718
522790BV00012B/78/P